Linda
D1760137

EDUCATION POLICY-MAKING IN WALES

EDUCATION POLICY-MAKING IN WALES

Explorations in Devolved Governance

Edited by

RICHARD DAUGHERTY, ROBERT PHILLIPS
and GARETH REES

*Published on behalf of the Board of Celtic Studies
of the University of Wales*

UNIVERSITY OF WALES PRESS
CARDIFF
2000

British Library Cataloguing-in-Publication Data.
A catalogue record for this book is available from the British Library.

ISBN 0-7083-1632-8

Typeset by Action Publishing Technology, Gloucester
Printed in Great Britain by Dinefwr Press, Llandybïe

Contents

Figures and Tables

List of Figures

List of Tables

Preface and Acknowledgements

In 1996, the editors received a small grant under the University of Wales Academic Collaboration Fund to organize a seminar series on education policy-making in Wales. Over twenty papers were given at two seminars held at Swansea and Cardiff. The range and breadth of papers reflected the depth of academic interest in education policy-making in Wales following the Education Reform Act, 1988. These papers provided the basis for the chapters which are included in this edited book.

The editors therefore wish to acknowledge the financial support received from the University of Wales, as well as that provided by the Board of Celtic Studies, which kindly provided the funding for the book. Finally, we wish to thank the University of Wales Press for publishing it.

List of Abbreviations

AAs	Associate Assessors
ACAC	Curriculum and Assessment Authority for Wales
ACCAC	Qualifications, Curriculum and Assessment Authority for Wales
AFE	advanced further education
BTEC	Business and Technician Education Council
CATS	credit accumulation and transfer scheme
CCW	Curriculum Council for Wales
CEF	College Employers' Forum
CISWO	Coal Industry Social Welfare Organisation
CNAA	Council for National Academic Awards
COSHEP	Committee of Scottish Higher Education Principals
CPS	Centre for Policy Studies
CR	contract research
CTCs	City Technology Colleges
CUV	Community University of the Valleys
CWB	Central Welsh Board
DACE	Department of Adult Continuing Education
DevR	development of research
DES	Department of Education and Science
DfE	Department for Education
DfEE	Department for Education and Employment
DMS	devolution of management to schools
ERA	Education Reform Act
ERDF	European Regional Development Fund
ESOL	English as a second language
ESRC	Economic and Social Research Council
ETAGW	Education and Training Action Group for Wales
EU	European Union
FAS	Funding Agency for Schools
FE	further education
FEDA	Further Education Development Association
FEFCE	Further Education Funding Council for England

FEFCW	Further Education Funding Council for Wales
FHE	further and higher education
FTE	full-time equivalent
GCSE	General Certificate of Secondary Education
GMS	grant-maintained schools
HE	higher education
HEFCE	Higher Education Funding Council for England
HEFCW	Higher Education Funding Council for Wales
HEI	higher education institution
HEQC	Higher Education Quality Council
HESA	Higher Education Statistical Agency
HMI	Her Majesty's Inspector/Inspectorate
IWA	Institute of Welsh Affairs
JRG	Joint Review Group
LEAs	local education authorities
LMS	local management of schools
NAB	National Advisory Board
NAGCELL	National Advisory Group for Continuing Education and Lifelong Learning
NAPS	National Assessment in Primary Schools
NATFHE	National Association of Teachers in Further and Higher Education
NC	National Curriculum
NCC	National Curriculum Council
NCIHE	National Committee of Inquiry into Higher Education
NCVQ	National Council for Vocational Qualifications
NDPBs	non-departmental public bodies
NIESR	National Institute for Economic and Social Research
NOMIS	National On-Line Manpower Information System
NPM	new public management
NTETs	National Targets for Education and Training
NVQ	National Vocational Qualifications
OFSTED	Office for Standards in Education
OHMCI	Office of Her Majesty's Chief Inspector of Schools
PACE	Primary Assessment and Curriculum Experience

PCFC	Polytechnics and Colleges Funding Council
PoW	Polytechnic of Wales
QAA	Quality Assurance Agency
QAC	Quality Assessment Committee
QCA	Qualifications and Curriculum Authority
QR	quality research
RAE	research assessment exercise
RFM	recurrent funding methodology
S4C	Sianel Pedwar Cymru
SATs	standard assessment tasks
SCAA	School Curriculum and Assessment Authority
SEAC	School Examinations and Assessment Council
TECs	Training and Enterprise Councils
TES	*Times Educational Supplement*
TGAT	Task Group on Assessment and Testing
TQA	Teaching Quality Assessment
TSI	Technology Schools Initiative
TTA	Teacher Training Agency
UCAC	Undeb Cenedlaethol Athrawon Cymru
UCC	University College of Cardiff
UFC	Universities Funding Council
UGC	University Grants Committee
UWIST	University of Wales Institute of Science and Technology
UWS	University of Wales Swansea
VET	vocational education and training
WAB	Welsh Advisory Board
WEA	Workers' Educational Association
WJEC	Welsh Joint Education Committee
WLB	Welsh Language Board
WLGA	Welsh Local Government Association
WO	Welsh Office
WOED	Welsh Office Education Department

Contributors

COLIN BAKER is Professor of Education at the University of Wales, Bangor, Director of Research Centre Wales, a Fellow of the British Psychological Society and a member of the Welsh Language Board. His books include *Aspects of Bilingualism in Wales* (1985), *Key Issues in Bilingualism and Bilingual Education* (1988), *Attitudes and Language* (1992), *Foundations of Bilingual Education and Bilingualism* (1993, second edition 1996), and the *Encyclopedia of Bilingualism and Bilingual Education* (1998 co-authored with Sylvia Prys Jones). He is Editor of the *International Journal of Bilingual Education and Bilingualism*.

THEO COX is Honorary Research Fellow in the Department of Education, University of Wales Swansea. His research interests have centred on educationally disadvantaged children. He has written a number of chapters, journal articles and books on this topic, as well as directing two funded research projects on disadvantage. His most recent publication is *Combating Educational Disadvantage* (Falmer, 2000). He has also published two books on the National Curriculum and primary education. He is a Fellow of the British Psychological Society.

RICHARD DAUGHERTY is Professor of Education and Dean of the Faculty of Arts at the University of Wales, Aberystwyth. His research interests are in the fields of assessment, education policy and geography education. A former President of the Geographical Association, Chair of the Curriculum Council of Wales and Chair of UCET Cymru, he is currently a member of the DfEE's National Educational Research Forum. Among his publications are a book on *National Curriculum Assessment: A Review of Policy 1987–1994* (Falmer, 1995).

DAVID EGAN is Head of the School of Education, University of Wales Institute Cardiff, and the current Chair of the Universities Council for the Education of Teachers, Cymru. His interests include the history of education and contemporary education policy in Wales. With Roy James (formerly Chief Inspector of Schools in

Wales) he is currently monitoring the work of the National Assembly for Wales education committees, as part of an Institute for Welsh Affairs/Centre for Welsh Governance research project.

JOHN FITZ is a Reader at the Cardiff University School of Social Sciences. He has undertaken funded research and published on a wide variety of areas in education policy, specifically investigations of the Assisted Places Scheme, grant-maintained schools policy, training for multi-skilling in post-compulsory education and training, school inspection and schools' ICT policy. His most recent research continued an earlier concern with school choice and social justice. In addition, he has conducted international comparative research and is a frequent visitor to the USA.

STEPHEN GORARD is a Reader at the Cardiff University School of Social Sciences. He has written over 100 academic publications on school effects, the social composition of schools, school choice, differential attainment by gender, the role of technology in education, methods for analysing large-scale datasets, the impact of target-setting, and patterns of participation in lifelong learning. He has recently produced reports for ACCAC ('The comparative performance of boys and girls at school in Wales') and the National Assembly for Wales ('Lifetime learning targets in Wales: a research summary'). The work represented here is dealt with in more detail in his new book *Education and Social Justice* (University of Wales Press, 2000).

ROB HUMPHREYS is Lecturer in Continuing Education, University of Wales Swansea, and from 1993 to 1998 was co-ordinator of the pioneering Community University of the Valleys scheme, in the Dulais Valley in south Wales. He co-edited, and was a contributor to, *Communities and their Universities: The Challenge of Lifelong Learning* (Lawrence and Wishart, 1996). With Hywel Francis, he was commissioned by NIACE Cymru to write the paper *The Learning Country: Citizenship and the New Democracy in Wales* (NIACE Cymru, 1999), and is co-author (with Michael Williams, Hywel Francis and Gary Rauter) of *Motivation and Efficacy: A Handbook for Trainers and Community Educators* (Wales Centre for Lifelong Learning, 1999).

MARTIN JEPHCOTE is a Lecturer in Education at Cardiff University School of Social Sciences where he is Director of Teaching and

Learning and Director of the PGCE. He teaches on the PGCE initial teacher-training programme for further education and contributes policy modules on the BA in Education. His recent research interests have focused on the impact of the incorporation of colleges of further education and he is generally interested in the process of policy-making and implementation.

GARETH ELWYN JONES is Research Professor of Education, University of Wales Swansea. His books include *Controls and Conflicts in Welsh Secondary Education, 1889–1944*; *Which Nation's Schools*; and *The Education of a Nation* (all published by the University of Wales Press), and *Modern Wales* (Cambridge University Press). His most recent book, edited with Dai Smith, is *The People of Wales* (Gomer Press, 1999), the BBC Radio Wales Millennium History.

STEVE MORRIS is a Welsh-speaker and lectures in Continuing Education (specializing in the Welsh language) at University of Wales Swansea. He has published several articles on adult learners of Welsh and Welsh for Adults as a component of language planning and policy in Wales. He is chair of the Welsh Language Board's Welsh for Adults Research and Resources Committee and will be editor of a collection of papers from the first ever research conference in the field held in June 2000.

ROBERT PHILLIPS is Senior Lecturer in Education, University of Wales Swansea. He has written extensively on the history curriculum, national identity and education policy. His book *History Teaching, Nationhood and the State* (Cassell) won the Standing Conference for Studies in Education prize for the best academic book published on education in 1998. He has just completed an edited book (with John Furlong) entitled *Education, Reform and the State, 1976–2001* (Routledge/Falmer, 2001) which analyses the politics of education policy in the twenty-five years since Callaghan's Ruskin College speech.

GARETH REES is a Professor at the Cardiff University School of Social Sciences, where he is also Deputy Director. He has carried out research and published very widely in the areas of: lifelong learning; the role of education and training in regional economic development; and the governance of education policy. He is currently completing an ESRC-funded project on the impacts of the

National Assembly for Wales on the governance of economic development. He is also finishing off a project for the OECD on 'learning regions'.

JANE SALISBURY is Co-ordinator of Postgraduate Studies at the School of Social Sciences, Cardiff University, where she lectures in education policy, qualitative research methods and post-16 education and training. She has published papers on classroom ethnography, vocational education and training along with the sociology of work and professions. Recent research for the EOC examined gender equality and educational reform in Wales. Other work on gender has resulted in an edited volume (1999), *Gender Policy and Educational Change: Shifting Agendas in the UK and Europe*, with Sheila Reddell.

SUE SANDERS is a Senior Lecturer in the Department of Education at University of Wales Swansea. She is co-author with Theo Cox of *The Impact of the National Curriculum on the Teaching of Five Year Olds* (Falmer). Her research interests include the effects of policy regarding subject knowledge on student teachers' self-efficacy. Her current work is exploring the relationship between government requirements and schools' expectations of newly qualified mathematics teachers.

DANNY SAUNDERS is Professor and Head of the Centre for Lifelong Learning at the University of Glamorgan He has published various books and journal articles on student-centred learning, game design, study skills and educational simulations. He is the chair of the Community University of the Valleys Planning and Co-ordination Group, and is a member of numerous community consortia including the Rhondda Cynon Taff Lifelong Learning Forum. Current projects include an Internet-based journalism activity for secondary-school children, developing learning and teaching strategies for community-based learning, and designing staff development activities in teaching and learning innovation.

GERRAN THOMAS is a Lecturer in Education at the University of Wales, Aberystwyth. He has published a number of research papers on policy-related matters, especially relating to curriculum-related issues and school inspections. He is qualified as an inspector of schools and has participated in many school inspections. His papers include: 'The new schools' inspection system: some problems and possible solutions' in *Educational Management and Administration*; 'A brief history of the genesis of the new schools' inspection system', in the *British Journal of Educational Studies*; and 'Some reactions to the teaching of Science using a modular scheme' in the *Educational Review*.

GETHIN WILLIAMS retired in 1996 as Deputy Principal of University of Wales College, Newport, after thirty-three years of service in higher education in Wales. He served on a number of bodies in Wales and the UK and in a variety of capacities including academic auditor, adviser and consultant. He undertook a number of assignments for the Welsh Office, HEQC, HEFCW and the HE Funding Councils which led to the publication of reports, monographs and articles. On his retirement he became Honorary Research Fellow at Cardiff University of Wales where he is engaged on a study of the impact of changes in government policy on the development of higher education in Wales since 1975, for which an ESRC award was made.

Introduction

RICHARD DAUGHERTY, ROBERT PHILLIPS
AND GARETH REES

With the establishment of a National Assembly in Wales, questions about the appropriate scope of policy-making in Wales have come to the forefront of political debate. More generally in the UK, the parallel processes of devolution in Scotland and Northern Ireland and the tentative moves towards regional government in England provide a wider context for considering the role of the 'national/regional' level in the formulation and implementation of state policy. It has been argued that the development of supra-national institutions within the European Community has had the effect, perhaps paradoxically, of increasing the significance of 'sub-national' units of government and the so-called 'hollowing-out' of the conventional national state.

Academic analysis in Wales has been relatively slow to take up the challenges posed by these developments. More specifically, little attention has been given to analysing those policy areas most directly affected by the current phase of devolution. One of the most significant of these is education, which occupies a central position in contemporary government policy in Britain and indeed in social democratic politics generally. Education policy is central not only to state strategy for economic efficiency and development but also in strategies for alleviating social exclusion and inequality. Important questions are therefore posed as the extent to which the National Assembly will be empowered to develop distinctive policies in those fields.

Education is one of the principal responsibilities of the Assembly and so provides a critical policy area for the analysis of devolved governance in Wales. What is happening now is but the latest stage in the history of education policy-making in Wales which has its origins in the end of the nineteenth century with the Welsh Intermediate Act of 1889 and the establishment in 1907 of the

Welsh Department of the Board of Education. In the 1990s there was a striking, and rather surprising development of administrative devolution to Welsh educational institutions. Not only did the Welsh Office assume responsibility for all aspects of education policy, including training and economic development, but there was also a proliferation of devolved institutions, which have taken over responsibility for implementation of education policies within Wales. These include, for example, the school curriculum, initially overseen by the Curriculum Council for Wales (CCW) a non-departmental public body (or 'quango') which would later be superseded by an organization with a wider remit, the Qualifications, Curriculum and Assessment Authority for Wales (ACCAC). In further and higher education, funding policy is in the hands of the Welsh Funding Councils.

This collection of essays aims to make two related types of contribution to a discussion of these and other important policy developments affecting education in Wales. First, it presents the most complete analysis to date of a major element of state policy in Wales. Each sector of the education system is represented, from primary schooling through to further, higher and continuing education. Contributors explore the development of an education policy system in Wales, which, it is argued, has become increasingly distinct from what was previously assumed to be a common 'England and Wales' context. They also examine the impact of policies on the nature of educational provision in Wales and their effects in terms of economic efficiency and social inequalities. Second, the collection aims to make a contribution to the analytical frameworks that will enable us to understand not only education policy in Wales, but also devolved governance more generally. As far as the structure of the book is concerned, we have decided to cluster the chapters thematically into four main parts entitled 'Orientation', 'Curriculum and Assessment', 'Effectiveness and Monitoring' and 'Post-Compulsory Education'.

In the first section, which sets out to orientate the reader analytically, the development of education policy-making in Wales is addressed through sociological perspectives. In chapter 1, Robert Phillips and Sue Sanders refer to a wide range of initiatives arising from the 1988 Education Act and subsequent legislation, which have prompted discussion about the emergence of a distinctive scenario for education policy in Wales. They identify some of the institutional, ideological and cultural factors that account for this development and consider some of the theoretical and conceptual tools that emerged in the 1990s in seeking to explain it. Phillips and Sanders argue that education policy in Wales is characterized by a complex set of policy-related dynamics centred on the mediation between external influences and local/regional imperatives. In chapter 2, John Fitz asks to what extent the Wales-based institutions and policy processes set the education system in Wales apart from the system in England. He argues that the creation of educational markets, and their articulation to an ensemble of controls operated by the state, embeds similar forms of governance across both systems. Nevertheless, Fitz suggests, the institutions in Wales have demonstrated an increasing willingness to interpret legislative and administrative frameworks to create educational identities somewhat different from their English counterparts.

The second section concentrates primarily upon curriculum and assessment issues, comprising mainly a series of empirical studies of aspects of policies affecting schools in Wales. In chapter 3, Gareth Elwyn Jones draws upon distinguished work in the field over many years to place current debates over education policy-making in Wales within a historical perspective. Starting with the 1889 Welsh Intermediate Education Act, he traces the nature of educational governance and policy-making in Wales over the next hundred years. Jones demonstrates that, whereas specific pieces of legislation like the 1889 Act gave Welsh institutions a limited measure of control, education policies in Wales were, in the main, initiated in England and geared towards priorities perceived to be relevant there. Theo Cox (chapter 4) draws on a study of the implementation of the National Curriculum (NC) in south Wales primary schools to trace the responses of teachers and headteachers to policy decisions taken at the national (England) and, to a lesser extent at the national (Wales) levels. Linking his evidence to that from other studies on the NC, Cox confirms that centrally imposed policies were modified through the professional practices, beliefs and ideologies of teachers. Richard Daugherty, in chapter 5, refers to the wider context of NC policy but focuses upon the evolution of the associated assessment policies in Wales, from being subsumed within the England and Wales debates of the early 1990s to the more recent scenario which has seen some distinctive assessment policies developed and implemented within Wales. In his review of policies on bilingual education in chapter 6, Colin Baker identifies three distinct perspectives: bilingual education as language planning, as pedagogy and as politics. He argues that these perspectives are often separate from, even in conflict with, each other but also that the changing political context provides an opportunity for a meeting of different perspectives and minds.

The chapters in section three consider two themes that have had a high profile in the education policy discourse of the 1990s, school effectiveness and school inspection. In chapter 7, Stephen Gorard points out that the effectiveness of schools in Wales, especially secondary schools, has been a matter for debate for at least the past thirty years. Whole programmes of target-setting and measures for school improvement have been predicated upon the notion that schools in Wales have been underperforming in comparison with schools in England. Utilizing new research data and alternative modes of analysis, Gorard revisits the 'schooled to fail' thesis and raises questions about the evidence and the arguments which have underpinned it. Gerran Thomas and David Egan, in chapter 8, present a brief history of school inspection in Wales before analysing, using evidence from interview data with key figures in the process, the way a different system of inspections was developed and then legislated for in the 1992 Education (Schools) Act. They point to ways in which inspection policy in Wales, though within a common statutory framework for England and Wales, has taken a somewhat different course from that in England as the separate Office of Her Majesty's Inspector in Wales (OHMCI) has adopted its own style of working and, to a limited extent, distinctive inspection procedures.

In the fourth section, the focus shifts away from schools towards the post-compulsory sectors. Martin Jephcote and Jane Salisbury (in chapter 9) suggest that, since the 1988 Education Act and the 1992 Further and Higher Education Act, the further education sector provides an illuminating example, illustrated by reference to three recurring themes, of the contemporary process of policy-making, policy implementation and the management of institutions. They show how the sector has embraced the trappings of the market but in other ways has become highly centralized. Their evidence leads them towards an actor approach to policy-making, with individuals and groups acting in their own interests, rather than a simplistic view of policies being developed, enacted and then implemented. In chapter 10, Gethin Williams gives an account of changes in government policy on higher education over the period from 1975 to the mid-1990s. He draws on research evidence to develop a conceptual framework for understanding the forces at work, at the national (Wales) level and within institutions, in shaping and implementing policies for this sector. The other two chapters in this section consider policies for adult and continuing education. Rob Humphreys and Danny Saunders (chapter 11) use a case study of the Community University of the Valleys as a starting-point for the development of an analytical framework for understanding the changing nature of what has traditionally been termed the adult education work of higher education institutions (HEIs) in Wales. They argue that, despite the emergence of lifelong learning as a major concern of government education policy, it is too soon to write the obituaries for adult education in HEIs. Writing about one specific aspect of provision for adults in further and higher education, Steve Morris (chapter 12) charts the development of the Welsh for Adults programme and considers its role in realizing the aims of the 1993 Welsh Language Act. He summarizes research evidence on student motivation and points to some of the tensions between organizations with responsibilities in this field.

In the concluding chapter, we attempt to provide an overview of the education policy context in Wales and identify the main ideas and some of the common themes which emerge from the chapters in the book. We also consider the broader context within which education policy debates and processes take place, as well as the relationship between Welsh education and the economy. We speculate here about the future of education policy in Wales and the UK under the changed climate of New Labour's so-called 'Third Way'. Finally, we also consider both the possibilities and limitations for further autonomous decision-making through the Welsh Assembly and the ways in which devolved governance is likely to influence the precise nature of education policies in Wales in the future.

I
Orientation

1

Contemporary Education Policy in Wales: Theory, Discourse and Research

ROBERT PHILLIPS AND SUE SANDERS

Introduction: different policies – new theories?

There has to be some sort of pragmatic imperative to produce an edited collection on education policies in Wales. This question has a particular resonance when we consider whether the book would have attracted the range, depth and brevity of chapters, say, ten years ago: we rather suspect that it would not have. Nevertheless, the task that we set ourselves when we embarked upon the project was a difficult one, as education policy analysis is notoriously messy and complicated (see Fitz, Halpin and Power, 1994). It is also essentially a disparate discipline, as the diverse set of chapters in the book illustrates. It is therefore notoriously difficult to offer universal and overarching theories to give it a firmer methodological orientation and it would be foolish to try. However, there may be some intellectual reference points which may help. In this sense, the words in the subtitle of our chapter provide a fairly accurate indication of what it sets out to achieve and explains our motivation in attempting to contribute positively to a book of this sort. Essentially, we want to examine some of the major features of the contemporary education policy scene in Wales and then consider their implications for the ways in which they are theorized and researched.

The following section therefore considers whether it is necessary to theorize in terms of distinctive education policies in Wales and whether it is therefore also necessary – and desirable – to consider particular analytical frameworks which both describe and explain them adequately. When we touch upon some of the most recent debates on this issue within our own research community (Williams,

Daugherty and Banks, 1992; Phillips, 1996a, 1996b; Delamont and Rees, 1997; Jones, 1997) this question becomes more complicated than it might at first seem. Our basic argument is that education in Wales is characterized by a complex set of policy-related dynamics, centred on the mediation between external influences and local/regional imperatives. As we comment in the conclusion, however, in some senses this makes Wales no different from any other part of the UK.

The next section goes on to consider some of the educational discourses which have emerged in Wales since 1988; we identify three for particular attention, namely restorationism, marketization and community. We shall try to argue that whilst many of these influences have had their origins (and by definition their own policy agendas) *outside* Wales, others have emerged *within* Wales, initiated by cultural, historical, political and institutional factors. The fact that these discourses are not natural bedfellows provides intellectual impetus – as it does in England – to the richness and complexity of policy-related debates in Wales at macro, meso and micro levels.

Our third aim is to consider the implications of these sorts of debates for future policy-related research agendas in Wales. If we accept both the complexity and the distinctiveness of the policy scene in Wales, then this inevitably leads to a whole set of research questions. It also centres upon issues relating to the particular orientation of such research agendas and what they are setting out to achieve. This inevitably leads us to consider the relationship of the academic research community in Wales with policy-makers in terms of identifying research priorities. It also forces us to consider our relationship with the education policy research community in other parts of the UK and beyond. Above all, what we shall be arguing is that there is a need for us to theorize – systematically and at times critically – the *origins, trajectories and outcomes* of education policies in Wales and to consider how they relate to the 'bigger picture' outside it.

Theorizing education policies in Wales

We need to begin this chapter with a brief reflective account (see Troyna, 1994) on the rationale for a collection of this sort. As (relatively) fresh-faced academics starting work in a Welsh education department some years ago, we were presented with the rather daunting prospect of establishing a master's module specifically concerned with education policy. For us, looking back, this was significant for two reasons. First, the fact that there had been no such module suggests that education policy studies was a relatively new development. This is now difficult to comprehend given the voluminous literature that has since built up concerned with the analysis of education policy in the UK (Halpin and Troyna, 1994; Ranson, 1995). Second, the fact that one of us was asked to teach the module because he was a historian was also significant. Education policy has often been the preserve of historians of education, particularly in Wales, and Gareth Elwyn Jones's distinguished career is testament to that (see Jones, 1997).

Therefore, the module began to be planned around an already very well established literature with a predominantly historical orientation. Gareth's own work on various aspects of the history of education policies in Wales was immensely helpful (some of which has recently been summarized: see Jones, 1997). Particularly helpful was the edited collection on *Education, Culture and Society* (Jones, 1991a), as was another edited volume by Gareth Evans which, interestingly, touched upon many of the issues which we will be discussing in this chapter, such as bilingual education, the inspectorate, post-16 education and examinations and assessment (Evans, 1990). Inevitably, our module focused upon a 'case study' of the controversial education policy-related debate over school performance, most commonly associated with the work of Reynolds (1989, 1990).

As the impact of the 1988 Education Act began to be felt and as distinctive education policy orientations in Wales began to emerge (see below), it became evident to us that there was potential for a particular policy-related research agenda which could explain them, and by which they could be *theorized*. At the time, Scotland and England were witnessing the emergence of an applied analytical framework to explain the education policy reforms there, namely policy sociology, defined by Ozga (1987: 142) as a research orientation that was: 'concerned with finding out how things are and how they came to be that way and is not concerned with a specific problem or its implementation'. Hence Phillips's desire through the pages of the *Welsh Journal of Education* (Phillips, 1996b) to suggest (perhaps rather crudely) that much of this theoretical work could usefully be employed to illuminate more effectively the policy scene in Wales in the late 1980s and early 1990s. Three elements of sociology policy analysis were particularly seductive as far as we were concerned. First was the view that education policy, particularly at a macro level, could only be understood by appreciating what McPherson and Raab (1988) have famously referred to as the 'assumptive worlds' of policy-makers. Hence, Ball's (1990) preoccupation with policy discourses in what he called the 'context of influence' concerning the Education Reform Act. Second, Ozga's (1987) call for theorists to link macro and micro policy contexts seemed particularly important, as was her definition of policy sociology cited above. Third, there was the view, illustrated by the 'case studies' undertaken by the King's College scholars (Ball and Bowe with Gold, 1992) that education policy created elsewhere could be recontextualized at a micro level, with local imperatives playing a vital role in the reformulation of policies.

Policy sociology – particularly associated with the work of Ball (see Hatcher and Troyna, 1994) – has come under intellectual scrutiny in a number of respects, not least because of its theoretical eclecticism. Nevertheless, the stress upon localized mediation, recontextualization or interaction of policy discourses originating elsewhere still seems useful to apply to the Welsh context. From a rather different theoretical perspective, Delamont and Rees (1997: 1) have articulated this eloquently and, in the process, provided the intellectual desire (which goes alongside the pragmatic imperative) to produce this book. This is the desire to

> define a research agenda which ... is able to theorise education (broadly defined) in Wales in ways which explore the interactions of general sociological analysis with the characteristic features of Welsh society. What is involved here, then, is both the application of general sociological analysis to the specific conditions of the Welsh social structure, as well as the development of the former through the engagement with the latter. This is an analytical enterprise which has the potential to develop comparatively, not only within the United Kingdom, but also more widely in (at least) the European context.

We want to return to these issues again at the end of this chapter. We first want to reflect on some of the education policy developments in Wales since 1988.

Education policies in Wales since 1988: different from the rest?

Few would have predicted the sheer pace and scale of the education reforms of the Thatcherite era, leading as Chitty (1992) and others have reminded us, to an education system 'transformed'. Yet few could have predicted either the variety (perhaps a better word to use here would be contradictions: see Whitty, 1990) or the unexpected outcomes of such policies. In particular, not even the wisest sage in the 1980s, faced with an apparently uncompromising, ideologically alien government, would have ventured to suggest that ten years after the most far-reaching and important Education Act of the second half of the twentieth century, Wales would have its own version of the 'National' Curriculum, with the *institutional and monitoring* systems to oversee it in the shape of the Curriculum Council for Wales (CCW) (later renamed ACCAC) and the Office of Her Majesty's Chief Inspectorate (OHMCI) respectively. Yet other flagship Thatcherite policies of the period – most notably the grant-maintained initiative – have in actual policy outcome terms been largely ignored in Wales and thus have had nowhere near the impact they have had in England (Fitz, Halpin and Power, 1993).

These unexpected ('contradictory') policy outcomes provided us in the late 1990s with the opportunity to discuss, in an intellectually honourable manner, whether it was possible to discuss education policies not necessarily from an 'England and Wales' but more often from an 'England or Wales' perspective. We want to argue that this can only be properly explained by the interaction between policy discourses originating elsewhere and the local mediation of such policies within Wales, caused by a range of cultural, social/economic and political factors. We want to illustrate what we mean by concentrating upon three policy discourses in particular: restorationism, marketization and community.

Restorationism

The Tory curricular reforms of the period drew ideological and philosophical inspiration, of course, from traditional notions of curricular thought (see Halpin, Fitz and Power, 1997). Ball (1993) has famously referred to this as the impact of cultural restorationism, defined as the 're-valorisation of traditional forms of education' most commonly associated with a classical education,

traditional subjects and conventional teaching methods. Ball himself
cites Jones (1989: 29) who describes this same ideological/educa-
tional orientation as regarding 'cultural cohesion as an essential
prop of state authority'. We want to argue that this reference to
cultural cohesion explains not only successful attempts to marginal-
ize alternative discourses of multiculturalism in England but,
intriguingly, also provided an opportunity for distinctively Welsh
alternatives. Let us spell out more precisely what we mean: whereas
cultural restorationists and their government allies strove for traditionally 'English' cultural representations through the curriculum,
they were prepared to countenance Welsh cultural curricular expression as it posed no threat (in contrast to multiculturalism or
anti-racism) to their vision of a culturally cohesive England.

We are suggesting that, in curricular terms, Wales has witnessed
its own brand of cultural restorationism, beginning with the publication in 1987 of the Welsh Office's own version of the NC (Welsh
Office, 1987) and has been most notably expressed in the announcement of compulsory Welsh, and in the distinctive statutory orders in
a range of NC subjects and above all, in the cross-curricular
discourse of the Curriculum Cymreig (CCW, 1993) which survived
the Dearing period.

It is important to stress here, however, two important points
about restorationism in Wales which need clarification. First, it
would be inaccurate to claim that the distinctiveness of the Welsh
curriculum emerged simply because of the policy vacuum created
by ideological circumstance. Those who wanted a distinctive Welsh
dimension had to work hard for it. Thus, as far as history was
concerned, the distinctive history curriculum came about as a consequence of the pressure exerted upon the Welsh Office and
government ministers by the Association of History Teachers in
Wales (see Jones, 1991b; Phillips, 1993). There were also, of
course, supporters within the institutional framework centred not
only in the Welsh Office, but CCW and OHMCI also. Second, as
one of us has argued elsewhere, the particular form which restorationism has taken in Wales is different from that in England, hence
for example the Curriculum Cymreig's emphasis upon regional
diversity and local difference (see Phillips, 1996b). Thus justifica-
tions for the compulsory teaching of Welsh are provided by
reference to the diversity of contemporary Europe and the wider
economic and social benefits of bilingualism (Bellin, 1994).

Similarly, Welsh history is to be taught within the context of wider British, European and world perspectives (Welsh Office, 1995a). In short, it could be argued that in Wales cultural restorationism has taken on a democratic spin with an orientation towards a wider Europeanism, reflecting perceived Welsh cultural, social and ideological realities.

Marketization

As a range of policy sociologists have reminded us, Thatcherism was characterized as much by Hayekian market choice as it was by state-centred preoccupation with cultural cohesiveness. As with the wider economy and society in the 1980s and 1990s, Welsh education has been weathering free-market gales.

One of the major advocates of the application of free-market principles to education was, of course, the erstwhile Secretary of State for Wales, John Redwood. Thus, competition, deregulation and privatization were to be the essential elements of a future prosperity in Wales in a mass, global market (Redwood, 1994a), implying the need for a variety of schools. These principles could apparently be applied in a relatively straightforward way to education; simple comparisons across schools needed to be encouraged and scrutinized through league tables in order to encourage efficiency and competition (Redwood, 1994b). The 'winners' within this free market needed to be rewarded for their efforts, hence the announcement of specific Welsh Office funding for 'popular' schools (Welsh Office, 1995b). In order to compete within the global market, reforms in education and training were required to link education with employers and industry (Welsh Office, 1995c).

We want to argue that, as with the wider economy, the effects of such policies have been mixed and again mirror local/regional imperatives. The policies most commonly associated with the polices of marketization as applied to education had their origins, of course, in the pages of the New Right pamphlets of the 1980s and have been difficult enough to apply even to apparently conducive contexts in England and elsewhere in the world (Henig, 1994; Halstead, 1994; Bridges and Husbands, 1996). In Wales, in terms of actual policy outcomes, certain elements of marketization – such as grant-maintained status (GMS) schools – were largely ignored, yet other aspects, such as the impact of league tables, have had to be lived with. These different policy outcomes can only be explained by the complex relationship between the 'bigger picture' and the local environment. Thus, whereas policies initiated from London have involved a degree of national compulsion, others which have required local discussion and decision-making to introduce them have been rejected, a vivid illustrative example of local mediation of national policy. Of course, these sorts of struggles have also occurred in England, but the extent of the rejection of GMS in Wales demonstrates perhaps the distinctiveness of the local policy context, which is sharpened also by the growth of bilingual schools. However, as a number of scholars have shown, the impact of marketization at the local level is even more complicated than our simplistic analysis has demonstrated here (see Fitz, chapter 2, for a more detailed analytical discussion).

Community

If restorationism and marketization have involved mediation and recontextualization of influences originating elsewhere, it could be argued that the third policy discourse identified in this chapter has distinctive characteristics most commonly originating within Wales itself. It has become fashionable in the age of the postmodern to deny the existence of Jurassic 'meta-narratives' such as community and indeed there are valid reasons why, in the age of globalization, there is a need to re-examine what the term actually means (Morley and Robins, 1995). However, the notion of community in its more conventional sense centred on the particular characteristics, traditions and values of the locality has undoubtedly been influential in specific areas. For example, it may account for the rejection of GMS referred to earlier, although this may need further empirical investigation.

Less contentious is the impact of community ideas upon specific policy initiatives in Wales and we want to use two examples to illustrate our point. The first takes us back to the early days of the creation of the NC. Whereas in England the National Curriculum Council (NCC) was developing the cross-curricular dimension of citizenship (NCC, 1990), the CCW was cultivating its own, very different and characteristic version named *community understanding* (CCW, 1991a, 1991b). This was significant for a number of reasons. The fact that it was different from its English equivalent was testament to the degree of institutional autonomy gained by the CCW, which was now attempting to mirror local (community) needs. Moreover, anyone who has read the *community understanding* documentation would have been struck by its radicalism in a profoundly conservative age. It referred to the need to introduce pupils to the complexity of community where people could be 'grouped in terms of class, gender, race and age', leading to 'differences between people that raise issues of diversity, inequality and prejudice' (1991b: 6). The same paragraph went on to stress that pupils should learn to question stereotypes and understand the ways in which cultural diversity could be celebrated and inequality and prejudice combated. It suggested that pupils be made aware of human rights, introduced to the range of democratic processes available to them and be made aware of the ways they could initiate change *either* as individuals *or* as members of groups. Finally, in a remarkably frank and bold paragraph, the document stated that 'pupils should know how and why wealth and resources are distributed unevenly between individuals, groups, nations and continents' (1991b: 9).

If the actual content of the documentation was remarkable, the disappearance of *community understanding* from official discourse is also significant – an issue which we want to return to at greater length below. Suffice it to say at this point, however, that *community understanding* would have been a useful contribution to contemporary debates relating to the relationship between the individual and society which have captured the headlines in recent years.

The second area where the specific needs of Welsh communities have initiated particular policy initiatives (especially within the south Wales context) is in the area of community education and lifelong learning. As Istance and Rees (1995:3) have demonstrated, various historical and cultural traditions, combined with social and economic factors most commonly associated with high levels of long-term unemployment mean that the need for lifelong learning is highly relevant to the Wales of the twenty-first century in order to promote both 'community interests *and* individual development' (their emphasis). Again, this regional imperative has initiated institutional response in the shape of the University of the Valleys initiative (Francis and Humphreys, 1996).

Future educational research and policy imperatives

In this final section, we want to consider some of the issues that may shape education policy agendas in the future within the context of this discussion. Inevitably, any crystal-ball-gazing is speculative and is itself influenced, at the time of writing, by immediate institutional and legislative developments, particularly the Welsh Assembly and White Papers (Welsh Office, 1997, 1999).

It may therefore be appropriate to begin by contemplating research which is concerned with the education policy scene at a macro level. There is plenty of potential, it seems to us, to undertake more systematic work on the ways in which important institutional frameworks within Wales operate. Whereas there have been some analytical studies of the role of local authorities in education policy (see Fletcher, 1996), as far as we know there have been no policy analyses of the role of the Welsh Office and, for example ACCAC, say on the lines of studies conducted on the DES in England. Our own instincts persuade us to believe that a historical analysis (combined with a social science orientation) of contemporary institutional developments associated with education would be 'illuminative' (Ozga, 1987), particularly for revealing the 'assumptive worlds' of policy mediators in Wales. Such an approach may well explain why certain policy discourses find official favour whilst others do not.

This reminds us once more of the relevance of the notion of recontextualization at the local level. Wales is a 'locality' in the general sense; therefore, some of the differences within Wales may be as interesting as those which characterize regional differences across the UK as a whole (Delamont and Rees, 1997). Moreover, the rural/urban dichotomy within Wales may only be one factor in exacerbating local difference. More sensitive and controversial local divergences centred upon language and culture. Thus a recent study of the implementation of the Curriculum Cymreig which reported a 'spirit of purposeful co-operation' (Jones and Lewis, 1995) in the schools that embraced it would have also been well advised to consider why other schools in Wales have largely ignored it. An even more sensitive – yet similar – issue relates to the contrasting regional implementation of the teaching of Welsh in schools (see Gorard, 1997a). Work of a critical, analytically informed nature is needed to explore how these meso and micro cultural/political struggles are taking shape. Similarly, work which considers the long-term cultural and ideological impact of recent (complex) changes to the curriculum in Wales on pupils' future perceptions of identity would also be interesting. This implies the need to engage objectively with the relationship between curriculum and nationalism (see Williams and Jones, 1994; Evans *et al.*, 1997).

The challenge here, as one of us has argued elsewhere, is how to ensure that the curriculum reflects how Wales really is rather than what somebody would wish it to be (Phillips, 1996a, 1996c). As Brian Davies (1991: 83) has perceptively suggested, there is a need to ensure 'international and cross-cultural access to differentiated experience which does not see a need to separate issues of identity, equality and worth'.

If there is a need to explore new research agendas, there is also need to go back to old ones. Delamont and Rees (1997: 12) have rightly reminded us that 'Wales certainly needs a new "policy sociology" but it needs a revitalised old-style sociology of education too', not least because it will 'contribute to the development of policies which address the manifest problems besetting the education system in Wales' (1997: 1). They suggest two areas where this is particularly needed. First, they argue that the whole question of educational attainment needs to be revisited; indeed, recent work which has explored once more the connection between social deprivation and attainment questions the myth of Welsh secondary school underachievement (see Bellin *et al.*, 1996; Gorard, 1997b). Second, they argue that public policy in Wales should reflect particular problems besetting the post-16 environment which in Wales are particularly associated with the relatively low take-up of education and training (Istance and Rees, 1994; Rees and Istance, 1997) and the relatively poor quality and availability of jobs (particularly high-quality ones) for school-leavers (Rees, Williamson and Istance, 1996; see also Gorard *et al.*, 1997).

All this reminds us again, of course, of the 'bigger picture' within which debates over policies take place. This realization should also encourage us to put post-1997 election policy proposals into their proper context. Whatever these proposals may say about the need for 'higher standards', the provision of 'new qualification routes' and the generation of 'motivation and self-belief' amongst pupils, future welfare and prosperity depend in Wales, as they have done throughout most of the twentieth century, upon wider structural factors associated with the economy and society (see the Conclusion for a further discussion of these issues). One of the reasons for the generation in recent years of debates which have emphasized distinctiveness is the belief that Welsh needs in this respect have been relegated (Bellin, Osmond and Reynolds, 1994; Reynolds, 1995; Barnes, 1996). Whether or not we agree with that analysis, the fact remains that under the new Welsh Assembly, autonomy concerning Welsh education policy-making is likely to be enhanced not diminished. This indeed provides intellectual food for thought for the type of chapter which will be included in collected volumes such as this in the future. The emphasis upon local/ regional diversity also has interesting and exciting implications for the ways in which Welsh education policies and educational change are theorized from a comparative perspective. Obviously, it is now necessary to make national *institutional* comparisons in the UK. But there is the opportunity also for regional comparative work on a wide range of educational policy issues not only in the UK but within Europe too. The ways in which the research community in Wales responds to this challenge will be an exciting research agenda in itself.

References

Ball, S. (1990) *Politics and Policy Making: Explorations in Policy Sociology*. London: Routledge.

Ball, S. (1993) Education, Majorism and the curriculum of the dead. *Curriculum Studies,* 1(2), 195–214.

Ball, S. and Bowe, R. with Gold, A. (1992) *Reforming Education and Changing Schools: Case Studies in Policy Sociology*. London: Routledge.

Barnes, D. (1996) A design for Welsh education. *Planet,* 119, 72–9.

Bellin, W. (1994) Language and education. In W. Bellin, J. Osmond and D. Reynolds, *Towards an Educational Policy for Wales*. Cardiff: Institute of Welsh Affairs.

Bellin, W., Farrell, S., Higgs, G. and White, S. (1996) Using census information to compare school performance. *Welsh Journal of Education,* 5(2), 3–25.

Bellin, W., Osmond, J. and Reynolds, D. (1994) *Towards an Education System for Wales*. Cardiff: Institute of Welsh Affairs.

Bridges D. and Husbands, C. (eds.) (1996) *Consorting and Collaborating in the Education Marketplace*. London: Falmer.

CCW (1991a) *The Whole Curriculum: Principles and Issues for Consideration by Schools in Curriculum Planning and Implementation.* Cardiff: CCW.

CCW (1991b) *Advisory Paper 11: Community Understanding: A Framework for the Development of a Cross-Curricular Theme in Wales.* Cardiff: CCW.

CCW (1993) *Advisory Paper 18: Developing a Curriculum Cymreig.* Cardiff: CCW.

Chitty, C. (1992) *The Education System Transformed.* Manchester: Baseline Books.

Davies, B. (1991) Welsh voices: more than just talk? In G. E. Jones (ed.), *Education, Culture and Society.* Cardiff: University of Wales Press.

Delamont, S. and Rees, G. (1997) *Understanding the Welsh Education System: Does Wales Need a Separate 'Policy Sociology'? Working Paper 23.* Cardiff: School of Education, University of Wales Cardiff.

Evans, G. (ed.) (1990) *Perspectives on a Century of Secondary Education in Wales, 1889-1989.* Aberystwyth: Dept of Education, University of Wales, Aberystwyth.

Evans, J., Davies, B., Bass, D. and Penney, D. (1997) Playing for position: education policy, physical education and nationalism in Wales. *Journal of Education Policy*, 12(4), 285-302.

Fitz, J., Halpin, D. and Power, S. (1993) *Grant Maintained Schools: Education in the Market Place.* London: Kogan Page.

Fitz, J., Halpin, D. and Power, S. (1994) Implementation research and education policy: practice and prospects. *British Journal of Educational Studies*, 42(1), 53-69.

Fletcher, J. (1996) Changing partners: education and the unitary authorities. *Welsh Journal of Education*, 5(2), 43-52.

Francis, H. and Humphreys, R. (1996) Communities, valleys and universities. In J Elliott, H. Francis, R. Humphreys and D. Istance (eds.), *Communities and their Universities: The Challenge of Life-Long Learning.* London: Lawrence & Wishart.

Gorard, S. (1997a) Paying for a 'Little England': school choice and the Welsh language. *Welsh Journal of Education*, 6(1), 19-32.

Gorard, S. (1997b) *'Schooled to Fail'? Revisiting the Welsh School Effect.* Cardiff: School of Education, University of Wales Cardiff, mimeo.

Halpin, D., Fitz, J. and Power, S. (1997) In the grip of the past? Tradition, traditionalism and contemporary schooling. *International Studies in the Sociology of Education*, 7(1), 3-20.

Halpin, D. and Troyna, B. (eds.) (1994) *Researching Education Policy: Ethical and Methodological Issues.* London: Falmer.

Halstead, M. (ed.) (1994) *Parental Choice and Education: Principles, Policy and Practice.* London: Kogan Page.

Hatcher, R. and Troyna, B. (1994) The 'policy cycle': a Ball by Ball account. *Journal of Education Policy*, 9(2), 155–70.

Henig, J. (1994) *Rethinking School Choice: Limits of the Market Metaphor*. Princeton, NJ: University of Princeton Press.

Istance, D. and Rees, G. (1994) Education and training in Wales: problems and paradoxes revisited. *Contemporary Wales*, 7, 7–27.

Istance, D. and Rees, G. (1995) *Life-Long Learning in Wales: A Programme for Prosperity*. Cardiff: NIACE.

Jones, B and Lewis, I. (1995) A Curriculum Cymreig. *Welsh Journal of Education*, 4(2), 22–35.

Jones, G. E. (1991a) *Education, Culture and Society*. Cardiff: University of Wales Press.

Jones, G. E. (1991b) Making history: a personal view of history in the National Curriculum. *Welsh Journal of Education*, 3, 3–9.

Jones, G. E. (1997) *The Education of a Nation*. Cardiff: University of Wales Press.

Jones, K. (1989) *Right Turn: The Conservative Revolution in Education*. London: Hutchinson Radius.

McPherson, A. and Raab, C. (1988) *Governing Education: A Sociology of Policy since 1945*. Edinburgh: Edinburgh University Press.

Morley, D. and Robins, K. (1995) *Spaces of Identity: Global Media, Electronic Landscapes and Cultural Boundaries*. London: Routledge.

NCC (1990) *Curriculum Guidance Number 8: Education for Citizenship*. York: NCC.

Ozga, J. (1987) Studying education through the lives of the policy makers: an attempt to close the macro–micro gap. In S. Walker and L. Barton (eds.), *Changing Policies, Changing Schools: New Directions for Schooling?* Milton Keynes: Open University Press.

Phillips, R. (1993) Reprieve from the 'sword of Damocles'? *Welsh Historian*, 19, 11–15.

Phillips, R. (1996a) Who am I and why are we here? Some Welsh reflections on culture, curriculum and society. Paper given at the SCAA International Conference on Culture, Curriculum and Society, February, also published in *Multicultural Teaching*, 14(3), 41–4.

Phillips R. (1996b) Education policy making in Wales: a research agenda. *Welsh Journal of Education*, 5(2), 26–42.

Phillips, R. (1996c) History teaching, cultural restorationism and national identity in England and Wales. *Curriculum Studies*, 4(3), 385–99.

Ranson, S. (1995) Theorising education policy. *Journal of Education Policy*, 10(4), 427–448.

Redwood, J. (1994a) Do we want a global market? *Guardian* (10 January).

Redwood, J. (1994b) *Views from Wales*. London: Conservative Political Centre.

Rees, G. and Istance, D. (1997) Higher education in Wales: the re-emergence of a national system? *Higher Education Quarterly*, 51(1), 49–67.

Rees, G., Williamson, H. and Istance, D. (1996) 'Status zero': a study of jobless school-leavers in south Wales. *Research Papers in Education*, 11(2), 219–35.

Reynolds, D. (1989) The wasted years: education in Wales, 1979–1989. *Welsh Journal of Education*, 4(2), 4–21.

Reynolds, D. (1990) The great Welsh education debate. *History of Education*, 19(3), 251–60.

Reynolds, D. (1995) Creating an educational system for Wales. *Welsh Journal of Education*, 4(2), 4–21.

Troyna, B. (1994) Reforms, research and being reflective about being reflective. In D. Halpin and B. Troyna (eds.), *Researching Education Policy: Ethical and Methodological Issues*. London: Falmer.

Welsh Office (1987) *The National Curriculum in Wales*. Cardiff: Welsh Office.

Welsh Office (1995a) *History in the National Curriculum: Wales*. Cardiff: HMSO.

Welsh Office (1995b) *A Bright Future: Getting the Best for Every Pupil at School in Wales*. Cardiff: Welsh Office.

Welsh Office (1995c) *People and Prosperity: An Agenda for Action in Wales*. Cardiff: Welsh Office.

Welsh Office (1997) *Building Excellent Schools Together*. Cardiff: Welsh Office.

Welsh Office (1999) *The BEST for Teaching and Learning: Building Excellent Schools*. Cardiff: Welsh Office.

Whitty, G. (1990) The New Right and the National Curriculum: state control or market forces? In M. Flude and M. Hammer (eds.), *The Education Reform Act, 1988: Its Origins and Implications*. London: Falmer.

Williams, M., Daugherty, R. and Banks, F. (eds.) (1992) *Continuing the Education Debate*. London: Cassell.

Williams, M. and Jones, B. (1994) Tensions between cultural restoration and nation building in the nationalised Welsh school curriculum. Paper presented at the European Curriculum Researchers' Network Conference, Enschede, Netherlands, August/September.

2

Governance and Identity:
The Case of Wales

JOHN FITZ

Introduction

Within the UK national system Wales has had its own educational
institutions for more than a century. The existence of the University
of Wales (established in 1889), a department of state, created in
1964, to administer – amongst other things – the provision of
education, a territorial schools' inspectorate, and its own further
and higher education funding councils provide some evidence for
the claim of a separate system. Moreover, the more recent restructuring of education in the UK can be interpreted as endowing Wales
with further capacity to manage its own affairs. The trend towards
greater territorial autonomy in education and other realms of public
policy has been consolidated by the constitutional changes which for
the first time provide for an elected assembly in Wales.

Distinctiveness and local identity are further enhanced by an
education system within which approximately 30 per cent of schools
educate students through the medium of Welsh, where Welsh is
taught in all maintained schools and is one of the four core subjects
in Welsh-speaking schools. The system is mature enough to have
generated its own 'myths' (see Gray, McPherson and Raffe, 1984),
which have had reverberations in policy, most notably in the belief
that Wales is a land where students have been 'schooled to fail' in a
system which has constantly been judged to be less effective than its
English counterpart (for example, Reynolds, 1989, but see Gorard
in chapter 7 below).

On the face of it there is evidence, then, to say that education
policy has been made in and for Wales for the best part of a
century. There are countervailing forces, though, which can be
interpreted as setting limits to the independence of action and the

policy-making capacities of territorial institutions, policy-makers and practitioners. Moreover, it can be argued that these have militated against the development of an education system that both reflects and responds to territorial needs and aspirations.

In constitutional terms, for example, the arena of *national* policy-making and the formulation of legislation remains English-based and London-centred (see Raffe, 1998). The other territorial 'home nations' (Northern Ireland, Scotland and Wales), by and large, interpret and 'recontextualise' (Bernstein, 1990, 1996) centrally generated policy frameworks. The process of recontextualization, which is founded on local economies, social histories, cultures, traditions, values, political alliances and institutional arrangements, is important. It gives rise to variations in the educational arrangements, contents and practices between the centre and the peripheral territories (see chapter 1 above).

Analysis of the balance between national policy frameworks and their local interpretation and recontextualization is the key theme of the exploration of the governance of education in Wales presented in this chapter. Drawing on research conducted primarily on school-centred policies in England and more recently in Wales, the chapter argues that systems of governance promoted by successive national governments, force, in Wales, considerable alignment to the goals, values and identities embedded in national policy frameworks. The latitude for local variation, under present arrangements, is relatively small. Moreover, it is proposed that recent restructuring of education and other public services has generated policy levers designed to constrain further local variations to national determined purposes, values and identities in education.

The data sources for this paper include research conducted by the author with other colleagues in the areas of self-managing schools and grant-maintained (GM) schools' policy (Fitz, Halpin and Power, 1993), school inspection policy (Fitz and Lee 1996), assessment policy (Fitz, Firestone and Fairman, 1999; Firestone, Winter and Fitz, 1999) and markets in education (Gorard and Fitz, 1998a, 1998b).

This chapter is arranged as follows. The first section sets out the theoretical underpinning which informs the analysis of the relationship between national policy-making and its interpretation at territorial level. The second outlines key elements of a new form of governance promoted via the restructuring of the public sector. The third relates this new form of governance specifically to education policy and notes its relative application in England and Wales. The last section considers the tasks ahead if Wales is to develop a distinctive vision of educational provision.

Policy: metaphors and narratives

For the purpose of this chapter, the policy process is conceptualized as a series of levels, hierarchically related. Each level is theorized as an ensemble of structured positions, occupied by institutions and agents, related through a struggle to become the authoritative shapers or interpreters of policy texts, within which are embedded specific purposes, contents and directives. Following Bernstein (1990, 1996), occupants in each successive level are engaged in the interpretation and recontextualization of the policy text made available and legitimate by the occupants of the preceding level. The model is predominantly top–down in character. Nevertheless, the policy process is characterized by inclusiveness, to the extent that the model embraces a recognition of all the agents and agencies, at each level, as contributors to the policy-making. Moreover, the idea of continuous interaction between agents and actors within and between levels is fundamental to the model.

The basic model proposed here has its metaphorical equivalents in Bernstein's 'fields' (1990, 1996) or 'arenas', from which it draws heavily, Firestone's 'ecology of games' (1989), the idea of 'levels' of Fitz, Firestone and Fairman (1999) and Ball and Bowe's 'policy cycle' (1992). Each of these metaphors is concerned with the fundamental problem of the relation between policies generated in one arena, as a set of ideas proposals or directions, designed to influence the ensemble of relations or practice in another, and their realization. They are also concerned to account for the passage of policy texts, through time and through space, and to recognize the lack of certainty that proposals will be adopted in the form in which they were intended.

I will focus here on the relationship between two levels. The first, the *national level*, denotes the institutional ensemble where policy is formulated, promulgated as legislation or as administrative action. In the UK, this includes the legislature, departments of state, English-based non-ministerial government departments such as the Office for Standards in Education (OFSTED) and agencies such as the Qualifications and Curriculum Authority (QCA), its predecessors, and the Teacher Training Agency (TTA) in England. The latter are included because they have exerted an influence beyond their 'English' territorial boundaries. Also included here are the various think-tanks associated with neo-liberal, neo-conservative politics and their more recent social democratic counterparts. The *territorial level* denotes the Welsh institutions involved in local planning, provision and regulation (education). This arena includes the Welsh Office (WO), the schools inspectorate (OHMCI), the Curriculum Council for Wales (CCW) and its successor bodies (ACAC, ACCAC), the Welsh Joint Education Committee (WJEC) and local education authorities and their associated professionals. Local teachers' unions and agencies such as the Institute of Welsh Affairs are also field occupants at the territorial level. These agencies and actors are primarily interpreters and recontextualizers in their mode of operation, engaged simultaneously in the evaluation of the national policy framework and scanning local conditions within which policies must be set and put in progress.

At the formal level, the transmission of national policy frameworks into the territorial context of Wales is relatively straightforward. Legislation is drafted jointly for England and Wales, often appearing in the same text. The Welsh dimension arises from, and the possibility for distinctive policies to emerge in, the powers given to the Secretaries of State to approve all legislation for Wales. On the advice of officials, they are able to adjust the implementation of such legislation in the light of local circumstances. This advice, though, as interviews with officials in the Welsh Office suggest, also has to be set alongside the convention of collective cabinet responsibility. Welsh Secretaries, then, have to make a case for variations to primary legislation as it applies to Wales. As Rees and others have argued, we have very little empirical research on the 'assumptive worlds' of Welsh civil servants and on the character and quality of the advice given, via the usual channels, to ministers (Rees, 1997). There is, then, a qualified constitutional recognition for a distinctive application of national policy in Wales. That situation applies to government agencies located in Wales. The latter, however, are constrained not only constitutionally but in their resources to forge innovative approaches to local policy issues. These limitations are evidenced when we consider the 'big picture' of public-sector restructuring over the last two decades. My argument here is that the principal changes wrought in the governance of the public sector, by national policies, apply as much in Wales as they do in England. These have undermined much of the distinctiveness of policies and policy-making in Wales.

Policy, governance and the public sector

For insights into forms of governance in the public sector that have been incrementally established since the early 1980s we can turn to writers in the fields of political science and public administration. Writers such as Gamble pointed to the seeming paradox of public-sector services being subjected to a 'free market' and a 'strong state' (Gamble, 1988). In the organization and provision of public-sector services, in Rhodes's words, 'fragmentation and centraliza-tion co-exist' (1997, p. 15). What he and others (for example, Hood, 1991; Ferlie *et al.*, 1996) in this genre suggest is that we understand that this is not a paradoxical or chaotic situation but an extremely flexible and powerful form of governing.

To paraphrase a complex argument, the reasoning runs as follows. The creation of free-standing, autonomous institutions, where available resources are tied to 'customer' use and satisfac-tion, has been accompanied by the embedding of an ensemble of ideologies and practices, loosely denoted as 'new public manage-ment' (NPM). In NPM three principal characteristics can be identified: managers are free to manage; managers have responsibil-ity for institutional survival; and institutions are accountable, up (via meso-level regulation) and down (via customer/client, prefer-ences). There are other versions of this but the broad combination of 'freedom', 'audit', 'accountability' and 'quality provision' are the key elements in these also. More sensitive accounts also note the restructuring of professions and professional practices within public institutions and also within private enterprise from which the models for public management were derived.

What Rhodes and others go on to argue is that what the combina-tion of 'autonomous institutions', strong central regulation and NPM gives rise to is a potent mix of self-surveillance and external regulation. Potent, because institutions and agents, at the 'hub and the rim', 'co-produce' the way public-service provision is organized, sustained and reproduced (see Offe, 1984). In this account, 'governance' of a new kind weakens boundaries between state and civil society, the professional and the personal. In Foucault's terms, what we have here is a very distinctive form of 'governmentality' (Foucault, 1977).

In practical terms, the writ for appointed government agencies, GP fundholding, hospital trusts and self-managing schools, set alongside increased ministerial powers to adjust policy and adjudicate policy issues, runs as strong in Wales as it does in England. The point to be made here is that while territorial agencies in their composition may have local appointees and personnel, at the structural level, the *mode of governance* and values associated with it permeate national borders. It is in this context that claims for a Welsh dimension have to be considered and moreover it is at this level that reformers will have to aim to in order to reconfigure the realm of policy and policy-making in Wales. What then have been the consequences for this restructuring for education in Wales?

New governance of education

The progressive attempts to restructure the UK national system of education commenced, in legislation, with the introduction of the Assisted Places Scheme in the 1980 Education Act, but were taken forward by the Education Reform Act, 1988, and subsequent Education Acts. The prolonged shift from locally planned and provided forms of schooling to an institutional arrangement compatible with a marketized system of provision is complex and contradictory. It has involved a reorientation not only of the postwar system of public-service provision but also the reorientation of 'citizens' as 'consumers', and a reshaping of what they can and ought to expect. My analytical framework for capturing the scope and character of the reform of education and the attendant reorientation is grounded in four linked concepts. This multi-theoretical – some might say *bricolage* – approach is not without its problems. It has, however, the merit, of emphasizing the complexity of a systemic change that has taken place at a number of levels. The four concepts are as follows.

Manufactured uncertainty, a term borrowed from Giddens (1994), is employed to describe the location of schools in education markets, the consequent shaping of schools' relations with each other and the impact of markets in the internal organization of schools (see also Halpin, Power and Fitz, 1997a). *Compulsory individualization* (Beck, 1994) suggests the reorientation of citizen consumers towards public-service provision organized along market principles. In Beck's terms it involves a process of disembedding individuals from 'traditional' communities and their re-embedding as agents required to make choices within and between publicly provided services, including education. *Redefining pedagogical authority* owes much to state theory and to Bernstein (1996) and denotes two things. First, the creation of a new layer of institutions within the central state and a subsequent redistribution of power and politics between these and conventional departments of government. Second, it refers to the increased central regulation of public meanings, discourses and institutional practices at the expense of local and community-generated systems and practices. The introduction of a National Curriculum and associated testing procedures, and its regulation via an expanded programme of school inspections is a notable example. *Standards driven reform* brings together statements about 'what every child should know' and what levels of attainment, as measured by national testing, each school should achieve. It is in this area that the Labour government has most extended a policy direction established under previous Conservative administrations.

The boundaries between the practices described by these concepts are somewhat fluid, sometimes overlapping, and in light of the constant changing policy goalposts, somewhat shifting. I also take it as axiomatic that each of these concepts denotes an associated discursive regime, embedded in policy texts which function to promulgate action, position institutions, agents and privilege regimes of truth, identify and legitimate particular sources of authoritative knowledge and prioritize certain voices.

Manufactured uncertainty

The deconstruction of the 1944 settlement and the concerted attack on professional groups thought to have a vested interest in its existence commenced within one year of Thatcher's first government, although the ground had been prepared well in advance (Edwards,

Fitz and Whitty, 1989). Policies which attempted to roll back the monopoly of LEA provision and producer control of education include the Assisted Places Scheme (1981), reformed governing bodies (1986, 1988), City Technology Colleges (CTCs) (1986), grant-maintained (GM) schools (1988), local management of schools (LMS) (1988) and open enrolment (1988) (see Maclure, 1988, 1998; Flude and Hammer, 1990; Pierson, 1998).

In brief, the organization of state education in England and Wales features:

(a) A high degree of institutional autonomy. All schools manage their own budget and their internal affairs (GM schools to a greater degree insofar as they owned their buildings and had the power of hire and fire).
(b) Schools are construed as individual cost centres that are market-driven by virtue of a per capita funding regime. Failure to recruit the planned number of students is intended to translate directly into reduced staff and resources.
(c) Schools exist primarily in a competitive not collaborative relation with each other. In this situation institutional survival is paramount.
(d) Published performance indicators – examination results and inspection reports – have been created to establish a hierarchy of relatively 'good' and 'poor' schools.

The privileged figure on the landscape is 'the parent', who is presented with a choice of schools in the state and the fee-paying sectors, which are intended to be diverse in terms of governance and in the education they offer.

How then does this arrangement articulate our organizing concept 'manufactured uncertainty'? That connection by David Halpin is made in an earlier paper, a section of which is quoted in some length here:

Anthony Giddens characterises 'manufactured uncertainties' as 'globalized forms of risk', the damage resulting from which is impossible to compensate for because 'their long-term consequences are unknown and cannot be properly evaluated' ... our starting point is the assumption that the education market place is a distributive mechanism premised on capitalistic economic principles. As such, it creates its own set of uncertainties which, like Giddens' 'global bads', willy-nilly interpenetrate peoples' everyday lives, especially teachers', parents' and children's, whose experience of the education service takes on a greater degree of indeterminacy than hitherto. What they previously regarded as a relatively stable and enduring service is now experienced as fallible and obdurately imperfectable. Thus headteachers can no longer assume a steady and ready supply of pupils to fill their schools; teachers no longer feel that permanency is written into their informal working conditions and they feel undermined professionally; parents can no longer be confident they will get the school of their choice or the education they want for their children; and pupils, faced with uncertain futures of their own, no longer accord schools the moral legitimacy which in a previous age could mostly be taken for granted. (Fitz, Power and Halpin, 1996: 4)

Thus, schools are faced with uncertainty and are required to manage risk in circumstances where their freedom to act without the constraints of LEAs is matched by the LEAs' diminished capacity to plan futures for schools or assist them if and when they are overtaken by turbulence or terminal crisis. Schools are expected to act like enterprises in the private sector but they also face the same problems of survival. And all the existing research on the impact of the 1988 Act suggests that schools are prepared to plot and scheme to preserve their 'market share' (for example, Fitz, Halpin and Power, 1993; Gewirtz, Ball and Bowe, 1995; Woods, Bagley and Glatter, 1998).

Manufactured uncertainty arising out of institutional reform has had an important effect not only on the culture of schools but also on their relationship with surrounding communities. Some GM schools, for example, changed their admissions procedures with relative ease, to become more academically selective but without consulting communities which traditionally used them as the 'local' secondary school. Others moved in the direction of 'cherry picking', selecting highly motivated students from across the ability bands whose parents were able to decode and willing to sign up to the schools' preferred missions and codes of conduct (Halpin, Power and Fitz, 1997a; Pennell and West, 1995).

The schools' interpretation of the market and their choice of survival strategies have to be located within an understanding that competition was imposed on an existing order of things in which some schools were more highly valued than others. The stratification of education has long been associated with, and determined by, a class structure in the UK, which has employed education as an element of social and cultural reproduction. In official discourse, at least, the curriculum and pedagogic modes employed by the independent and selective schools in the education of, predominantly, the upper and middle classes, are those most closely associated with a 'good education'. Some schools then enjoyed initial advantages in the newly created market, and have sought to sustain them. Others, and most notably GM schools, because they have had the greater capacity to recast themselves, have increasingly moved towards this model (Halpin, Power and Fitz, 1997a).

'Manufactured uncertainty', then, provides schools with choices. There are alternative futures, there is potential to project new educational identities, and indeed some schools, the CTCs, are obligated to move in this direction. I suggest, however that institutional reform has contributed to a retreat into the past. Schools have become risk-averse, opting, we argue, for safe, conventional images, curriculum, pedagogies and pupil identities. In a period of risk and uncertainty what is observed is the reinvention of 'tradition' and 'traditionalism' as a market strategy (Halpin, Power and Fitz, 1997b; Fitz, Halpin and Power, 1997a).

It can be argued that educational markets in Wales are somewhat different from those in England. For example, the independent sector in Wales is less prominent than its English counterpart; the latter educates about 8 per cent of students compared with less than 2 per cent in Wales. There are no CTCs in Wales and GM schools account for about 1 per cent of students in the maintained sector compared with about 4 per cent in England. Only one maintained school (GM) selects students on the basis of academic ability compared with the 166 grammar schools in England. On the other hand, in Wales, the market includes a choice for parents between Welsh- and English-medium schools and, under measures promoted by Welsh Secretary John Redwood's 'Popular Schools Initiative', funds were made available for 'popular' or oversubscribed schools to expand their accommodation in order to admit more students.

These local features establish the extent to which education markets in Wales are local and different from, say, the urban areas of England. In some respects, however, empirical work on educational markets in Wales remains relatively thin. For example, there is no published evidenced-based research on GM schools policy in Wales which would adequately account for its poor showing, nothing on the absence of CTCs and no studies of the impact of the Popular Schools Initiative. On the basis of small-scale comparative research conducted in Cardiff and Bristol, there is evidence though that 'manufactured uncertainty' applies to maintained schools in urban south Wales as well as in England. Maintained schools in Wales are equally concerned about the long-term future; they are concerned about their performance in public examinations and how these will be interpreted by parents. They are also conscious of and concerned about attracting students who perform well academically. There is no evidence yet on the relative effects of market principles on schools and their operation in the more rural areas of Wales nor of the extent to which 'manufactured uncertainty' impacts on the organization, curriculum and admissions policies in rural schools.

Compulsory individualization

In his analysis of the lineaments of the modern social order Beck identifies individualization as one of its key features (Beck, 1994). Individualization in his terms is used in a precise way to denote: 'first, the disembedding, and second the re-embedding of industrial society ways of life by new ones, in which the individuals must produce, stage and cobble together their biographies themselves' (Beck, 1994: 13). The process of disembedding and re-embedding, he goes on to argue, takes place as the certainties of industrial society disintegrate, to be replaced by new forms, policies and rules of social order (Beck, 1994). But it is not a process subjects freely enter. He argues that people are condemned to individualization. Individualization is a compulsion but a compulsion for manufacture, self-design and self-staging, 'under the overall models of the welfare state, such as the education system (acquiring certificates), the labour market, labour and social law, the housing market and so on' (Beck, 1994: 14).

As individuals create new styles, networks and biographies, they are required to take risks and acquire new responsibilities. Drawing on Beck's conceptual analysis of globalization, risk and individualization, it can be argued that compulsory individualization is the obverse of manufactured uncertainty. The marketization of institutional forms correspondingly requires individuals, whether they wish to or not, to make selections between forms of public service which formerly were provided in the context of a network of a local, connected, planned system of provision. Not that choice did not exist previously, rather, the aggregate of choices now has the capacity to reshape or destroy local institutional forms. Moreover, people are not only required to choose, they are also compulsorily expected to be responsible, in ways unspecified, for the choices they make. This was most certainly the position of parents in the order of things set out in the Education Acts of 1988 and 1993 and in the last Conservative government's 1996 White Paper proposals which specifically laid emphasis on 'choice and diversity'.

One of the effects of open enrolment is that parents may select any school in the state sector, providing it has the physical capacity to accommodate their children, whether this school lies within their own local authority or not. Parents have been re-embedded in circumstances where they are required to undertake a complex process of decoding what will be a good education for the child, what time and financial resources they can devote to getting children to and from school and in devising strategies to secure the school of their choice (see Gewirtz, Ball and Bowe, 1995). They are also expected to bear the burden of responsibility if they make the 'wrong' choice. And part of this responsibility lies in compulsory individualization, in the creation of biographies and identities which match the selection criteria of schools, especially popular or oversubscribed schools. This is borne out in research on school choice in the post-1988 context. British research has argued that while some parents have the financial, cultural and educational resources to decode what the education market means, to devise strategies and to construct identities to achieve their educational goals, others do not or cannot (Gewirtz, Ball and Bowe, 1995; Pennell and West, 1995; Reay 1995; Gorard 1997; Glatter, Woods and Bagley, 1997 and Woods, Bagley and Glatter, 1998). There is now strong evidence to show that those advantages probably operate only in the short term (Gorard and Fitz, 1998a).

The relatively small amount of school choice research conducted in Wales tends to support a view that compulsory individualization applies in Wales as well as in England, but with a territorial twist. The existence of Welsh-medium schools adds a further dimension in that parents have some degree of choice in what linguistic and cultural contexts they will educate their children and, therefore, what forms of educational identities will be given prominence.

It remains the case that circumstances where individuals compete for scarce resources historically militate against the construction of

forms of schooling dedicated to the provision of education appropriate to community needs, collectively defined. The process assists in
taking forward the competitive agenda at the heart manufactured
uncertainty. Moreover, re-embedding parents as customers or
consumers of education renders the schools themselves vulnerable
to parentally determined policies and pedagogic programmes. Thus,
for example, child-centred pedagogies are under attack, in official
discourse, the media, and via middle-class families exerting pressure directly on schools (see Reay, 1995).

Redefining pedagogic authority

Perhaps the most striking and potentially far-reaching consequences
of institutional reform run somewhat counter to the trends we have
so far identified. First, there has been a transformation of the state
both in terms of institutional arrangements and an increase in the
capacity that this new ensemble has to regulate the various activities
of schools. There has been the creation of a *meso-state*: non-
elected, ministerially appointed agencies, responsible for the
provision of aspects of education, social and welfare services. They
are accountable upwards to ministers but have no clear lines of
accountability downward, to citizens and electors. In England the
funding of GM schools, and progressively, of LEA schools was
determined by the Funding Agency for Schools (FAS). Teacher
education is decided by the TTA, while the QCA monitors the
National Curriculum (NC) and the national testing of students. Her
Majesty's Inspectorate (HMI) in England and Wales has been
succeeded by, respectively, the Office for Standards in Education
(OFSTED) and the Office of Her Majesty's Chief Inspector of
Schools (OHMCI) as the agencies responsible for the inspection of
schools and teacher education.

There has been, then, a proliferation of what might called in
Bernstein's terms official pedagogic (re)contextualizing agencies
(Bernstein, 1990, 1996), each concerned with a specific domain of
education policy and practice. Inevitably, there has been an increase
in the 'noise' as educational policy-making has been reconstituted,
and as institutions have been repositioned. The prominence of the
co-ordinating role of Prime Minister and his policy unit alongside
the Education Secretary and the DfEE is one of the key features to
emerge from these changes. Whatever the prevailing state of play,
it is now clear that the central state has established a formidable

institutional complex with which to regulate curriculum and pedagogic practices in schools. Central direction is conducted through:

(a) A National Curriculum (NC) which all maintained schools are required to teach, and associated testing procedures, in which children undertake national tests at ages 7, 11 and 14.
(b) Inspection, on a four-year cycle in England and a five-year cycle in Wales, by OFSTED in England and OHMCI in Wales. Inspection reports are available to parents.
(c) Guidance on pedagogy, mainly a strong steer to adopt a more teacher-centred approach to classroom transmission, via government-sponsored reports and by increasingly interventionist programmes such as the national literacy and numeracy strategies in England. (HMCI, 1995; DfEE, 1998)

There is strong evidence that educational professionals have challenged, subverted and adapted centrally generated curriculum and pedagogic policies and indeed have buffered students from the worst effects of the assessment policy (Ball, 1994; Gipps, Brown, McCallum and McAllister, 1995; Pollard, Broadfoot, Croll, Osborne and Abbott, 1994). Nevertheless, theirs is primarily a response to an agenda and to a dominant official discourse emanating from the centre. The wider implications of the central regulation of education, however, are to be found in the range of educational identities that are projected in the combination of curriculum, pedagogic and inspection policy.

In general terms the educational identities constructed in and through the NC, the inspection process and pedagogic guidance correspond with what Bernstein calls retrospective identities: 'These . . . are shaped by national, religious or cultural grand narratives recontextualized to stabilise a past in the future . . . With these identities the collective base is foregrounded much more than the exchange value of the identity' (Bernstein, 1996: 411). In this respect, though there are important differences between England and Wales in terms of what constitutes the NC, the English version emphasizes a subject-based curriculum, the insistence that Shakespeare and other writers in the 'canon' be taught in NC English, that history should be about statecraft and the dissemination of British (read English) traditions, the requirement that schools will be inspected on students' spiritual, social, moral and cultural development (evidence of which in part will be a daily collective act of religious worship, broadly Christian in character), and a steer towards strong framing in classrooms can be interpreted as the revitalization of nationalism and traditionalism. Alongside this, however, the government has attempted to foster modernization, via the inclusion of technology as a NC subject and has invited schools to adopt a technology focus through the Technology Schools Initiative (TSI) (Fitz, Halpin and Power, 1997a). It can be argued that many of these fundamental principles also operate in Wales. Children in Wales, however, have progressively been given the opportunity to explore their own national identity via curriculum programmes which introduce them to Welsh, Welsh history, geography, literature and music – the Curriculum Cymreig. These are important departures from England's NC and may well prove vitally important in the claim for building distinctive programmes of teaching, learning and assessment in and for Wales.

The trend towards the regulation of education, via meso-level agencies, applies in Wales. Not all English meso-level institutions have Welsh counterparts. A case in point here is the FAS. The funding of GM schools took place through the Welsh Office while the planning and provision of schools remained the province of LEAs, unlike in England where the FAS had a role now in a number of local authorities. There are territorial differences also regarding the introduction of the TTA and the National Literacy and Numeracy Strategies (DfEE, 1998, 1999). For example, while the centrally defined and closely prescribed specifications of the national literacy and numeracy strategies are being implemented in England, schools in Wales are being offered more general guidance on ways of developing pupils' literacy and numeracy. The local view, though, that these, in reality, are no more than English creations imposed on Wales, was summed up by one delegate at a conference on education policy in Wales, who made plea that such agencies should be rather more than sub-Post Office branches of the one in London.

There is some evidence that these territorial agencies have developed policies, values and operations somewhat different from the English counterparts. The schools' inspectorate in Wales (OHMCI) is one notable example. All maintained schools in Wales are subject to full inspections, on a fixed cycle, conducted by contracted teams of inspectors led by a registered inspector. The contracting process, quality monitoring and the interpretation and reporting of inspection data upwards to the policy-makers remains the responsibility of HMI, OHMCI's professional officers. This mode of inspection is very similar to that in operation in England. In most respects then, inspection processes, purposes and effects are very similar. Indeed, the framework documents, upon which inspections criteria and judgements are based, were written primarily by HMI in England.

Local adjustments were made in response to OHMCI's assessment of what would work best in the Welsh context. To reduce pressures on small schools it was decided that the inspection cycle would be every five and not four years. In addition, HMI still undertake section 10 inspections and they are also able to scrutinize and follow up school responses to inspection reports. Teachers in Wales are graded on a five–point scale, compared with seven points in England and grades at either end of the scale are notified to heads orally and not in writing as in England. One notable contrast also is the care that successive chief inspectors have taken to report positive aspects of the performance of schools and have avoided the headline-grabbing spin of their English counterpart's sharp criticism of teachers. The gentler touch may well reflect the longer involvement of the territorial inspectorate in offering direct advice to schools aimed at increasing schooling effectiveness and improvement. Nevertheless, it remains the case that inspection in Wales is very different, say, from the system in Scotland and, in most key respects, resembles that in England (see also chapter 8 by Thomas and Egan).

Standards-driven reform
This development has a somewhat longer history in Wales than in England. Since the publication of the Loosemore Report in 1981, one policy thrust in Wales has been the determination that levels of attainment in schools should at least match those achieved in England. That refrain is to be found in later policy programmes such as *A Bright Future* (Welsh Office, 1995, 1997a), *Building Excellent Schools Together* (Welsh Office, 1997b) and the Education and Training Action Group for Wales (ETAGW) Report (1998). The discourse of these documents is founded on claims that children in Wales perform less well than children in England and that its schools are less effective than similar schools in England. The 'schooled to fail' myth has been finally laid to rest in some

powerful research by Gorard (1998, and chapter 7 below). The 'underachievement' claim, though, gave successive Welsh Secretaries a powerful lever to argue for school effectiveness and improvement policies designed to drive up school performance. It also enabled them to sidestep policies which might have involved some form of wealth and income redistribution, or policies aimed at changing the social mix of schools. A similar strategy can be observed under the present Labour administration.

At the national level, the School Standards and Effectiveness Unit of the DfEE is emblematic of the government's main policy direction. In England, in association with their LEAs, schools are now required to set targets for attainment in public examinations. The top–down approach is not so evident in the implementation of target setting in Wales, where schools were invited to establish their own targets which were then modified where necessary by LEAs and then agreed by the WO. Target setting in both contexts has to be set alongside the threat of 'zero tolerance' for schools deemed to be 'complacent' or underachieving. Responsibility for raising standards then lies with school and with teachers. Little attempt has thus far been made to address the external factors which four decades of research suggest have a determining effect on student performance. Centrally determined standards, performance indicators and sanctions have become powerful policy levers to make schools accountable upwards to the centre and measures through which the scale and pace of pedagogic change can be regulated. There are acknowledged variations in how these operate territorially, and these variations are important, but it can be argued that the mode of governance embedded in these policies operates in Wales to much the same degree as in England.

On the arguments presented above, what has been witnessed in Wales over the past decade or so has been a new form of regulation by successive national governments. This, it can be argued, has two elements: regulation via markets and regulation through the state. It is not difficult to overlook how market forms, whether these operate in the wealth-creating or the public-sector arenas, act as constraints on the ensemble of relations into which actors and agencies may enter and on the values which are esteemed. Competition, choice and diversity in education then motivate schools and parents to act in ways which are not always necessarily self-seeking but they nevertheless limit the kinds of relations these schools and communities have with each other.

Moreover, in a situation of 'manufactured uncertainty', it is difficult to consider what counts as a 'good education' outside the quantum of test results and school reputation.

The creation of self-managing schools which enjoy different degrees of autonomy from LEAs is an arrangement which head-teachers and other members of the teaching profession would seek to defend on the basis of efficiency gains. That has to be set alongside the corollary of the diminished powers elected local authorities have to plan and provide a coherent local system responsive to local needs. Schools still have some powers to change the goalposts on admissions policies, student grouping practices, and curriculum and assessment initiatives without consultation with LEAs or indeed with the communities with which the schools are associated. It has yet to be demonstrated that schools in Wales act differently from those in England. My own small-scale studies suggest they do not. The combination of the struggle for institutional survival and surveillance and regulation via performance indicators, inspections and tough sanctions ensures a considerable alignment in management strategies and pedagogic practice between schools.

In a very perceptive article on the devolution of management (DMS) to Scottish secondary schools, McPherson in 1989 suggested that the proposed education reforms, including DMS, amounted to 'social engineering', 'designed to stimulate, and later perhaps consolidate an accelerating programme of economic and social change' (McPherson, 1989: 87). The aim of educational and other social legislation, he argued, was to engineer a society of increasing opportunity, but not of equality of opportunity, a smaller state but not necessarily a less powerful state, and to craft a permanent electoral majority for the Conservative Party (1989: 92). While he was not wholly right about electoral politics, he went on to add a new and rarely reported dimension to the decentralization debate, namely that the 1988 and subsequent legislation constrains the further development of separate and different systems of education in Scotland. The same analysis can be applied to Wales. What McPherson reminds us is that we are not simply addressing here issues of institutional and administrative arrangements but also their capacity to structure opportunities, shape expectations and embed particular values.

Conclusions

On the analysis presented above, two broad conclusions can be drawn. The first relates to the tasks facing the policy community in Wales. The second relates to the work ahead for policy researchers. From the arguments presented above, the capacities and resources of the recontextualizing agencies in Wales are demonstrably weak. For the most part, the big picture of restructuring the public sector has been replicated in Wales. The mode of governance which combines market regulation, disciplines and values alongside a powerful and an increasingly interventionist state is as much in evidence in Wales as it is in England. The centrally determined focus on standards and the strategies devised to raise these operate territorially as well as nationally. Putting aside the impact of poverty on patterns of educational opportunity and achievement, and emphasizing instead the importance of school-related factors in the quest for higher levels of performance, is as well advanced in Wales as in England. At the moment then, the meso-level recontext-ualizing agencies are unable or unwilling to identify and promote alternative strategies or provide new visions of a future. This is the level where an elected assembly could have some impact and relatively quickly.

The other feature of the mode of governance may well be more difficult to address primarily because of its appeal to educational professionals. They will, I believe, not give up easily the idea of self-managing schools. The research evidence points in the direction of heads and teachers not wishing to return to the days of pre-1988 LEA control. Many would urge, though, an expanded role for LEAs, both in terms of their planning functions and in their capacity to support schools responding to curriculum development and change. The other key components of 'manufactured uncertainty', choice, per capita funding and, relatedly, school-based admissions policies, do have a considerable impact on how schools organize themselves and on how they relate to each other and the wider community. The relationship between choice, competition and high standards quite simply remains unproven. That schools spend valuable resources on promoting themselves and cultivating reputations designed to attract parents of particular kinds of students, however, has been well documented. If we follow research evidence about policies which have increased opportunities for all students, then the way forward here is in the direction of academically balanced intakes in schools across local systems, and away from streaming and setting, at least in primary schools and in the non-examination years in secondary schools. Such policies are unlikely to be popular either with schools or with parents who have invested heavily, in different ways, in the opposite direction.

This leads on to the second conclusion and the place of research. Phillips and Sanders are right to argue for more policy research in Wales (chapter 1, above). Policies with a strong Welsh dimension – the local response to GM schools, the absence of CTCs and the impact of the Popular Schools Initiative, for example – do need further investigation. Moreover, for all the assertions, I am not aware yet of any study of the pedagogy of Welsh-medium schools which is underpinned by a robust theory of the kind proposed, say, by Bernstein, which identifies what works and what does not and what has more general application.

There is a larger task, though, and that is to alert the policy community that our research focus and commitment will never correspond with theirs. For sure, evidence will emerge which will be directly helpful to them, in terms of providing data about the relative benefits of this or that policy, and may well be of assistance in the determination of new ways forward. From a researcher's point of view, however, it remains the case that the policy-makers and policy processes are also legitimate and important areas of disinterested study. By comparison with our colleagues in Scotland and England this is an area that remains underdeveloped and in which much work remains to be done.

References

Ball, S. J. (1994) *Education Reform: A Critical and Post-structural Approach.* Buckingham: Open University Press.

Ball, S. J. and Bowe, R. (1992) Subject departments and the implementation of the National Curriculum: an overview of the issues. *Journal of Curriculum Studies*, 24(2), 97–115.

Beck, U. (1994) The reinvention of politics: towards a theory of reflexive modernisation. In U. Beck, A. Giddens and S. Lash (eds.), *Reflexive Modernisation.* Cambridge: Polity Press.

Bernstein, B. (1990) *The Structuring of Pedagogic Discourse.* London: Routledge.

Bernstein, B. (1996) *Pedagogy, Symbolic Control and Identity: Theory, Research and Critique*. London: Taylor & Francis.

Department for Education and Employment and Welsh Office (1996) *Self-Government for Schools*. London: HMSO.

Department for Education and Employment (1997) *Excellence in Schools*. London: DfEE.

Department for Education and Employment (1998) *The National Literacy Strategy*. London: DfEE.

Department for Education and Employment, (1999) 'The Standards Site' @, http//:www.standards.dfee.gov.uk/library/publications/development.

Education and Training Action Group for Wales (1998) *An Education and Training Action Plan for Wales: A Draft for Consultation*. Cardiff: Manweb PLC.

Edwards, T., Fitz, J. and Whitty, G. (1989) *The State and Private Education: An Evaluation of the Assisted Places Scheme*. Basingstoke: Falmer.

Ferlie, E., Asburner, L., Fitzgerald, L. and Pettigrew, A. (1996) *The New Public Management in Action*. Oxford: Oxford University Press.

Firestone, W. A. (1989) Educational policy as an ecology of games. *Educational Researcher*, 18(7), 18–24.

Firestone, W. A., Winter, J. and Fitz, J. (2000) Different assessments, common practice? Mathematics testing and teaching in the United States and England and Wales, *Assessment in Education*, 7(1), 13–37.

Fitz, J. and Lee, J. (1996) The fields of inspection. Unpublished paper, presented at the British Educational Association Annual Conference, Lancaster, September.

Fitz, J., Firestone, W. A. and Fairman, J. (2000) Local leaders: local education authorities, schools and policy implementation. In K. Riley and K. Seashore Louis (eds.), *Leadership for a Change*. London: Falmer Press.

Fitz, J., Halpin, D. and Power, S. (1993) *Grant-Maintained Schools: Education in the Market Place*. London: Kogan Page.

Fitz, J., Halpin, D. and Power, S. (1997a) Between a rock and a hard place: diversity, institutional autonomy and grant maintained schools. *Oxford Review of Education*, 23(1), 17–30.

Fitz, J., Halpin, D. and Power, S. (1997b) The limits of educational reform in the UK: the case of grant-maintained schools. *International Studies in Educational Administration*, 25(1), 60–7.

Fitz, J., Power, S. and Halpin, D. (1996) School autonomy as a policy instrument: the case of grant-maintained schools. Unpublished paper presented to the British Educational Association Conference, Lancaster, September.

Flude, M. and Hammer M. (eds.) (1990) *The Education Reform Act, 1988:*

Its Origins and Implications. London: Falmer.

Foucault, M. (1977) *Discipline and Punishment, the Birth of the Prison*. Harmondsworth: Penguin Books.

Gamble, A. (1988) *The Free Economy and the Strong State: The Politics of Thatcherism*. London: Macmillan.

Gewirtz S., Ball S. and Bowe R. (1995) *Markets, Choice and Equity in Education*. Buckingham: Open University Press.

Giddens, A. (1994) Living in a post-traditional society. in U. Beck, A. Giddens and S. Lash (eds.), *Reflexive Modernisation*. Cambridge: Polity Press.

Gipps, C., Brown, M., McCallum B. and McAllister, S. (1995) *Intuition or Evidence?* Buckingham: Open University Press.

Glatter R., Woods P. A. and Bagley C. (eds.) (1997) *Choice and Diversity in Schooling: Problems and Prospects*. London: Routledge.

Gorard, S. (1997) *School Choice in an Established Market*. Aldershot: Ashgate.

Gorard, S. (1998) Schooled to fail? Revisiting the Welsh school effect. *Journal of Education Policy*, 13, 115–24.

Gorard, S. and Fitz, J. (1998a) The more things change . . . the missing impact of marketization. *British Journal of Sociology of Education*, 19(3), 365–76.

Gorard, S. and Fitz, J. (1998b) Under starter's orders: the established market, the Cardiff study and the Smithfield project. *International Studies in the Sociology of Education*, 8(3).

Gray, J., McPherson, A. and Raffe, D. (1984) *Reconstruction of Secondary Education: Theory, Myth and Practice since the War*. London and Boston, MA: Routledge & Kegan Paul.

Halpin, D., Fitz, J. and Power, S. (1994) Self-governance, grant-maintained schools and educational identities. Unpublished Economic and Social Research Council end of award report (R00233911501).

Halpin, D., Power, S. and Fitz, J. (1997a) Opting into the past? Grant-maintained schools and the reinvention of tradition. In R. Glatter, P. A. Woods and C. Bagley (eds.), *Choice and Diversity in Schooling: Perspectives and Prospects*. London: Routledge.

Halpin, D., Power, S. and Fitz, J. (1997b) In the grip of the past? Tradition, traditionalism and contemporary schooling. *International Studies in the Sociology of Education*, 7(1), 3–19.

Hardman, J. and Levačić, R. (1997) The impact of competition on secondary schools. In R. Glatter, P. A. Woods and C. Bagley (eds.), *Choice and Diversity in Schooling: Problems and Prospects*. London: Routledge.

HMCI (1995) *Annual Report of Her Majesty's Chief Inspector of Schools: Standards and Quality in Education 1993/4*. London: HMSO.

Hood, C. (1991) A new public management for all seasons? *Public*

Administration, 69 (Spring), 3–19.

John, P. (1998) *Analysing Public Policy.* London and New York: Pinter.

Lee, J. and Fitz, J. (1998) Inspection for improvement: whose responsibility? *Journal of In-service Education,* 24(2), 239–53.

Maclure, S. (1988) *Education Re-formed.* London: Hodder & Stoughton.

Maclure, S. (1998) Through the revolution and out the other side. *Oxford Review of Education,* 24(1), 5–24.

McPherson, A. (1989) Social and political aspects of the devolved management of Scottish secondary schools. *Scottish Journal of Education,* 21(2), 87–100.

Offe, C. (1984) *Contradictions of the Welfare State.* London: Hutchinson.

Pennell, H. and West, A. (1995) *Changing Schools: Secondary Schools' Admissions Policies in Inner London in 1995.* Clare Market Papers, 9. CRE: London School of Economics.

Pierson, C. (1998) The new governance of education: the conservatives and education 1988–1997. *Oxford Review of Education,* 24(1), 131–42.

Pollard, A., Broadfoot, P., Croll, P., Osborne, M. and Abbott, D. (1994) *Changing English Primary Schools?* London: Cassell.

Raffe, D. (1998) Does learning begin at home? The use of 'home' international comparisons in UK policy making. *Journal of Education Policy,* 13(5), 591–602.

Reay, D. (1995) Contextualizing choice: social power and parental involvement. *British Educational Research Journal,* 22, 581–96.

Rees, G. (1997) The educational policy process in Wales. Unpublished paper, presented to the Scottish Educational Forum seminar, Educational Policy Processes of the UK, Edinburgh, October.

Reynolds, D. (1989) The wasted years: education in Wales, 1979–89. *Welsh Journal of Education,* 1(1), 39–46.

Rhodes, R. A. W. (1997) *Understanding Governance.* Buckingham: Open University Press.

Steinmo, S., Thelen, S. and Longstreth, F. (eds.) (1992) *Structuring Politics.* Cambridge: Cambridge University Press.

Welsh Office (1995) *A Bright Future: Getting the Best for Every Pupil in Wales.* Cardiff: HMSO.

Welsh Office (1997a) *A Bright Future: Beating the Previous Best.* Cardiff: Welsh Office.

Welsh Office (1997b) *Building Excellent Schools Together.* Cardiff: HMSO.

Whitty, G., Power, S. and Halpin, D. (1998) *Devolution and Choice in Education: The School, the State and the Market.* Buckingham: Open University Press.

Woods, P., Bagley, C. and Glatter, R. (1998) *School Choice: Markets in the Public Interest?* London: Routledge.

II
Curriculum and Assessment

3

Policy-Making in Welsh Education: A Historical Perspective, 1889–1988

GARETH ELWYN JONES

Introduction

In the summer of 1997 the government published a White Paper, *Building Excellent Schools Together*, which applied only to Wales. This was unprecedented and a reminder that only once in the history of Wales has there been an Act of Parliament devoted to meeting Welsh educational needs alone. It is a reminder, too, that an understanding of the Welsh Intermediate Education Act of 1889, along with intervening devolutionary measures, is relevant to analysis of present-day devolutionary processes in education. For example, its passing provided almost unprecedented recognition in modern times of Wales as a national community. It was overtly a class measure in a Victorian society which openly acknowledged the class structure of education in a way which governments have become increasingly reluctant to do, though it remains entrenched. Also, the class underpinnings of the curriculum were taken for granted and can the more easily be analysed. Why should this acknowledgement of the separate needs of Wales have come about and why should other pressures towards Welsh educational independence have punctuated our history since that time? This exploration will be in three chronological sections.

From 1889 to the end of the First World War

An analysis of the political forces at work in 1889, and the social imperatives which impelled recognition of Welsh needs, provides a significant pointer to the way in which policies have developed in Wales subsequently. It is, of course, a truism to point out that the

Welsh Intermediate Education Act was a political measure possible only with the consent of both Houses of Parliament. Such treatment of Wales was a break with the tradition of centuries. After the Acts of Union in the sixteenth century, Wales as a separate legal and political entity had virtually ceased to exist. The state which exercised political power over the people of Wales was that of 'England and Wales'. Of course, the political structure changed over the centuries, particularly as modifications to the economic base fed through into the politics of the state. The most dramatic example was the impact of the industrial revolution in the nineteenth century.

Gradually, the new wealth of industry influenced the political system, and accompanying demographic and employment patterns produced new pressures. Eventually, and very tentatively, this was reflected in greater democratization. The 1867 Reform Act nearly doubled the size of the electorate. With the 1884 Reform Act a majority of men, at least, had a vote by secret ballot. At more local level, there had also been greater democratization, largely through the school boards. These changes at local and national level provided some means for the popular will to be expressed, however entrenched the forces of traditional society – especially the landed aristocratic influence – still were.

The history of state education points up as dramatically as any aspect of government the way in which the popular will is filtered not only through politicians who interpret it in a representative democracy, but also, and crucially, the bureaucracy which administers subsequent policies. The history of civil service manipulation of the education system according to its own priorities and prejudices is a window into class attitudes and occupational prejudices. Two outstanding examples are provided by Sir Robert Morant in the early twentieth century and Sir Maurice Holmes in the 1940s (Simon, 1965; Gosden, 1976). Welsh education provides an even more interesting case study. Clashes between the Welsh Department and the parent body occurred regularly and, indeed, are still inevitable. While the Welsh Office (National Assembly) Education Department can occasionally win a battle, it has never yet won a war over the parent department in Whitehall.

Then, as now, there were pressure groups of varying effectiveness, with the religious bodies being among the most significant in terms of education policy and legislation. Governments had to be extremely wary of channelling state funds into education without the consent of religious leaders and there was a fundamental complication because of the intense rivalry between the Church of England and the Nonconformist denominations. In this respect, of course, the Welsh situation was particularly complex because of its considerable Nonconformist majority.

We sometimes forget, indeed in some quarters it has been fashionable to forget, that the ideas which resulted in change were articulated by individuals. Whatever wider forces were at work in the second half of the nineteenth century there still had to be leaders and channellers of public opinion who could exert political pressure. An excellent example in Wales was Hugh Owen, who imbibed contemporary idealistic opinion which preached that social stability and well-being could only be achieved when there was a harmonious relationship between the individual and the community, which included the national community of the state (Webster, 1990). To Owen, this communal cement was provided by a well-informed middle class for whom there were so few formal educational opportunities in Wales. The state must intervene.

This brief background comment can only begin to reflect the complexities of educational policy-making in late nineteenth-century Wales, with its communal and class connotations. Even so, it is a necessary reminder that the remarkable legislation of 1889, and subsequent changes, were – and are – the result of layer upon layer of argument, influence, bargaining and the exercise of power by diktat. Traditional historiography has often oversimplified the processes of educational legislation and policy-making, then and now. On the other hand, I believe that modern policy analysis can sometimes be based on too formulaic a structure, leaving too little scope for the role of the individual, opportunism and sheer accident.

The complexities of policy- and decision-making emerge in full measure in the legislation of 1889. There had been one Act of Parliament only since the sixteenth century – if we exclude the Cromwellian era – which had applied solely to Wales and seemed to provide separate treatment. But the 1881 Act which provided for Sunday closing of public houses in Wales must be seen in the context of a parliamentary vote in 1880 which endorsed local options. The Welsh Intermediate Education Act was a far more dramatic testimony to what might be achieved if the kind of individual, social and political interplay to which I have referred coalesced in an expression of national will. It has happened rarely in Wales but it is possible.

In so many ways it was a paradigm for future principles and tactics for those with the educational interests of Wales at heart. The Act recognized the existence of Wales in law. It recognized distinctive Welsh educational needs. It involved the newly created local authorities in the planning of education through their part in joint education committees. It channelled government money into state secondary education, not only surmounting traditional Treasury opposition to spending money in general but also in creating a precedent for doing so in England. It was, as Webster said, 'an astonishing achievement' (1990: 12).

Why should this have come about against the odds? The shortcomings in Welsh secondary education provision, particularly since the establishment of the University of Wales in Aberystwyth in 1872, had become impossible to ignore. There was an insufficient supply of students with an education adequate for a conventional university course. There was especially derisory provision of grammar-school education in those counties which had experienced such dramatic industrial and demographic growth. Welsh politics may have become overwhelmingly Liberal but all the political parties in Wales were now campaigning for an injection of state funds into Welsh secondary and higher education.

The Aberdare Report of 1881, out of which the 1889 Act grew, stressed the lack of adequate secondary education in Wales, which was only highlighted in a particular economic and social context. That social context not only decreed that an educational catalyst for ensuring the production of a Welsh middle class was essential, but also that particular kinds of schools were necessary to ensure this. The Aberdare Committee recommended three types of schools following the strict hierarchy of the Taunton Commission of 1868: first grade schools preparing pupils for Oxford and Cambridge, second grade schools preparing pupils for the Welsh university colleges and higher elementary schools for working-class pupils in the industrial areas.

By 1882, therefore, there was a blueprint in existence for the restructuring of school and university education in Wales, though it was a long way from here to the passing of the necessary legislation. Although university colleges were soon established (Williams, 1993, 1997), the prospects for intermediate schools were less promising. Treasury opposition seemed insurmountable, despite the fervent support of the Victorian version of an Education Minister, A. J. Mundella (Allsobrook, 1989). Even so, intermediate education in Wales remained a major concern of the increasingly vociferous Welsh Parliamentary Party and, interestingly, a Conservative government ceded ground. Then, historical accident meant that, with the creation of county councils after the Act of 1888, a relatively uncontroversial method of control existed.

What we have then, in 1889, is a case study of how education in Wales can be shaped. Economic and social forces create the environment, as do contemporary views on class and culture, but these have to be articulated and realized in a specific institutional context. That in turn is subject to the usual individual and bureaucratic political decisions which can themselves be influenced by varieties of pressure-group politicking.

At that point individual leaders of Welsh opinion, Sir Arthur Acland, Sir Henry Jones and T. E. Ellis, all steeped in Idealist philosophy and also particularly sympathetic to Welsh cultural and communal traditions, provided the template for development of the county schemes. Anxious to ensure coherence, they convened a conference of all the north Wales joint committees, later extended to all the Welsh counties (Webster, 1990). Similarly, by manipulating the county schemes, Acland brought about the creation of the Central Welsh Board which became a national institution in Wales (Evans, 1997). Here was an example of an unplanned devolutionary measure arising out of the creation of distinctive Welsh state secondary schools.

Welsh cultural nationalism, a strong-running tide at the time, spurred further changes. Drafts of the intermediate education bill had included a Board of Education for Wales, but it proved politically unacceptable. A similar fate awaited more grandiose plans for a National Council for Education for Wales which had the backing of Lloyd George but got nowhere in the turbulent wake of the 1902 Education Act and its bitter aftermath in Wales. Even so, the Liberal government in 1907 did provide one of the most significant devolutionary measures of the first half of the twentieth century when it created the Welsh Department of the Board of Education. It would appear, therefore, that in this fusion of long-term trends and an immediately favourable political climate an education system relevant to Welsh needs had been created, along with a concomitant system of controls which represented Welsh cultural achievement against a background of unparalleled economic vibrancy. But the waters now become particularly muddy. In this most favourable of climates, in the context of a dramatically revived cultural nationalism we would expect these new Welsh schools, and indeed colleges, to reflect these prevailing cultural values of language and heritage in their curriculum. This is precisely what did not happen.

So what shaped the curriculum of the new schools, if not the Act (Allsobrook, 1990)? Following the practice of the time, the Act laid down the parameters but the formula of Latin, Greek, modern languages, mathematics and science was supplemented by catch-all phrases such as 'the higher branches of knowledge'. The fact that schools could also benefit from the Technical Instruction Act of the same year meant that, in Webster's phrase, 'within such a framework almost any subject was possible' (1990: 22).

In the end, the county schemes made only English, mathematics, Latin, a foreign language, natural science, vocal music and drill compulsory. Welsh was optional and there was no great demand for it to be compulsory. There was also a whole range of optional practical and technical subjects. We have only to look at the range of examination subjects offered at School Certificate level by the Central Welsh Board (CWB) to see that, for example, metalwork or dairywork were on offer but had very few takers. The Welsh intermediate schools, once in existence, were moulded less by government than by contemporary views on the way in which social class should be reflected in the content of education and this content, in turn, determined status. At the school level, such thinking found expression in the policies of headmasters – there were few headmistresses – who inevitably wanted the highest status for their schools and therefore endorsed those subjects which would ensure this. Parents, insofar as they had a voice, were of similar mind because their objective for their children, particularly boys, was a secure, non-manual job to which the best route was the traditional academic curriculum. So the pattern was set for the academic curriculum of what, in institutional terms, have been the most Welsh of schools in our history. It was certainly not a curriculum which was Welsh in language or in culture (Jones, 1982).

War brought no diminution of devolutionary zeal, but with a different emphasis. In the middle of the war, with government apprehension about the perceived shortcomings of British technical education at its height, a commission was set up under Lord Haldane to investigate the University in Wales. In 1916, when the commission began its work, Wales was of central importance to the British economy, both in coal-mining and in metallurgical industries. The commission saw Wales as an economic entity and regarded it as axiomatic that the kind of education provided by the University of Wales was vitally important for the well-being of the Welsh economy. Evidence to the commission indicated that neither the University nor industrialists were sufficiently aware of this mutual responsibility. There was some positive result in that Swansea Technical College, with close contacts with local metallurgical industries, at last got its university status in 1920. The irony was that, under the impact of the Depression, by the outbreak of the Second World War there were more arts graduates from Swansea than science (Williams, 1997). Even so, with the creation of the School of Mines in 1912 and the links which Cardiff's University College had with technical colleges in Cardiff, Swansea and Newport, the Commission was able to recommend a university board of technology for Wales. It did not come about. In 1918 A. T. Davies, Permanent Secretary at the Welsh Department, used the commission as an excuse to press Lloyd George to create a national body in Wales to co-ordinate elementary, technical, secondary and university education – the Welsh Department writ large, of course. The idea got nowhere. The significant point is that such a body was discussed at the highest levels of government on three occasions between 1887 and 1918.

The perennial rivalry between central and local government, not to mention the ambitions of the University of Wales, ensured that no unified national control of the education system came about. In 1916 the CWB tried to seize the initiative from the Welsh Department in its misleadingly titled *Referendum*. Two proposals were for a Parliamentary Secretary for Wales and a Council of Education for Wales. The latter kept alive the proposal in the 1906 bill and the public backing given by Lloyd George to Welsh educational autonomy in 1913. The tragedy was that the two national educational bodies in Wales saw themselves as embryonic national councils and were at each others' throats.

The inter-war period

Against a background of economic disaster for much of the inter-war period, parents and pupils in Welsh schools and colleges were preoccupied with survival. The attention of their political masters, if it strayed to Wales at all, was centred on how to alleviate the worst forms of distress and, in the later 1930s, to begin a modest restructuring of Welsh industry.

At the same time it is easy to underrate the devolutionary measures which regularly punctuated the period. It is true that the Welsh Department of the Board of Education continued to operate at a considerable distance from Wales, and after 1920 lost not only the dynamic of Sir Owen Edwards but his post of chief inspector as well. The major initiative of the Welsh Department to implement a multilateral pattern of schooling was brushed aside imperiously by the Board of Education. Yet there was regular recognition of the distinctive needs of Wales.

What becomes interesting is the nature of perceptions of the Welsh dimension in this completely changed economic and political context. In political terms the great Liberal radical causes of the late nineteenth century either had come to fruition or were of no consequence in dramatically different economic circumstances. Radicalism in Wales was increasingly the preserve of the Labour Party. But the stark reality was that there was to be no Liberal government in this period and only two short-lived and ill-fated Labour governments. In terms of school reorganization, therefore, there was little change despite the 1926 Hadow Report which served to reinforce the stratification of education and its class underpinning. Nor was there any radical rethinking of the curriculum which differentiated the schools and continued in large measure to be controlled by central government. When the Welsh Department of the Board of Education was forced by the Hadow Report to consider ways of reorganizing secondary education it was impelled to the radical conclusion that the only way to adapt successfully in rural Wales was to establish common secondary schools. The Board of Education showed precisely where power in the system lay by ensuring that this proposal got nowhere. Radicalism in educational policy in Wales did emerge from time to time in the ideas of people like W. G. Cove, MP for Aberavon, and some of the biggest local authorities strove to maximize educational opportunity for the mass of young people, but the main concern was to protect the school system in circumstances in which central government was intent on cutting back on costs (Jones, 1982).

Stressing only the negatives, prominent as they were, is distorting. The Welsh education structure remained distinctive and government recognized this distinction more directly than is the case now. For example, in July 1919, Fisher, president of the Board of Education, set up a departmental committee to be chaired by the Hon. W. N. Bruce, to

> inquire into the organisation of secondary education in Wales, and to advise how it may be consolidated and co-ordinated with other branches of education with a view to the establishment of a National system of public education in Wales, regard being had to the provisions of the Education Act, 1918, and to the recommendations of the Royal Commission on University education in Wales ... (*Report*, 1920a)

There could be no more explicit acknowledgement by central government that national control of education in Wales was a realistic goal.

The committee investigated the burning issues of the moment such as examinations, inspection and the shortfall of places in the secondary schools. But the most significant conclusion from our point of view is that the committee's report recommended yet again the establishment of a National Council of Education in Wales, with the majority of members to be drawn from local authorities. The Council would take over the responsibilities of the CWB and the Court of the University of Wales. Its remit beyond this was fascinating. Admittedly the report referred to the proposed council's 'advisory and deliberative role', but it was intended, within broad guidelines laid down by the Board of Education, to be responsible for 'the framing and administration of regulations for secondary schools', the conduct of school examinations and to have a role in implementing a unified inspectorate for Wales.

Soon after the end of the First World War, therefore, the relationship between the coalition government and Wales in terms of education was similar to that which had developed under the pre-war Liberal government. It caused no stir that Wales should have its own government-sponsored investigation into secondary education. The call for a National Council to run all education in Wales, though it did not come about, was still part of the official discourse. Central government also recognized that, when wider issues were discussed, Wales deserved separate treatment. In the Young Report into scholarships and free places, published in 1920, there was a section devoted specifically to Wales (*Report*, 1920b). The achievements of 1889 and 1907 are too often seen in isolation. The Bruce and Young Reports between them provided an exciting blueprint for a specifically Welsh education to be developed after the war, both administratively and in terms of school development. They provide a glimpse of what might have been.

Of course, the agenda changed during the remainder of the inter-war period for economic, social and political reasons which are too well known to rehearse here. But even in these adverse circumstances, recognition of specifically Welsh educational needs, and some administrative obeisance towards them, did not stop. The reasons again have a bearing on developments to our own time. First, once bodies like the Welsh Department are created they have a life of their own and ambitions to expand their empires. Second, and underpinning this, there continued to be distinctive needs in Wales, associated for example with school organization and the Welsh language, as well as the enormous strains on the system consequent on the special circumstances in Wales of the Depression.

What did change in this new climate was concern with the nature of the curriculum in Welsh schools. The humanist curriculum of the secondary school became even more of a symbol of escape from the industrial and agricultural collapse which now beset the Welsh economy. But individuals matter in systems. With the death of Sir Owen Edwards in 1920 Wales lost an educationalist with a vision, if a contentious one. His post was combined with that of Permanent Secretary. Neither A. T. Davies nor his successors showed any interest in the curriculum except in so far as it impinged on the authority of the Welsh Department.

Inevitably, the focus of concern over what constituted a Welsh education changed, but it was no less potent an issue. For example, it was the theme of Walter Jones's presidential address to the Welsh Secondary Schools Association in 1926 in which he argued that the stress on secondary school success had resulted in schools in Wales being indistinguishable from those in England. He was concerned not only at the neglect of the Welsh language in school but also at the low priority given to Welsh history and the Welsh heritage (Jones, 1926). For the first time there was serious research into bilingualism, though its findings were not what we would now term 'politically correct'. Welsh was still the first language of a very substantial minority of pupils – over a third of the population of Wales spoke Welsh – while the education which they received was almost wholly through the medium of English. One of the initiatives planned by the Welsh Department in 1923 was the establishment of a departmental committee into bilingualism, prompted both by the University of Wales and the Central Welsh Board. This was one of the rare occasions in Welsh educational history when educational research had a direct impact on policy, because recent work seemed to indicate that bilingualism had an adverse effect on what was termed 'mental development'. That a departmental committee might come up with the same conclusions – politically unacceptable – gave the Welsh Department considerable qualms. The result was that an inquiry into bilingualism turned into an inquiry into the place of the Welsh language in education and the means by which its study might best be promoted. What is so significant, though, is that no sooner had one major investigation been completed than another was instituted. In 1927 Lord Eustace Percy, President of the Board of Education, set up a departmental committee of enquiry into education in rural Wales – and how best to meet the needs of a general education, rural industries, business and professions and life in a rural community. Here was another major policy initiative, and a reminder that the poverty of rural Wales was, if anything, more insidious in its effects on education than the more dramatic deprivation of industrial Wales in the inter-war period.

It is true that the practical effects of these reports were limited indeed compared with the impact of central government economies. When, in 1932, the government replaced free places with special places in the secondary schools, a policy which could hardly have been less popular across much of Wales, it was implemented by a separately numbered Welsh circular – a form of play-acting which has continued. Here was the perennial modern paradox of the Welsh situation, a circular emanating from the Welsh Department which provoked a national outcry. Even so, the reports represented highly significant government recognition of the special needs of Wales. With unemployment in Wales rising to 31.2 per cent in 1930 there was recognition also of the disaster of industrial Wales and in that year the Board of Education instigated an inquiry into the educational problems of the south Wales coalfield, published in the following year. This was eventually complemented by the establishment of two nominated bodies, an advisory council on technical education in south Wales and one for north Wales.

The idea of a National Council for Education in Wales was not dead. The pressure groups responsible were the Central Welsh Board, the Federation of Education Authorities and the University of Wales, and a representative delegation met the President of the Board of Education in 1927. Percy offered, or rather offered to consider, a Welsh Advisory Council to advise him on matters concerning Welsh education. This was rejected. The Welsh Department was not best pleased at the offer. Two years later there was a parliamentary initiative, when a bill was presented in the House of Commons proposing a National Council. The problem was that neither of the main protagonists, Llewellyn Jones and Megan Lloyd George, had any political clout. The main difference in the inter-war period was that, while ideas on increasing Welsh educational autonomy were by no means dead, Wales was no longer of any great political account, except as an economic and social problem. So a pattern began to emerge with which we are very familiar. There were educational initiatives which applied solely to Wales. There was incremental, creeping devolution. There were political gestures. Economic disaster in rural and industrial Wales promoted specific interest in education's inter-relationship with the regional economy. But the macro-economic and political climate was such that on major issues of policy, for example, the structure of secondary education, Wales had neither the power nor perhaps the energy to create the kind of furore which accompanied the 1902 legislation.

From 1944 to 1988

It is well known that the Second World War quickly prompted theories as to how the education system should adapt to the new society which would emerge (Gosden, 1976; Lowe, 1988). The responses in Wales now followed an established pattern. The Welsh Secondary Schools Association wanted reformed education for adolescents. The CWB wanted a National Council for Education –

and a Secretary of State for Wales. The Welsh Teachers' Union wanted special treatment for Wales in any education bill – and a system of multilateral schools. A number of Welsh Members of Parliament pressed for the Welsh Department to be transferred to Wales to carry out there all those duties normally undertaken by the Board of Education. Of course, Board of Education officials reacted with classic civil service obfuscation, stressing all the reasons why this was impractical. But, as seems to the the way with devolution, a minor concession emerged: the Permanent Secretary would meet local authorities in Wales and not drag them to Bournemouth, to which the Welsh Department, with the Board, had been evacuated. This changed practice very little, but it altered perceptions since it was now put about that the Welsh Department would conduct its business in Wales, a myth which had some potency. In the broader political spectrum, positions had changed. The Welsh Labour Party was at one with the Federation of Education Committees in wanting a Secretary of State for Wales. The new President of the Board of Education, R. A. Butler, was totally opposed and was considering only an Advisory Council for Wales in the 1944 legislation, along- *misleading* side those for England and Scotland. When Butler met a delegation from the CWB, the Federation of Education Committees and the University he easily diverted talk of national independence for Welsh education into acceptance of the idea of a nominated central advisory council. There is nothing new about nominated bodies influencing Welsh education. This advisory council, comprising ten teachers, ten local authority and governing body representatives and ten others was to be the nearest thing to a Welsh educational voice for many years, and then sporadically and at the whim of central government. Some consolatory powers were reserved for the Welsh Joint Education Committee, created in 1949, including the functions of the north and south Wales advisory committees on technical education.

From 1944 to the mid-1980s the matter of independence of control for Welsh education paradoxically assumed a lower profile than it had since the late nineteenth century, for two main reasons. First, the impotence of the Welsh in matters educational was demonstrated as conclusively as ever in the wake of the 1944 Education Act but with scarcely any political fall-out, either nation- ally or locally. The 1944 Act was welcomed in Wales because it coincided with Welsh priorities such as free secondary education

(Jones, 1990). What the Welsh public was unaware of was the power struggle between the larger local authorities and the Labour government over the structure of secondary education. Only the development plan files, available since the mid-1980s, have revealed how bitter were these struggles and how powerful the armoury of central government and civil servants in imposing a system of grammar/secondary modern schools in Wales.

Second, in unprecedented fashion, power over the detail of school organization and curriculum was diffused from central government to local authorities and teachers. With the coming of comprehensive education, and the consequent disappearance of the eleven-plus examination, freedom in the primary and lower secondary schools reached its apogee. It was not long, of course, before the backlash of the mid-1970s, but for a heady period the Welshness of education had to be fought for on more minor fronts. Indeed, most of the energy towards any Welsh distinctiveness was channelled into the movement for Welsh-language schools and consequent negotiations with local authorities. There was unprecedented growth in the provision of Welsh-language education, of course, and the Welsh Department took as much credit as it decently could. It is in these contexts that devolutionary increments of the period must be seen. Their significance not so much immediate as in having potential for action when central government once more asserted its authority over the education system.

What were these devolutionary steps? Under the 1944 Act Wales got its Central Advisory Council. It did some sterling work but its limitations were quickly apparent. In 1949 there was a report on the future of secondary education in Wales. Like its Scottish counterpart the Council advocated multilateral and bilateral schools, and justified them on grounds of Welsh communal solidarity (CACW, 1949). Unlike its Scottish counterpart, its schemes were almost wholly abortive. Best known of its reports was that produced in 1967 on primary education in Wales, known as the Gittins Report (CACEW, 1967). Here was a significant acknowledgement of both the different kinds of problems which confronted primary schools in Wales and of the administrative division epitomized in the existence of the Council. What we do not know is how much freedom of manœuvre was available to the Welsh Committee in coming to conclusions which, in teaching philosophy, were very similar to those of the associated Plowden Report.

Then, when the Schools Council was created in 1964, there was some recognition of the separate curricular needs of Wales with the establishment of the Committee for Wales. However, one of the most significant omissions in the work of the Schools Council was an investigation of the whole school curriculum, in Wales. It was not that the Committee had nothing to say. In 1974, it produced an excellent discussion paper on the nature of a Welsh curriculum, but this was the era of the curricular 'secret garden' and any hint of forced entry would have been counterproductive. So the same fate awaited this document as had befallen that excellent statement of Welsh curricular priorities published by the Welsh department of the Ministry of Education in 1953 (Jones, 1997).

In retrospect the most significant devolution was administrative. The publicity accorded to the evacuation of the Welsh Department of the Board of Education to Bournemouth during the war had its impact. Two years after the end of the war the Welsh Department opened a permanent office in Cardiff. Five years later 80 per cent of Welsh department work was transferred to Cardiff. The year before the creation of the Welsh Office the permanent secretary of the Welsh Department took up office in Cardiff. The creation of a Secretary of State for Wales in 1964 was of immense significance – six years later responsibility for all primary and secondary education functions in Wales was vested in that office.

Of course, there were still no powers of primary or secondary law-making; nor was there any national democratic accountability within Wales. But as the grip of central government tightened in its reassertion of control over the curriculum and organization of schools in a process which continues to the present day, the existence of a WO Education Department, with its own civil servants and an associated Welsh inspectorate, provided more avenues than previously for pressure groups to influence this process. Precedent also decreed that when the Central Advisory Councils atrophied and the Schools Council was killed off, the new instrument of government control, the Schools Curriculum and Assessment Authority, should be paralleled by the Curriculum Council for Wales (CCW).

A century after the Welsh Intermediate Education Act of 1889, Kenneth Baker's Education Reform Act of 1988 proved to be, in wholly different form, another watershed in the history of Welsh education. The way in which that most important of Acts, for Wales as for England, was made to apply in the special circumstances of Wales indicates that little had changed in the catalogue of influences which are brought to bear on education policy-making. Wales had no say over policy at the macro level. The twin policy prongs of a NC and its assessment, together with local management of schools, owed nothing to input from Wales; but because the Act reasserted state control over the detail of school organization and curriculum unequivocally, however dressed up in the rhetoric of the market, the institutions of government in Wales assumed a new degree of importance.

State control has not only continued but has been inexorably extended, a process which showed no sign of diminution with the change of government in 1997. Given the scale and scope of legislation, government inquiries and the responsibilities of quangos, the involvement of government appointees and civil servants in the education process is more significant than at any time since the war. Pressure-group influence has diversified rather than diminished, extending now to such bodies as teacher unions, subject associations and parents of pupils in Welsh-language schools, as well as a 'think tank' like the Institute for Welsh Affairs. The 1988 Act and its aftermath have demonstrated that the cocktail of control has not changed in essence, however much the mix may have been modified. Power lies overwhelmingly with central government, though it has chosen occasionally to disperse fractions of it. In this dispersion the Welsh voice has been heard both institutionally, in the CCW and its successor, and through individuals like (Sir) Wyn Roberts, but never statutorily. The mix allowed relatively enlightened policies for Welsh education from 1988 to 1992, then imposed some wholly inappropriate ones. Since 1997 the lottery of party and individual combination has been emphasized by the new Minister of State implementing policies which have emphasized a distinctive Welsh educational system. We would do well to remember that such individual concern with the needs of Wales is not unprecedented. That it may not this time be so easily cast aside as in some previous Welsh Office regimes will be due to an entirely new element in the system of control, the National Assembly.

References

Allsobrook, D. (1989) A benevolent prophet of old. *Welsh Journal of Education*, 1(1), 1–9.

Allsobrook, D. (1990) Technical education in Wales: influences and attitudes. In O. E. Jones (ed.), *The Welsh Intermediate Education Act of 1889: A Centenary Appraisal*. Cardiff: Welsh Office, pp. 27–42.

Central Advisory Council (Wales) (1949) *The Future of Secondary Education in Wales*. Cardiff: HMSO.

Central Advisory Council for Education (Wales) (1967) *Primary Education in Wales*. Cardiff: HMSO.

Evans, W. G. (1997) *An Elected National Body for Wales: The Centenary of the Central Welsh Board*. Cardiff: WJEC.

Gosden, P. H. J. H. (1976) *Education in the Second World War*. London: Methuen.

Hadow Report (1926) *The Education of the Adolescent: Report of the Consultative Committee*. London: HMSO.

Jones, G. E. (1982) *Controls and Conflicts in Welsh Secondary Education, 1889–1944*. Cardiff: University of Wales Press.

Jones, G. E. (1990) *Which Nation's Schools? Direction and Devolution in Welsh Secondary Education*. Cardiff: University of Wales Press.

Jones, G. E. (1997) *The Education of a Nation*. Cardiff: University of Wales Press.

Jones, W. (1926) Presidential Address. *Welsh Secondary Schools Review*, 13(1), 8.

Lowe, R. (1988) *Education in the Post-War Years*. London: Routledge.

Report (1920a) *Report of the Departmental Committee on the Organisation of Secondary Education in Wales*. London: HMSO.

Report (1920b) *Report of the Departmental Committee on Scholarships and Free Places*. London: HMSO.

Simon, B. (1965) *Education and the Labour Movement, 1870–1920*. London: Lawrence & Wishart.

Webster, J. R. (1990) The Welsh Intermediate Education Act of 1889. In O. E. Jones (ed.), *The Welsh Intermediate Education Act of 1889: A Centenary Appraisal*. Cardiff: Welsh Office, pp. 12–26.

Williams, J. G. (1993) *The University Movement in Wales*. Cardiff: University of Wales Press.

Williams, J. G. (1997) *The University of Wales, 1893–1939*. Cardiff: University of Wales Press.

4

The Impact of the National Curriculum upon Primary Education in Wales

THEO COX

Introduction

This chapter presents research findings concerning the impact of the National Curriculum (NC) upon primary education in Wales, drawing in particular on the author's own longitudinal study of the views of class teachers and headteachers in a representative sample of primary and infant schools in a south Wales LEA. It also presents findings from other research studies carried out in England and Wales, and official reports concerning the implementation and review of the NC. Selected curricular, pedagogical and policy issues arising from the research are briefly discussed.

The passing of the Education Reform Act (ERA) in 1988 marked a strikingly new phase in British state education characterized by the reassertion of central government control of the content of the curriculum across the five to sixteen year age range. This was coupled with a deliberate weakening of the powers of local government in education, through the enforced delegation of their responsibilities to schools.

A major element in the ERA was the introduction of a statutory NC and its associated assessment framework for all pupils between the ages of five and sixteen in state schools in England and Wales. This curriculum was broken down into eleven subjects in Wales, comprising 'core subjects' (English, mathematics, science and Welsh in schools teaching through that medium) and 'non-core' foundation subjects (design/technology, history, geography, art, music, physical education and Welsh, in schools where it is not a core subject).

For each subject a set of statutory attainment targets was specified and a national programme of assessment of the targets in the core subjects was instituted, through a combination of standard assessment tasks (SATs) and teacher assessment. The specification of curriculum content in each subject was in the form of programmes of study. The NC and its assessment framework was couched in terms of four key stages of learning, with Key Stages 1 and 2 covering the primary school stage (five to eleven years).

After a brief period for consultation with teachers and others, the NC was introduced into all state primary, junior and infant schools from September 1989 for Year 1, Key Stage 1 pupils, with a staged introduction of the curriculum at the later key stages in subsequent years. In 1993, following overwhelming evidence of the unmanageability of the NC, especially at Key Stages 1 and 2, which was produced by HMI and other bodies, the government commissioned Sir Ron Dearing to carry out a wholesale review of the NC and its assessment in England, with a view to streamlining and simplifying it. A parallel revision was carried out in Wales by the then Curriculum Council for Wales (CCW). Both reviews were remarkable for the emphasis they placed upon consultation with teachers and others, with the aim of tapping their experience and views of the NC. For example, in addition to the formal consultation procedures via questionnaires to schools and specially convened meetings arranged by the curriculum bodies in England and Wales, Sir Ron Dearing openly invited readers' responses to a series of articles on the NC and related matters which he published in the *Times Educational Supplement* in the autumn of 1993 (see Dearing, 1993, for the first of these). In Wales the review process was divided into four main age phases, each phase involving consultation with teachers and others involved in education in Wales. Reports on this work were published by the CCW in July 1993 and December 1993, and by the curriculum and assessment body which replaced it, the Curriculum and Assessment Authority for Wales (ACAC), in September 1994.

Dearing's (1994) final recommendations for the revision of the NC in England, and those for Wales (CCW, 1993), were accepted by the government. This led to a more detailed review of the content and assessment of each NC subject by the curriculum bodies for England and Wales respectively, the main aims of which were to focus the curriculum requirements on the essentials of each non-core foundation subject in order to improve their manageability and to give primary teachers more time to concentrate on the teaching of the 'basic skills' of literacy and numeracy. A further aim was to set higher attainment standards, especially in key aspects of the core subjects. Following a further process of consultation the final curriculum recommendations of the School Curriculum and Assessment Authority (SCAA) in England, and of ACAC in Wales, were accepted by the government and revised orders for the NC came into force on 1 August 1995 for Key Stages 1–3. Also, in keeping with Sir Ron Dearing's recommendation, a five-year moratorium on any further change in the NC was declared, with the aim of ensuring that teachers enjoyed a period of stability in which to implement it.

While endorsing the present NC the Labour government elected in 1997, in its White Papers for England (DfEE, 1997) and Wales (Welsh Office, 1997a) respectively, argued that it needed to be more sharply focused on giving all children a 'proper grounding in the basics within a broad and balanced curriculum' (DfEE, 1997: 22). Accordingly it asked SCAA's successor, the Qualifications and Curriculum Authority (QCA), and ACAC's successor, the Qualifications and Curriculum Authority for Wales (ACCAC), to examine how a sharper focus on literacy and numeracy in primary schools could be achieved. It also set in train, through these two bodies, a full review of the NC to take effect from the year 2000.

The distinctiveness of the National Curriculum in Wales

There are certain differences between the NC in Wales from that in England which, taken together, constitute a distinctive Welsh dimension or Curriculum Cymreig (see CCW, 1991). The most important of these is the fact that, in Wales, the Welsh language is an additional subject, either core or non-core, depending upon the cultural and linguistic orientation of the particular school. This of course means that the curriculum load imposed by the NC is significantly greater in Wales than in England. In addition four non-core subjects, history, geography, art and music, have subject orders which are distinctive to Wales and contribute to the Curriculum Cymreig. The NC assessment framework is broadly the same in both countries.

It is interesting to note that an interim review of the present NC, with regard to the period September 1998 to August 2000, was conducted in different ways in Wales and England. In the latter case the Secretary of State for Education simply suspended the subject orders for the six core foundation subjects in order to give teachers more scope to concentrate on teaching the basic skills, whilst still 'having regard to' the orders for the non-core subjects. This decision was endorsed in the subsequent statutory consultations with teachers and others carried out by the QCA. In Wales, however, the Secretary of State put forward several alternative proposals for the required review, only one of which involved a suspension of the non-core subject orders, and these were duly considered by teachers and others through ACCAC consultation procedures. The consultation led that body to recommend to the Secretary of State that certain parts of the subject orders be retained in their statutory form whilst other specified parts could be regarded as optional by teachers. This recommendation, subsequently accepted by the Secretary of State, appears to have been guided by a desire to protect the Welsh dimension of the NC and also to ensure curricular continuity and progression between Key Stage 2 and subsequent stages. It appears from this that, at least in regard to the interim review, teachers and others involved in education in Wales played a greater part in the decision-making than their counterparts in England.

Research on the impact of the National Curriculum on primary education in Wales

There appears to have been relatively little systematic or sustained research on the impact of the NC upon primary education in Wales, in contrast to England, where the Primary Assessment and Curriculum Experience (PACE) Project has been conducted, at Key Stages 1 and 2, at the Universities of Bristol and the West of England (Pollard et al., 1994, Croll, 1996). Also the 'National Assessment in Primary Schools: an Evaluation (NAPS) Project' has studied teachers' assessment practices in primary schools in England (see Gipps et al., 1995). In addition, as part of the Leverhulme Primary Project carried out at the University of Exeter, a questionnaire survey of the views of teachers on the NC was carried out in 1989 (Wragg et al., 1989). Although the sample for this survey included teachers in Wales, the results of this were not presented separately for teachers in England and Wales.

In Wales itself some reports concerning the ongoing implementation of the NC and the views of teachers and other interested parties have been published by the curriculum agencies for Wales and also by the schools inspectorate in Wales (OHMCI), based upon their own surveys and school inspections. For example, the OHMCI published a report describing and evaluating practices in classroom organization, teaching methods and leadership in primary schools in Wales, in relation to the NC, based upon school inspections and visits and a special survey of a sample of schools (OHMCI, 1994). However, such studies have not generally been based upon controlled sampling or research procedures.

The Swansea University Impact Study

A research study carried out by the present author studied the views of headteachers and Year 1 class teachers in a controlled sample of primary and infant schools in one LEA in south Wales. The study, carried out in the spring and summer terms 1994, was a follow-up phase to an original study of the impact of the NC on the teaching of five year olds carried out from 1989 to 1991, that is, during the initial stage of the introduction of the NC into primary schools. The aim of that study was to obtain the views of primary headteachers and Year 1 class teachers on the NC and how it was working. For convenience the study in both phases will be referred to as the 'Swansea University Impact Study'.

Early implementation (1989–1991)
In the original study evidence was drawn from a random sample of twenty-six primary and infant schools (approximately one school in five) in a south Wales LEA. The sample was judged to be representative of the LEA schools in terms of size, ranging from fewer than 100 pupils to over 400 pupils, and social catchment area, ranging from middle class to lower working class. The geographical area of the study was predominantly urban but included some rural areas containing well-established village communities. Two of the schools were voluntary aided, with the rest being state maintained. In two schools teaching was conducted through the medium of Welsh at

Key Stage 1, one of them being an officially designated Welsh-medium school. In both of these schools Welsh was taught as a core subject rather than a non-core foundation subject, as in the remaining schools.

Interviews of the headteachers and Year 1 class teachers, those teaching children in Year 1 of the NC (aged five to six years), were carried out by the Project's research officer, an experienced primary teacher. These were based upon questionnaires, with separate versions for head and class teachers. Interviews were conducted during the summer terms of 1989 and 1990, that is, spanning the first year of implementation of the NC, and teachers in the sample were asked to complete a short written follow-up questionnaire in the summer of 1991. In 1989 the sample comprised twenty-six head teachers and thirty-one class teachers.

Full details of the findings of this study can be found in Cox and Sanders (1994) but the main conclusions were as follows:

1. While there was a general welcome by the teachers for the clear planning framework provided by the NC, this was offset by their widespread concern at its overloaded nature, with the sheer number of attainment targets threatening the depth and quality of children's learning.

2. Teachers at Key Stage 1 reported a significant increase in their workloads following the introduction of the new curriculum and a strong feeling of being under constant pressure to meet the many attainment targets relevant to their pupils. They believed this pressure to be adversely affecting the teaching of slower learners and also of children under five, because of a reduction in their opportunities for play-based, experiential learning.

3. The assessment and record-keeping requirements of the NC were a major focus of the concerns of the class teachers and head-teachers alike, because of the demands they made upon the time and managerial skills of class teachers at the expense of their teaching time. This deep concern was coupled with a view of the majority of teachers that the formal assessment of children's educational attainments at age seven was educationally unsound.

4. Teachers' use of cross-curricular, topic-based work changed over the period of the research. Topic work became more structured to take in as much of the NC as possible. Topics became more focused with a trend toward science-led topics. There was also

something of a move away from cross-curricular work, even at this key stage.

Follow-up study (1994)

A follow-up extension to the original study was carried out in 1994, five years after the introduction of the NC at Key Stage 1, in order to monitor any changes in the views of the teachers about the working of the new curriculum. Twenty-three of the original twenty-six schools agreed to take part, providing a sample of twenty-three headteachers and thirty Year 1 class teachers. Ten of the headteachers had taken part in the original study but only nine of the original thirty-one class teachers took part in the follow-up. As before, the teachers' views were gathered through structured interviews based upon questionnaires circulated to the schools beforehand.

By the time of the follow-up study the full range of eleven NC subjects had been introduced in Wales, plus religious education. During the summer term all schools and LEAs in Wales were engaged in a consultation exercise mounted by ACAC, as described earlier in this chapter. A full report of the 1994 study can be found in Cox (1996) but the following is a summary of the main findings:

1. Although a majority of headteachers and Year 1 class teachers expressed themselves as 'fairly happy' with the NC, since it provided a helpful planning framework, there was strong criticism of its overloaded content and of the perceived over-emphasis on assessment and record-keeping which was felt to place an undue burden upon class teachers.

2. Teachers anticipated that the forthcoming revision of the NC would reduce pressure on both teachers and children since it would become more manageable and should lead to improved quality of teaching and learning. The burden of assessment and record keeping was also expected to be reduced, releasing more time for teaching the basic skills, which was a major concern of the teachers. Some doubt was expressed by a small number of teachers as to whether the content of the Revised NC, then in draft form, had been suffi-ciently reduced to improve its manageability.

3. Contrary to the trend towards more subject-focused teaching at Key Stage 1, reported during the original study, the evidence from the follow-up study indicated that the balance between

thematic and subject-specific teaching had not shifted in the majority of classes at Key Stage 1, although it appeared to have done so at Key Stage 2.

4. There was some disagreement among headteachers regarding the effects of the NC on children under five. The majority judged that these children had not been noticeably affected but there was a minority view that they had been adversely affected by downward pressure from the NC, resulting in reduced opportunities for free play and in the formalization and tighter teaching control of these children's learning activities. However, the majority of headteachers agreed that there had been a broadening of the curriculum, with more structure, more focused work and more collaborative planning among early years teachers.

The main findings of the 1994 follow-up study largely echoed those of the original study during the introduction of the NC, namely that there was a general welcome among the teachers for the clear planning framework provided by the NC, tempered by their concern about curriculum overload and the perceived over-emphasis upon assessment and record-keeping. The finding that the NC appeared to have brought some curricular benefits for children under five, but at the expense of some loss of flexibility and informality in teaching, and a reduction in such children's opportunities for play-based, experiential learning was also in line with the earlier findings. In these respects, therefore, the teachers' views of the NC in the research sample did not appear to have changed significantly over the five-year study period.

Other studies of the impact of the National Curriculum

The findings of the Swansea University Impact Study are largely in accord with those from the PACE project at the Universities of Bristol and the West of England. This was based on a sample of forty-eight primary schools drawn from eight LEAs in England and covers both Key Stages 1 and 2, using a combination of interviews with teachers and some pupils, written questionnaires for teachers and some classroom observation. The study findings regarding the impact of the NC at Key Stages 1 and 2 are reported in Pollard *et al.* (1994), and Croll (1996), which support those of the Swansea study in showing that the teachers were broadly positive about the NC and appeared to regard it as a worthwhile educational development, particularly with regard to its clarification of teaching aims and the provision of an overall curriculum structure which could facilitate planning for progression.

However, the teachers in the PACE study expressed serious misgivings about particular aspects of the NC, especially its overloaded content and inflexibility which was felt to restrict the teachers' capacity to adapt their teaching to their children's needs. In response to the pressures of the NC, teachers appeared to be adapting by tightening their classroom control and providing more direction to children's activities. Classroom observation showed the dominance of work in English and the preponderance of work in the core subjects, especially English and mathematics. Evidence from the study of whole school changes showed that there was a steady move away from teachers working with their own individual planning systems toward more co-ordinated school approaches, using the structure provided by the NC.

Teachers also showed much concern about aspects of the assessment and record-keeping requirements of the NC as they perceived them, notably their very time-consuming nature and the weight given to formal, summative assessment, which posed a severe challenge to their existing practices and beliefs. Despite this somewhat negative reaction, the study found some evidence for the emergence of improvements in teachers' assessment knowledge and practice as they gained in confidence and learned to mediate the external requirements towards their own professional ends.

Like the PACE and Swansea University studies, the NAPS study (Gipps *et al.*, 1995) found some evidence for negative feelings among a sample of Key Stage 1 primary teachers towards aspects of the NC assessment programme. In particular there was anger and guilt about the publication of test results, feelings of dissonance and alienation because of the perceived invalidity of the testing programme and concern about the impact of testing on young children. However, this negative feeling was strongly offset by the encouraging evidence for a steady improvement in the quality and rigour of the Year 2 teachers' practice and understanding of assessment.

On the question of teachers' views on the proposed revision of the NC in 1994, following the reviews by Dearing and by the

CCW, a report published by ACAC (1994) on the consultations carried out in Wales showed that the majority of primary schools expressed reservations about teaching the statutory curriculum within the recommended time (80 to 85 per cent of available teaching time), especially at Key Stage 2. At Key Stage 1 respondents identified higher expectations of children's performance in English as a particular concern which could result in a disproportionate allocation of time to the subject, thereby affecting the manageability of the whole curriculum. Results from parallel consultations in England were very similar (SCAA, 1994). While individual subjects were judged to be manageable by teachers with particular subject interests, the curriculum as a whole was felt by many primary teachers to be too heavy, particularly at Key Stage 2.

Despite such reservations the annual report of OHMCI in Wales for the year 1995–6 claimed that the schools had welcomed the implementation of the new statutory orders for the NC and asserted that 'The revision has made the NC more manageable and more realistic to teach in the time available' (OHMCI, 1997: 5). The chief inspector also reported improvements in the quality of teaching in primary schools as teachers enhanced their subject knowledge and came to grips with the revised NC. The chief inspector's report for the following year 1996–7 (OHMCI, 1998) asserted that the improvement in the quality of primary teachers' curriculum planning, teaching and assessment and record-keeping had continued. Such improvements appeared to be reflected in raised levels of attainments in literacy and numeracy at Key Stages 1 and 2, according to the judgements of the school inspectorate and also to the recent evidence provided by the NC national assessments in the core subjects in Wales (Welsh Office, 1997a, 1997b, and 1997c).

Discussion

In a discussion of the possible roles of teachers in relation to educational policy, Croll (1996) argues that, far from being mere implementers of centrally formulated educational policies such as the NC, teachers act as policy-makers in practice, that is, the nature of professional activities such as teaching necessarily involves the mediation of policy through professional practice in ways which amount to policy creation. Drawing upon evidence available from the PACE study, he claims that, even in the case of a very tightly constrained policy such as the NC, the policies have been changed in practice in several respects. With regard to curriculum coverage for example, the PACE research team (Pollard *et al.*, 1994) showed that teachers were devoting a higher proportion of time than in the past to the basic subjects of English and maths, even though the explicit aim of the NC was to broaden curriculum coverage. 'Faced with the pressure of covering the programmes of study for the core subjects, teachers responded in a way that, unintentionally, reversed part of the policy' (Croll, 1996: 18, 19). He also claims that the teachers' practical operation of standardized NC assessments had made them less objective and independent measures than the government policy-makers intended.

Whether or not one agrees with Croll's description of such professional practice as policy creation, it is certainly the case that, where centrally imposed policies are seen to be in opposition to the existing educational ideologies and practices of schools and teachers, the implementation of such policies will be influenced to some degree by the latter, especially over a period of time. This was apparent in the Swansea University Impact Study in respect of a number of pedagogical and curricular matters. First, with regard to the practice of cross-curricular teaching, the traditional practice in most primary schools before the NC was to combine the subject-specific teaching of English and mathematics with an approach to curriculum planning and teaching through thematic or topic work which embraced other subjects to a greater or lesser extent, a cross-curricular approach. It appeared that, in the first two or three years of implementing the NC, the schools in the study may have reduced their use of the cross-curricular approach under the pressure of the new subject orders but, by the time of the follow-up phase of the study in 1994, that shift of balance appeared to have been corrected as the teachers became more familiar and confident with those orders. This trend applied more at Key Stage 1 than at Key Stage 2, where it appeared that the cross-curricular approach was proving more difficult to sustain under the greater weight of the science and non-core subject knowledge required at this stage.

The continued adherence to a cross-curricular approach by many teachers in the Swansea study, at least at Key Stage 1, was maintained despite the fact that the NC was conceived and promulgated in the form of separate subjects, each with their own distinctive core of knowledge and skills. Moreover the cross-curricular approach came under strong attack on the grounds that the subject knowledge required by the primary teacher made it unlikely that the generalist teacher would be able to teach all of the subjects to the depth required (Alexander, Rose and Woodhead, 1992). That case, in what came to be known as the report of the 'three wise men', was made in a document commissioned by ministers in England. It is worth noting in the context of education policy in Wales that neither the parallel document from HMI in Wales (1992) nor subsequent annual reports from the OHMCI (for example, OHMCI, 1997) were as critical of a cross-curricular approach to planning and teaching in the primary school.

A study carried out by Maynard (1996) shows how it may be possible to modify primary teachers' professional beliefs and ideologies in a more positive way than by hostile criticism or government fiat. Maynard describes how some primary teachers took part in a research programme of mentoring their Primary PGCE students during their teaching practice placements, and how they gradually appeared to change their attitudes to the status of subject knowledge. Their developing awareness of the key importance of such knowledge challenged their previous adherence to a 'child-centred' philosophy of teaching which did not accord it such status.

The gradual process of reconciling apparently opposing policies by primary teachers was also evident in the Swansea Impact Study with regard to the relation between the NC and the curriculum for children under five, particularly those in infant reception classes. It was found that a minority of teachers and headteachers judged that the quality of the education of their under-fives had been adversely affected by downward pressure from the NC, leading to reduced opportunities for children's free play and the formalization and tighter control of the children's learning activities by their teachers. These concerns received support from an HMI Wales survey of educational provision for under-fives during 1994–5 (OHMCI, 1995). However, at the time of the follow-up phase of the study, some of these headteachers indicated that they had actively resisted these curricular pressures which they saw as threatening the educational needs of these children. The headteacher of a large primary school serving a socially disadvantaged area expressed the following view:

We have made a conscious decision that the National Curriculum will not be introduced into the reception class. In other schools reception children receive a watered down version of the National Curriculum. We adopt an early years approach through structured play. The National Curriculum has compartmentalized things and children don't learn in this way. At first the National Curriculum challenged the confidence of teachers regarding their philosophy but now teachers are taking a more relaxed view of it.

Such a response is a good example of what Broadfoot and Pollard (1996), writing in the context of their PACE study, describe as the successful mediation of change in which teachers feel sufficiently confident in their knowledge, skills and abilities to be able to adapt to imposed changes and to develop practices which accord with their professional values and circumstances.

In the context of this discussion it is interesting to note that the *Desirable Outcomes* policy document produced by ACAC (1996) concerning the education of under-fives makes no explicit link between those educational outcomes and the attainment targets of Key Stage 1 of the NC, in contrast to the equivalent document published by SCAA (1996). It also puts much greater emphasis upon the importance of play in the learning of young children than the latter. This suggests that the statutory body advising the Welsh Office on curriculum policy, ACAC, was more concerned than its counterpart in England, SCAA, to protect the child-centred nature of early years teaching from undesirable pressures from the NC, although the evidence from the Swansea Impact Study indicated that Key Stage 1 primary class teachers and headteachers were more divided on this issue.

Conclusions

In conclusion it appears that, as in England, the introduction of the NC in Wales has had some clear benefits at the primary education stage, including the provision of a clear curriculum planning framework to facilitate progression throughout Key Stages 1 and 2, a considerable expansion of whole school collaboration in curriculum and policy planning between teachers, and the provision of a broadly based curriculum to pupils as a matter of entitlement, although the latter has recently been weakened by the recent interim changes to the NC, especially in England. In addition more recent reports by the schools inspectorate in Wales have attributed the raising of standards of pupil attainment, particularly in the core subjects, to the introduction of the NC (OHMCI, 1997, 1998). However major concerns remain about the manageability of the curriculum in this phase, especially with the even greater emphasis now being placed by the present government upon raising standards of numeracy and literacy, and also the possible narrowing and over-formalization of education during the pre-compulsory years under the influence of the NC.

The NC and its assessment framework, as part of the ERA, were centrally imposed upon schools in England and Wales by the then Conservative government. In its drive to raise educational stan-dards, particularly in the basic skills, the Labour government, elected in 1997, has continued in the same centralist, strongly direc-tive tradition of educational policy-making, for example, in regard to increasing the amount of time to be allocated to the teaching of English and mathematics, and in regard to target setting for schools in these subjects. Although the Labour government extended its use of policy directives to include methods of teaching literacy and numeracy, it was also interesting to note during 1998 another example of the approach to policy issues differing in Wales. Whereas great emphasis was placed in England (though without statutory force to back it) on schools and teachers adopting the methods embodied in national projects on literacy and numeracy (DfEE, 1997), the Welsh Office's way of dealing with the same policy issues relied more on advocating a collaborative approach to the raising of standards (Welsh Office, 1998).

The evidence from the PACE study in England and from the Swansea University Impact study is that the implementation of the centrally imposed NC has been mediated through the professional practices, beliefs and ideologies of the teachers, in ways that may have modified that curriculum in some respects. It is also argued that the adoption by government of a more consultative, less managerial model for the development of educational policies would be more effective in practice, not least because it would recognize teachers' professional status. The conduct of the 1998 statutory consultation in Wales on the proposed changes to the Key Stage 1 and 2 programmes of study for the years 1998 to 2000 provides a good example of a more collaborative and potentially more fruitful approach. Such an approach still allows the government to retain its leadership role in the formulation of policy but it gives greater scope for teachers and others involved in children's education to make meaningful contributions to the process and it is likely to generate a stronger commitment by teachers to effective policy implementation. Bines (1998) argues that, although teachers have accommodated a huge amount of change over the past twenty years, often with enthusiasm and commitment, there is not enough genuinely open discussion of the content and possible outcomes of some policies. In her view (government) policies still seem to be based on the belief that, in the interests of raising standards, teachers, teacher trainers and education authorities need to be told how to do their work. Croll (1996) similarly argues that, given the inevitability of teacher involvement in the practical determination of policy and the difficulties which have arisen from the refusal to consult at a representative level, or respond to teachers' concerns, government may find a partnership model more effective in getting educational change to happen than a model based upon the view of teachers as implementers.

While there have been several instances of primary curriculum policies being framed differently from the equivalent policies in England, the main conclusion to be drawn from the research evidence in Wales is that policy-making is a process in which both policy-makers at a national level and teachers in schools play an active part. Even if, as a consequence of devolution in education policy-making, there is to be an increasingly distinctive policy-making process at the all-Wales level, those who are engaged in the process will need to be aware of the central importance of teachers both in the shaping of policy and in its implementation.

References

ACAC (1994) *The National Curriculum Proposals in Wales: Report on the Consultation, Summer 1994.* Cardiff: ACAC.

ACAC (1996) *Desirable Outcomes for Children's Learning before Compulsory School Age.* Cardiff: ACAC.

Alexander, R., Rose, J. and Woodhead, C. (1992) *Curriculum Organisation and Practice in Primary Schools: A Discussion Paper.* London: HMSO.

Bines, H. (1998) *Times Educational Supplement* (22 May), 15.

Broadfoot, P. and Pollard, A. (1996) Continuity and change in English primary education. In P. Croll (ed.), *Teachers, Pupils and Primary Schooling*. London: Cassell.

CCW (1991) *The Whole Curriculum 5-16 in Wales*. Cardiff: CCW.

CCW (1993) *The National Curriculum and Assessment Framework in Wales: Final Report*. Cardiff: CCW.

Cox, T. (ed.) (1996) *The National Curriculum and the Early Years: Challenges and Opportunities*. London: Falmer Press.

Cox, T. and Sanders, S. (1994) *The Impact of the National Curriculum on the Teaching of Five Year Olds*. London: Falmer Press.

Croll, P. (1996) Practitioners or policy makers? Models of teachers and educational change. In P. Croll (ed.), *Teachers Pupils and Primary Schooling*. London: Cassell.

Dearing R. (1993) Have your say. *Times Educational Supplement* (17 September), 21.

Dearing R. (1994) *The National Curriculum and its Assessment: A Final Report*. London: SCAA.

DfEE (1997) *Excellence in Education* (Cm. 3681). London: HMSO.

Gipps, C., Brown, M., McCallum, B. and McAllister, S. (1995) *Intuition or Evidence? Teachers and National Curriculum Assessment of Seven-Year-Olds*. Buckingham: Open University Press.

HMI (Wales) (1992) *Classroom Organisation and Teaching Methods in Primary Schools in Wales*. Cardiff: Welsh Office.

Maynard, T. (1996) The missing element? Early years teachers' attitudes to subject knowledge. In T. Cox (ed.), *The National Curriculum and the Early Years: Challenges and Opportunities*. London: Falmer Press.

OHMCI (1994) *Classroom Organisation, Teaching Methods and Leadership in Primary Schools in Wales*. Cardiff: HMSO.

OHMCI (1995) *Report by Her Majesty's Inspectors: A Survey of Provision for Under-Fives in the Playgroup and Maintained Sectors in Wales 1994-95*. Cardiff: HMSO.

OHMCI (1997) *Education in Wales: A Summary of the Annual Report of Her Majesty's Chief Inspector of Schools in Wales 1995-96*. Cardiff: HMSO.

OHMCI (1998) *The Annual Report of Her Majesty's Chief Inspector of Schools in Wales 1996-97*. London: HMSO.

Pollard, A., Broadfoot, P., Croll, P., Osborn, M. and Abbot, D. (1994) *Changing English Primary Schools? The Impact of the ERA at Key Stage One*. London: Cassell.

SCAA (1994) *The Review of the National Curriculum: A Report on the 1994 Consultation*. London: School Curriculum and Assessment Authority.

SCAA (1996) *Nursery Education: Desirable Outcomes for Children's Learning on Entry to Compulsory Education.* London: School Curriculum and Assessment Authority.

Welsh Office (1997a) *Building Excellent Schools Together* (Cm. 3701). London: HMSO.

Welsh Office (1997b) *National Curriculum Assessment Results in Wales: 1997. Key Stage 1.* Cardiff: Welsh Office.

Welsh Office (1997c) *National Curriculum Assessment Results in Wales: 1997. Key Stage 2.* Cardiff: Welsh Office.

Welsh Office (1998) *National Year of Reading: Getting Ready.* Cardiff: Welsh Office.

Wragg, E. C., Bennett, S. N. and Carré, C. G. (1989) Primary teachers and the National Curriculum. *Research Papers in Education,* 4, 17–37.

5

National Curriculum Assessment Policies in Wales

RICHARD DAUGHERTY

This chapter reviews how one area of policy, the assessment arrangements linked to a National Curriculum (NC) for schools in Wales, has evolved in the period since the Education Reform Act of 1988. Its focus is on the formulation of policy, concerned more with what Ball (1994) refers to as the contexts of influence and of text production than with the contexts of practice and of outcomes. As in other areas of education policy where the relevant legislative framework is on an England and Wales basis, one question to be explored is the extent to which a distinctive policy process, perhaps leading to distinctive policy outcomes, can evolve in circumstances where the policy agenda is typically set and developed in England. In particular, this chapter examines how policies for assessment of the NC have been developed differently from policies for the curriculum to which the assessment relates.

Theoretical insights into the formulation of education policy can be drawn from policy sociology studies (see chapters 1 and 2). However, account must also be taken of the potential for such studies to be 'both limited and limiting' (Troyna, 1994: 70) and of the need to draw on other approaches to the analysis of policy, in particular from political science and from social administration (Fitz, Halpin and Power, 1994). In their study of policy on school inspections in Wales, in a reference to the article by Phillips (1996a), Fitz and Lee argue (1997a: 4): 'Policy sociology of the kind described by Phillips remains the best proven way of "getting inside" the policy process. But that process is crucially shaped by the rules, regulations, practices and procedures of those institutions.' The analysis in this chapter centres on two types of institution with roles in the policy process, the Welsh Office and the statutory bodies which are responsible for advising the Welsh Office on policy. The Welsh Office is at the centre of the policy-making process in Wales. Whatever the influences on policy formulation may be (from within Wales and from England), formal responsibility for policies on the school curriculum and assessment in Wales during the period under review has rested with the Secretary of State for Wales. An important source of institutional influence is the relevant non-departmental public bodies (NDPBs), popularly known as 'quangos'. They are statutory bodies established by government to advise on specific areas of policy and to be responsible for policy implementation. Several have played their part in policy-making over the period in question.

Following the demise of the Schools Council in 1983, successive governments were concerned to avoid establishing an education quango which, by taking responsibility for both curriculum and assessment policy, might be seen as an over-powerful successor to the Schools Council. Thus, in 1983, separate quangos for curriculum and for assessment were established, each with responsibility for policy in both England and Wales: the School Curriculum Development Committee and the Secondary Examinations Council. When the 1988 Education Reform Act replaced these organizations, the separation of assessment policy from curriculum policy was maintained but the idea that policy advice and implementation in both England and Wales should be the responsibility of a single organization was retained only in relation to assessment. The School Examinations and Assessment Council (SEAC) was the body given statutory responsibilities covering all aspects of school examinations in England and Wales as well as the NC assessment arrangements which were among the other provisions of the 1988 Act. Though assessment policies were still to be dealt with on an England and Wales basis following the 1988 Act, responsibility for advising on curriculum policies in Wales was given to a separate Wales-only quango, the Curriculum Council for Wales (CCW), with statutory duties broadly comparable to those of its counterpart in England, the National Curriculum Council (NCC).

It would be more than five years on from 1988, when the education quangos were once more reconstituted, before Wales would have a statutory body responsible for both curriculum and assessment policies. Only since April 1994 has there been a Curriculum and Assessment Authority for Wales, usually referred to by its Welsh acronym ACAC, in a direct relationship with the Welsh

Office without necessarily any reference at all to the policy advice of its counterpart in England, the School Curriculum and Assessment Authority (SCAA). Yet another change in these institutional structures occurred in 1997 as a consequence of the integration into the work of ACAC and SCAA of duties formerly undertaken by the National Council for Vocational Qualifications (NCVQ). Since October 1997 Wales has had its own Qualifications, Curriculum and Assessment Authority (ACCAC) alongside the Qualifications and Curriculum Authority (QCA) in England.

Education policy-making in Wales

Before narrowing the focus to consider the evolution of assessment policies in Wales since 1988 and, in particular, the role of successive quangos in that evolution, it is necessary to establish in outline the nature of the process of education policy-making in Wales during the period under review.

The key decision-maker was the Secretary of State for Wales, a member of cabinet alongside the minister with equivalent powers in England, the Secretary of State for Education. In practice, to an extent for which empirical evidence is not available, decisions on education policy may well have been taken by a junior minister in the Welsh Office who, like the Secretary of State, had education as one element in a wider brief.

Closest to ministerial decision-making were Welsh Office officials who acted, as civil servants, in support of the process leading up to the taking of decisions. Again, more empirical evidence would be needed than is currently available in order to establish how far that closeness of officials to policy decisions brought with it a substantial influence on the nature of those decisions.

Outside the Welsh Office were the statutory bodies which, because legislation stipulates that they must, ministers were required to consult before arriving at decisions on policy. In this category were not only the education quangos referred to above but also the school inspectorate in Wales, though the formal relationship between inspectorate and the Welsh Office changed after the setting up of OHMCI (Wales) in 1993 (see chapter 8 by Thomas and Egan, below). Quangos with briefs extending beyond education policy, such as the Welsh Language Board, also fall into this category.

Beyond the inner circle of officials, quangos and inspectorate, the sources of influence on policy are many and varied. Some are overt and direct in seeking to shape policy. On any major education policy decision, organizations representing particular constituencies of interest can be expected to present their views. The Welsh Local Government Association (WLGA), the Welsh Joint Education Committee (WJEC) and the teacher associations fall into this category along with many other organizations. In addition, other interest groups and individuals submit their views to the Welsh Office on matters which concern them, either by making use of the statutory consultations which precede many major policy decisions or simply by taking up with ministers and/or officials a matter of immediate concern to them. Finally, and by its nature the most difficult to describe, there is the covert process of lobbying whereby individuals and organizations with informal access to ministers and/or officials will, either in addition to overt lobbying or as an alternative route to influence, make their views known and thus seek to shape policy decisions.

In the absence of research evidence which can throw light on policy formulation within the Welsh Office, it is not easy to go beyond this sketch of how decisions were made and who was involved in making them. However, there are a number of features of the policy process in Wales in the period under review which are sufficiently clear to an observer of that process to be worth noting before proceeding to study one area of policy in greater depth.

The first of these features concerns the decision-makers themselves, ministers in a government which, in education as in any other area of policy, might find it difficult to defend differences in policy which, though relating to different parts of the UK, are associated with the same legislative framework. Since, with the one notable exception of more than a century ago, the Welsh Intermediate Education Act of 1889, all education legislation affecting Wales has been developed as subsections of Acts which are mainly concerned with England, any policy decision relating to Wales has potential echoes for the equivalent policy as it affects England. With a system of collective cabinet responsibility and with ministers in England likely to find their flanks exposed if policy in Wales follows a route which a government's critics in England could use to embarrass it, the scope for independent decision-making on education policy matters by Welsh Office ministers has often seemed to be strictly limited.

The second feature affecting the policy process in Wales is the relative smallness of the Welsh Office as a government department and its place on the periphery, psychologically as well as geographically, of a London-centred civil service. The government department responsible for education policy in England (successively in the period under review, the DES, the DfE and now the DfEE) employs a relatively large number of civil servants, typically grouped so that several officials may be working on the same policy area. In those circumstances and in the different context of policy-making in England, officials in the DES and its successors have been viewed as a distinct source of policy ideas and influence, generating proposals and seeking to ensure that their preferred option finds favour. In contrast, in the different culture of the Welsh Office and with each official required to cover several areas of policy, each of which would have a team working on it in London, the Welsh Office has not been viewed as an initiator and promoter of particular policy options. This is not to suggest that Welsh Office officials are not potentially significant influences on policy decisions but rather to propose that their influence is more likely to be felt in reaction to policy proposals developed elsewhere.

A third feature may, in part, be a consequence of the second. Policy development in England has often seen the schools inspectorate, in addition to being an important source of evidence to guide ministerial decision-making, as a distinct source of policy proposals. This tendency has increased since the establishment of the Office for Standards in Education (OFSTED) as an independent non-ministerial department and has been further emphasized by the predeliction of a particular chief inspector for public pronouncements aimed at promoting a particular personal policy agenda. In contrast, the role of the inspectorate in Wales has been both less public and also less distinct from the department to which its advice is directed. Studies of policy on school inspection by Thomas and Egan (chapter 8) and by Fitz and Lee (1997b) reveal differences between Wales and England in this respect.

A fourth feature worthy of note, as it affects education policy-making in Wales, relates to the lobbying of ministers and officials by organizations and individuals. Insofar as such lobbying is evident to an observer of education policy-making, it would seem that

Welsh Office ministers are subject to fewer external lobbying pressures than are their counterparts in England. From time to time on specific policy issues there has been very public pressure which has received a considerable amount of media attention in Wales. However, the relative lack of a developed lobbying system in Welsh politics, the fact that many of the relevant organizations (including all but one of the teacher associations) are England-based, and the fact many people in Wales respond to the English media are all factors which appear to affect the nature and extent of lobbying on education policy matters in Wales.

Curriculum policy: the main scenario

Any discussion of policy-making in relation to NC assessment arrangements must take account of the main scenario, the policies on the curriculum which those arrangements are intended to assess. Indeed, the broader field of curriculum policy-making in Wales over the period since 1987 is potentially a major field of study in itself. A series of episodes, each concerning an aspect of curriculum policy, has drawn attention to the potential, within the framework of England and Wales, for policies on the curriculum to diverge in Wales.

Even before the Education Reform Bill had completed its passage through parliament, the Welsh Office was beginning to articulate what a NC for Wales might mean when it published its own policy statement (Welsh Office, 1987) on broadly the same lines as that from the DES earlier in the year (DES and WO, 1987) but with short sections dealing with what the authors of that document saw as the distinctiveness of the curriculum in Wales. Over the same period, the Minister of State responsible for education policy in the Welsh Office, Wyn Roberts, has subsequently reported that strenuous efforts were made (including a meeting with the Prime Minister, Margaret Thatcher) to ensure that Welsh would have the status of a core subject in the legislation for a NC.

During 1990 and 1991, pressures were exerted on the Welsh Office with a view to developing a partially distinctive curriculum for the study of history in Wales and to make equivalent but more modest distinctive provision for geography. The process by which distinct subject orders were settled upon in art and music during

1992 and 1993 would also repay study as an example of how Welsh Office ministers have been, under certain circumstances, ready to make policy decisions which lead to educational provisions in Wales differing from the equivalent provisions in England. More broadly, policy decisions during the early 1990s on a Welsh dimension to the whole curriculum of schools in Wales, such as the decision to support the development of a Curriculum Cymreig, from its origins in the CCW's policy statement on *The Whole Curriculum from 5 to 16* (CCW, 1991) through development funding (CCW, 1993) to its status as one of the 'common requirements' in all NC subject orders in Wales since 1995, reveal something of the extent to which the curriculum policy process in Wales has been distinctive.

However, on most curriculum policy matters the Welsh Office has been in an essentially reactive mode, responding to policy initiatives in England in which it had no part and of which it has often been given very little notice. The primary curriculum review of 1992, the review of the English order in the same year and the Dearing review of the overall framework in 1993 all reveal something of how the policy process in Wales reacts when responding to high-profile initiatives which have no necessary relevance to the situation in Wales but into which, since the policy agenda is an England and Wales one, Wales finds itself drawn.

Academic studies of these rich pastures for those interested in education policy in Wales have been few in number, offering an overview of trends (Jones, 1994; Jones, G., 1997) or some insights into policy implementation (Jones and Lewis, 1995; Cox, in chapter 4 above) rather than focusing on policy formulation. There are a few notable exceptions to that generalization, including Elfed-Owens's thesis (1996) tracing the development of the Curriculum Cymreig and work by Evans and his colleagues (1997) on physical education and nationalism in Wales. For the most part, those interested in education policy in Wales have had to content themselves with incidental evidence drawn from accounts of curriculum policy-making in England (see, for example, Phillips (1996b; 1998) on NC history and Cox (1996) on the NC for English).

There is much still to be done if we are to gain a fuller understanding of how the policy decisions which have had such a major impact on the curriculum of schools in Wales over the period since 1988 were made. However, three points do emerge from this brief outline of events. First, curriculum policy has been seen from the outset as an area in which the Welsh Office can be expected, to a limited extent, to take a distinctive policy stance. Second, the aspects of curriculum policy in which such distinctiveness has been accepted by ministers and officials (in England as well as in Wales) are those where there is an acknowledged cultural dimension to policy, the Curriculum Cymreig, Welsh as a subject on the curriculum and a minority of other NC subjects, notably history. Third, the working through of this policy agenda has been facilitated by the establishment from the outset in 1988 of a separate Wales-based quango to advise the Welsh Office on curriculum policy and to oversee implementation.

National Curriculum assessment policy

Research into this area has either ignored Wales (Daugherty, 1995) or focused on implementation and impact (Daugherty *et al.*, 1997; Daugherty and Freedman, 1998) rather than on the origins of the policies concerned. What is attempted here is a study of policy-making on NC assessment in Wales which makes use of official policy statements and other public documents to develop a tentative hypothesis about the role of education quangos in policy formulation.

Across England and Wales, government policy on the assessment arrangements introduced within the terms of the 1988 Education Reform Act can be understood as falling into three broad, relatively distinct phases (Daugherty, 1997a). The first phase, from the consultation papers of 1987 through to the middle of 1991, saw an attempt, by government and by the teaching profession, to formulate and to implement assessment policies based mainly on the blueprint supplied by the government-appointed Task Group on Assessment and Testing (TGAT) (DES and WO, 1988). A series of major policy changes during the second half of 1991 heralded the abandonment of much of what TGAT had proposed and its replacement by new policies in relation to public examinations as well as to NC assessment; this can be regarded as a being the start of a second phase of policy development. A speech by the Prime Minister, John Major, to the Centre of Policy Studies (CPS) in July 1991 was followed shortly afterwards by the appointment of the CPS chairman, Brian Griffiths, to chair the assessment quango, SEAC. A new era of less GCSE coursework, 'pencil and paper' NC tests, publication of performance tables and much consequential conflict with organizations representing teachers had begun. That phase continued until 1993 when the man who has since become the government's favourite education policy troubleshooter, Sir Ron Dearing, was called in to rescue a policy in crisis. Since that time, whilst many of the assessment policies introduced during the period from 1991 to 1993 remain largely unchanged, successive governments have moved more cautiously and thus avoided another major conflict with the teaching profession.

Where was assessment policy in relation to Wales in all this? During the first two phases, covering the period from 1987 to 1993, it would seem that policy-making in relationship to Wales was largely concerned with the Welsh language. Tests and classroom tasks to assess pupil attainment in the language were developed to match the generally well-received subject order for Welsh. Major development contracts were allocated to agencies to design tests and tasks to be used to measure attainment in Welsh, in the words of the 1988 Act, 'at or near the end of each key stage'. Substantial funding was committed to curriculum and assessment materials in support of the development of Welsh as a second language. In addition, some innovative work was undertaken on the 'parallel development', in Welsh and English, of tests in mathematics and science (Wiliam, 1994; Jones D., 1997).

But if, as is apparent throughout the period from mid-1991 to Easter 1993, there were major battles over the fundamentals of NC assessment policy taking place in England, there is no evidence that those battles were also raging, whether on parallel or on different lines, in Wales. It is tempting to suggest that this was, at least in part, a consequence of the configuration of educational quangos during the period in question. The Welsh Office was as responsible for policies on assessment as it was responsible for policies on curriculum. But, under the provisions of the 1988 Act, while its statutory advisory quango on curriculum (CCW) was Wales-based with a membership drawn entirely from Wales, the equivalent quango for assessment (SEAC) was London-based with only one of its Council members, supported by a small secretariat, being from Wales. SEAC had in 1988 established an Advisory Committee for Wales comprising individuals nominated by the Welsh Office to represent educational institutions in Wales. Its agenda included items on broad policy issues as well as items referring to assessment of, and through the medium of, Welsh but it would seem that the Committee's views did not carry any real weight in influencing what was seen, by the Welsh Office as well as by the DES/DfE, as an England and Wales system of NC assessment.

A further factor which would have inhibited a distinctive approach in Wales to NC assessment during this second phase of the system's development was the fact that the government was unlikely to allow its high-profile push to introduce a more traditional testing regime in England, led by Kenneth Clarke as Secretary of State for Education and Brian Griffiths as chairman of SEAC, to be compromised by the development of potentially embarrassing alternative approaches in Wales.

As explained above, there was over the same period a series of episodes which resulted in distinctive positions being established in Wales on several aspects of curriculum policy (Welsh, history, geography, art, music, the Curriculum Cymreig). In each case, while the Welsh Office did relatively little to generate a distinctive policy position, it was, in the end, ready to accept that in important respects the NC should take a somewhat different form in Wales. Even in areas where the stance on curriculum matters taken by its curriculum advisory body, CCW, was at odds with the stance taken by its counterpart in England (NCC) on the primary curriculum and on the English order, the Welsh Office did not immediately bow to what can be assumed were pressures from the DES/DfE to follow the policy line being taken by ministers in England.

However, though the configuration of, and the approach taken by, educational quangos during the first two phases of implementing NC assessment would seem to have had an effect on decision-making, it cannot be accepted as a full explanation of the apparent readiness of those involved in policy-making in Wales to accept that assessment policies should, with the exception of those relating to the Welsh language, be common to England and Wales. Were there any pressures on the Welsh Office and/or SEAC to develop a different approach in Wales? If such pressures were being brought to bear at that time they were so low-profile as to be invisible. In effect, those individuals and organizations in Wales concerned about the direction which NC policy was taking tended to join forces with like-minded organizations in England and try to influence policy-making there. It is likely that the Welsh Office will have been in receipt of some such representations but few would have seen the Welsh Office as having any significant influence on the policy line being taken in England.

That situation began to change with the government announcement in March 1993 of a major review of NC and the associated assessment arrangements, to be undertaken by Sir Ron Dearing personally in England and by CCW in Wales. During the period leading up to the publication of parallel reports in December 1993, Dearing collaborated closely with CCW in order to build a common position on both curriculum and assessment matters which, while being acceptable to government, would also go some way to meeting the objections of teachers which had brought the system to crisis point earlier in 1993. That process of review can be regarded as the start of a third phase of assessment policy as it affects both England and Wales. However, there was little as yet which was distinctive about assessment policies in Wales; the only substantial differences between Dearing's final report and the parallel report from CCW relate to the Welsh language.

The third phase in relation to NC assessment policy in Wales is probably better defined as beginning in April 1994 with the establishment of a new quango, the Curriculum and Assessment Authority for Wales (ACAC). For the first time curriculum and assessment policies for Wales could be developed together by a Wales-based statutory advisory body.

ACAC's first opportunity to develop a coherent set of policies, embracing both curriculum and assessment, came with the parallel reviews of assessment policy, initiated jointly by ministers in the Welsh Office and the DfEE and undertaken by the authority in Wales and by SCAA in England. In the reports of these parallel reviews can be detected the first glimmering of a distinctiveness to thinking about assessment in Wales which extends beyond matters relating to the Welsh language.

SCAA's report of its *Review of Assessment and Testing* (SCAA, 1996) in England is, in effect, a restatement of most of the policy stances taken on assessment in the course of the 1993 Dearing review. Though the 1996 report made sixty-four recommendations, it is difficult to detect any serious rethinking on the many topics covered by the review: the statutory framework, fitness for purpose, teacher assessment, the use of assessment data. If there is a theme running through the review it is a preference for seeking to squeeze more from the expensively gathered and extensively collated masses of attainment data which NC assessment was making available. Hence the inclusion of school improvement indices, age standardized scores and management information systems among SCAA's recommendations to the DfEE.

The DfEE, no doubt relieved that SCAA had avoided recommending anything which might challenge the primacy of the evaluative purpose of NC assessment, published its response in February 1996. Some sense of the bland and inconsequential nature of this set of proposals can be gained from the first paragraph: 'SCAA has recommended that the summative and formative purposes should continue to be the foundation for NC assessment. The Secretary of State agrees' (DfEE, 1996: 3). The underlying message is clear: any serious rethinking of NC assessment would not be contemplated at least until the major review of the NC scheduled for the year 2000 following Dearing's five-year moratorium on change.

In Wales, there were two major differences apparent in the way the parallel review was undertaken. ACAC proposed that the review in Wales should be in two stages, the second of which would not be completed until December 1996, giving ACAC an opportunity to take further any matters left unresolved after the first phase. A second difference between the review in Wales and its counterpart in England lay in the adoption by ACAC of an overarching aim for its review:

ACAC's overall aim in conducting this review is to produce a coherent and integrated curriculum and assessment framework which meets the needs of pupils, has the confidence of the teaching profession, parents, governors, and the wider public, raises standards of achievement and widens educational opportunity. (ACAC, 1996: 2)

The ACAC review prompted the Welsh Office to agree to some differences emerging on the details of NC assessment policy. For example, a co-ordinated strategy, involving HMI and Welsh Office as well as ACAC, was agreed to strengthen the teacher assessment side of the system, so often overshadowed by the end of key stage tests (Daugherty, 1996). Another divergence of policy concerned the publication of performance data derived from the testing of eleven year olds at the end of Key Stage 2. From 1996 the assessment results were published by the DfEE for each state school in England but the Welsh Office published only summaries of the results for each LEA.

ACAC's report on the second phase of its review was submitted to the Welsh Office in January 1997, *Getting the Best from the National Curriculum Assessment Arrangements in Wales* (ACAC, 1997) and the Welsh Office's response was circulated for consultation in March (Welsh Office, 1997a). The Welsh Office endorsed ACAC's aim of producing 'a coherent and integrated curriculum and assessment framework', linking that with its own initiative to improve school standards in Wales, *A Bright Future* (Welsh Office, 1995). The election of a Labour government in May 1997 intervened to change the political context in which these policies were being developed. In the first year of the new government there was little evidence, for example in the White Paper for Wales published in July 1997 (Welsh Office, 1997b), of any new thinking about assessment policy and no sign that the Welsh Office was contemplating taking a different position on policy in this area from that set out in the parallel Education White Paper in England (DfEE, 1997).

However, it may in time prove to be the case that the different emphases in the ACAC advice (ACAC, 1997), when compared with the advice given by its English counterpart (SCAA, 1996), will have signalled some changes, modest but significant, in the details of assessment policy in Wales. For example, ACAC appears to give more weight to improving statutory teacher assessment than does SCAA and the former subsequently developed optional assessment materials to support everyday teacher assessment whilst the latter put its funding into optional end-of-year tests. The decision by ACAC to appoint separate test development agencies with effect from the 2000 tests also leaves open the possibility that a distinctive style of testing of the core subjects could emerge in Wales.

Discussion

What does the available evidence and the above analysis reveal about the formulation of education policy in Wales in relation to NC assessment? Given the analysis's reliance on public policy statements as evidence from which to draw inferences about policy-making, any conclusions are necessarily provisional, subject to being tested against substantive empirical evidence. There are, however, several features of policy formulation in this area which can be said to offer insights into the policy process in Wales.

First, in matters relating to the Welsh language, there has from the beginning been little inclination on the part of policy-makers in England, even during the five years when an England and Wales quango had the lead in these matters, to interest themselves in the way in which assessment policies concerning Welsh have developed. This has led to important differences, largely unrecognized in England, between the ways Welsh is assessed at the end of each key stage and the ways English is assessed (in Wales as in England). The use of classroom tasks as a major component in the assessment of Welsh was retained without any obvious controversy during the second phase of policy development, when equivalent assessment procedures were being axed from the testing of English, mathematics and science.

Second, the role of the Welsh Office as essentially reactive to policy initiatives originating elsewhere is underlined by the evidence from the above analysis. Through each of the phases of policy evolution since 1987 the Welsh Office has typically responded to policy positions taken by others, including, since 1994, the Wales-based quango which now has a policy role in relation to assessment. It has been argued (see chapter 3, above) that the Welsh Office has won a few education policy battles in other fields when it has been in conflict with England, but never a war. There is no evidence from this study of the Welsh Office engaging in more than the occasional defensive skirmish, still less of it declaring a policy war with England. It can, of course, be argued that a reactive stance is the proper role for a government department to take in policy formulation but, irrespective of propriety, such a stance has left the Welsh Office vulnerable to being carried along on a wave of unstoppable initiatives emanating from England.

Third, there is little evidence from this study of policy-making in Wales having been shaped either by a Wales-based debate about the issues or by lobbying directed at ministers in the Welsh Office. There have been several assessment matters which have been hotly debated in Wales during the period in question; the defence of the WJEC's Certificate in Education in the early 1990s was one such matter and the extension by UCAC of its boycott of NC tests into

1995 when other teacher organizations had agreed to co-operate was another. What has been absent has been a more broadly based debate in Wales about possible alternatives to the current policy orthodoxy and therefore any general pressure on the Welsh Office to consider adopting a position which differs fundamentally from that being taken in England.

In contrast there has been a debate, relatively well developed within the education sector if not in a wider public context, about the school curriculum. The CCW policy statement on the whole curriculum (CCW, 1991) may have of necessity been an attempt to develop a post-hoc rationale for a statutory curriculum which was already in place but it did involve a wide-ranging discussion to which teachers, schools and other interested organizations contributed. The case for a school curriculum developed in Wales was strongly put (Daugherty, 1993) and widely accepted within Wales. In relation to specific subjects, arguments about the NC orders for history, art, music, geography and English have at regular intervals revisited the question of the nature of Welshness in the school curriculum. In the late 1990s the prospect of an elected Assembly reinvigorated the debate in Wales about the school curriculum (Daugherty, 1997b; Jones, 1998; Jones and Reynolds, 1998).

Fourth, the role of quangos in policy-making has been shown as one significant variable in the policy process. It is especially notable in the second phase referred to when the contrast between a degree of distinctiveness in Wales in relation to curriculum policy and a seeming acceptance in Wales of a series of changes to assessment policy, clearly ideologically based as well as England-based, is very obvious. But it is also apparent that, in the most recent phase of the evolution of assessment policy, the existence of a Wales-based quango since 1994 has contributed to changes in the specifics of policy if not in the fundamentals. It can be argued that, in a country whose political institutions are underdeveloped and where the political agenda is often set from across the border, an indigenous quango may find itself becoming more influential than it would otherwise be.

Conclusion

It may be helpful to distinguish three types of policy development process in education policies for Wales. 'And Wales' policies are those where all the assumptions and priorities derive from London; Wales, if considered at all, is an 'add-on' element in such policies. 'In Wales' policies are those where, within an England and Wales policy framework and within strictly defined parameters, policy is formulated and implemented to some extent distinctively in Wales. Policies on the NC in Wales have on several occasions been of the 'In Wales' type whereas, until very recently, the associated assessment arrangements have been viewed by almost all concerned as being most appropriately developed on an 'And Wales' basis.

The third category of policy development might be termed the 'From Wales' type, where policies are formulated, developed and implemented in Wales without there necessarily being an equivalent policy-making process in England. This has occurred only rarely in the curriculum policy field, associated in particular with the Welsh language and the Curriculum Cymreig. There is no sign as yet of policies on NC assessment being seen as meriting a 'From Wales' approach to policy-making.

Further studies are needed before a fuller picture of policy formulation in relation to NC assessment can be firmly established. What, for example, has been the role of the school inspectorate in Wales in influencing assessment policy? What part have individuals played, at any level in policy-making from ministers down, either in establishing distinctive policies in Wales or in ensuring that the Welsh Office follows the line taken in England? However, the evidence on assessment policy in Wales that is available to us points to a conclusion similar to that reached by Fitz and Lee from their work on school inspection policy:

> Our study suggests that the convention of Cabinet collective responsibility tends to override other powers conferred on the Secretary of State [for Wales] to shape independent policy for Wales. This convention is likely to constrain the development of new and different initiatives in Wales. (Fitz and Lee, 1997a: 9)

The setting up of a democratically elected Assembly in 1999 will change the process of education policy formulation in Wales. Whether the allocation to that Assembly of a major role in education policy can change the underlying policy question from 'To what extent can policies in Wales diverge from those in England?' to 'Which policies are appropriate for Wales?' is less certain.

Note

The author was a member of the Curriculum Council for Wales from 1988 until 1993 and its Chairman from 1991 to 1993. He was also a member of the School Examinations and Assessment Council from 1988 until 1991.

References

ACAC (1996) *Review of National Curriculum Assessment Arrangements: First Phase.* Cardiff: ACAC.

ACAC (1997) *Getting the Best from the National Curriculum Assessment Arrangements in Wales.* Cardiff: ACAC.

Ball, S. (1994) *Education Reform: A Critical and Post-structural Approach.* Buckingham: Open University Press.

CCW (1991) *The Whole Curriculum from 5 to 16 in Wales.* Cardiff: Curriculum Council for Wales.

CCW (1993) *Developing a Curriculum Cymreig.* Cardiff: Curriculum Council for Wales.

Cox, B. (1996) *Cox on the Battle for the English Curriculum.* London: Hodder & Stoughton.

Daugherty, R. (1993) Why policies must be made in Wales. *Times Educational Supplement* (22 October), 18.

Daugherty, R. (1995) *National Curriculum Assessment: A Review of Policy 1987–1994.* London: Falmer Press.

Daugherty, R. (1996) In search of teacher assessment – its place in the National Curriculum assessment system of England and Wales. *Curriculum Journal*, 7(2), 137–52.

Daugherty, R. (1997a) National Curriculum Assessment: The experience of England and Wales. *Educational Administration Quarterly*, 33(2), 198–218.

Daugherty, R. (1997b) *A School Curriculum for a Future Wales.* Milton Keynes: British Curriculum Foundation.

Daugherty, R. and Freedman, E. (1998) Tests, targets and tables: the use of Key Stage 2 assessment data in Wales. *Welsh Journal of Education*, 7(1), 5–21.

Daugherty, R. *et al.* (1997) *Evaluation of Key Stage 2 Assessment in Wales 1996: Summary Report.* Cardiff: Curriculum and Assessment Authority for Wales.

DES and WO (1987) *The National Curriculum 5–16: A Consultation Document.* London: Department of Education and Science and Welsh Office.

DES and WO (1988) *National Curriculum Task Group on Assessment and*

Testing: A Report. London: Department of Education and Science and Welsh Office.

DfEE (1996) *Review of Assessment and Testing: Consultation Paper*. London: Department for Education and Employment.

DfEE (1997) *Excellence in Schools*. London: Department for Education and Employment.

Elfed-Owens, P. (1997) The implementation of the National Curriculum in Wales. Unpublished Ph.D. thesis, University of London Institute of Education.

Evans, J., Davies, B., Bass, D. and Penney, D. (1997) Playing for position: education policy, physical education and nationalism in Wales. *Journal of Education Policy*, 12(4), 285–301.

Fitz, J. and Lee, J. (1997a) Contrary voices? Education policy and school inspection in England and Wales. Paper presented at a seminar on Culture, Curriculum and Community: Education Policy in Wales, Swansea.

Fitz, J. and Lee, D. (1997b) HMI and OFSTED: evolution or revolution in school inspection? *British Journal of Educational Studies*, 45(1), 39–52.

Fitz, J., Halpin, D. and Power S. (1994) Implementation research and education policy. *British Journal of Educational Studies*, 42(1), 53–69.

Jones, B. and Lewis, I. (1995) A Curriculum Cymreig. *Welsh Journal of Education*, 4(2), 22–35.

Jones, D. (1997) Bilingual mathematics: development and practice in Wales. *The Curriculum Journal*, 8(3), 393–410.

Jones, E. P. and Reynolds, D. (1998) Education. In J. Osmond (ed.), *The National Assembly Agenda*. Cardiff: Institute of Welsh Affairs, pp. 230–44.

Jones, G. (1994) Which nation's curriculum? The case of Wales. *Curriculum Journal*, 5(1), 5–16.

Jones, G. (1997) *The Education of a Nation*. Cardiff: University of Wales Press.

Jones, G. (1998) *Growing Up at Last? Education and the National Assembly*. Talybont: Y Lolfa.

Phillips, R. (1996a) Education policy making in Wales: a research agenda. *Welsh Journal of Education*, 5(2), 26–42.

Phillips, R. (1996b) History teaching, cultural restorationism and national identity in England and Wales. *Curriculum Studies*, 4(3), 385–99.

Phillips, R. (1998) *History Teaching, Nationhood and the State*. London: Cassell.

SCAA (1996) *Review of Assessment and Testing*. London: School Curriculum and Assessment Authority.

Troyna, B. (1994) Critical social research and education policy. *British Journal of Educational Studies*, 42(1), 70–84.

Welsh Office (1987) *The National Curriculum in Wales*. Cardiff: Welsh Office.

Welsh Office (1995) *A Bright Future: Getting the Best for Every Pupil at School in Wales*. Cardiff: Welsh Office.

Welsh Office (1997a) *Assessment and Testing 7, 11 and 14 year olds: Consultation on the Secretary of State for Wales' Proposals*. Cardiff: Welsh Office.

Welsh Office (1997b) *Building Excellent Schools Together*. Cardiff: Welsh Office.

Wiliam, D. (1994) Creating matched National Curriculum assessments in English and Welsh: test translation and parallel development. *Curriculum Journal*, 5(1), 17–29.

6

Three Perspectives on Bilingual Education Policy in Wales: Bilingual Education as Language Planning, as Pedagogy and as Politics

COLIN BAKER

Introduction

In the last five decades in Wales, bilingual education has grown rapidly in a remarkably short period of time. In Wales, there has been a reversal from an almost entirely monolingual education in English to Welsh, as a subject, being compulsory for all children in the National Curriculum (NC). Bilingual education has risen from small origins in Aberystwyth half a century ago to approximately one in five primary schools using both English and Welsh to transmit the curriculum. This chapter suggests that there are three policy perspectives that underlie such a rapid expansion.

First, there is the viewpoint of language planners (for example, in Wales, Ireland, Catalonia and the Basque country) who believe that bilingual education is one essential means of language maintenance, language revitalization and reversing language shift. Second, there is a different perspective from educationalists who see bilingual education as effective pedagogy. Such a viewpoint has particularly been championed by language activists, but has also been implemented by enthusiastic, innovatory and visionary inspectors, advisors and practitioners at school and classroom level. Third, the chapter will suggest that bilingual education cannot be understood purely in terms of its value in language planning, nor in terms of its effectiveness as a system of education. Bilingual education can only be fully understood in relation to political ideology, movements in political ideas and political opportunism. These three perspectives will be presented in turn. The conclusion returns to a central issue about whether the three perspectives integrate or whether they are separate and in conflict.

Bilingual education as language planning

In recent decades in Wales, there has been both a latent understanding and an increasingly articulated plea that bilingual education is essential to maintaining the Welsh language. Statistics from the 1991 census illustrate how important bilingual education is for the maintenance of the Welsh language.

At the 1991 census, 18.7 per cent of people aged three and over were returned as speaking Welsh. Across Wales, only 16.5 per cent of households could potentially reproduce the language in their children, by one or both parents being able to speak the language to their children.[1] Thus, there is the probability of the Welsh language being insufficiently reproduced in the home (intergenerational transmission) for the language to be maintained in its current density among the population. In 11.6 per cent of households in Wales both partners speak Welsh, but 8 per cent of those Welsh-speaking parents do not speak Welsh to their children. When the father and not the mother is Welsh-speaking, there is only a 48.8 per cent chance of their child or children becoming Welsh-speaking. If the mother is Welsh-speaking and not the father, there is a 53.5 per cent chance of their child becoming Welsh-speaking (at home or at school – the census does not discriminate). Also, according to the 1991 census figures, 36.1 per cent of all children who are Welsh-speaking come from homes where neither parent speaks Welsh. That is, approximately one in every three children learn to speak Welsh (according to the census) outside the family. Such children probably acquire Welsh through *ysgolion meithrin* or the statutory school system. The above figures indicate how important bilingual education in Wales is in language regeneration. Bilingual education in Wales is essential in Welsh-language maintenance because language reproduction in the family is occurring at too low a level.

Welsh Office statistics gathered from primary schools every year tell a slightly different story. Census data does not distinguish various levels of fluency. Therefore, 'Welsh-speaking' in the census includes those who are fluent and those who have much lower levels of fluency, and probably includes children who only speak

Welsh in school lessons. According to returns from schools to the Welsh Office, 6.3 per cent of pupils in Wales speak Welsh at home; 8.1 per cent of pupils speak Welsh fluently due to bilingual education and not via the home; 27.9 per cent of pupils speak Welsh but not fluently (Welsh Office, 1997). Thus, a slightly higher percentage of pupils appear to acquire Welsh via bilingual education than via the family. The conclusion from both census figures and Welsh Office statistics is that bilingual education in Wales is essential in Welsh-language maintenance.

Yet, in the history of Welsh-language maintenance in the twentieth century, language planning has often been concerned with matters other than bilingual education. The symbolic and linguistic importance of the language of signposts, the 'status' importance of a Welsh-language television channel, and the recent successful campaign for rights to use the Welsh language enshrined in the 1993 Welsh Language Act, each locate recent emphases of Welsh language activism. While minority-language mass media, language rights enshrined in law, the standardization of Welsh through literacy, radio and television are all important, even essential parts of language planning, they are each (and cumulatively) insufficient.

For a language to survive and revive, it has to be lived and loved. Daily language use and a consistently favourable attitude to a language are all important. While it is implausible, imagine a minority language with rights to use enshrined in law, with radio and television, CDs and computer programs in that minority language, bilingual signposts, but everyone using the majority language at home, when experiencing the mass media, in leisure and religious activities, in employment and in all daily social interaction. It is theoretically possible to have many support systems for a language, but for the language to be dying because it is not used in families and communities. Therefore, at the heart of language planning is planning for usage. This suggests that language rights, mass media, signposts and many other strategies and actions are not of first-order importance in themselves. While each contribute to the status and institutionalization of a language, they are ultimately important to the extent to which they contribute to four priorities discussed below.

It is argued here that there are four major priorities that directly relate to the survival and strengthening of any minority language, and in our case, the Welsh language: (1) language reproduction in the family; (2) language production from pre-school education through formal schooling to adult education; (3) using Welsh for economic purposes; and (4) social, cultural and leisure participation through the medium of Welsh. These four priorities will now be briefly considered, particularly because they relate to future language policy in Wales, and how bilingual education fits into that schema.

Language reproduction in the family

Minority languages decline when families fail to reproduce the language in their children. No minority language has a secure future without parents raising their children through that language. For example in Wales, if a substantial or even a moderate proportion of Welsh-speaking parents raise their children through the medium of English, neither Welsh-medium education nor eisteddfodau and chapels could do enough to arrest the decline of the language. Family language planning is a top priority; quintessential but insufficient by itself.

One basic performance indicator of the future of a language is age trends. Where and when much higher proportions of older people speak Welsh than younger age groups, the language is in danger. Where and when younger age groups are in larger proportions than older speakers of the language, a positive sign for the future of the language is present.

Language production through bilingual education

Examples of Welsh parents or mixed-language marriages not reproducing the Welsh language in their children immediately highlight the need for language production to occur also through informal and formal education means. Language learning at *ysgolion meithrin*, in primary and secondary schools, at further and higher education level, and in adult language learning classes becomes essential to increase the supply of Welsh-speakers.

Future Welsh-language reproduction in the family seems unlikely to produce the same number or densities of speakers as at present. Therefore, making up the shortfall, and increasing the stock, requires language acquisition and language learning through informal and formal education.

The shift from a pre-war system that replaced Welsh with English to a system that, in 1999, made it compulsory for all children in Wales to learn Welsh from the age of five to sixteen, is a revolution. While there are many advances that are needed in bilingual education in Wales, nevertheless a strong foundation for learning Welsh and learning through the medium of Welsh is already in place. Language planning through bilingual education has succeeded in Wales and becomes an accompanying foundation for language revitalization.

Using Welsh in the economy

As essential as it is for language reproduction to occur in the home and for language production to occur in education, neither secures a strong future for a minority language. Having the ability to speak Welsh does not mean that it will be used in adult life. Some children leave school speaking Welsh fluently and are literate in Welsh, yet do not use the language thereafter. The family and education provide a potential, not a promise of Welsh-language maintenance. Neither parents nor pedagogues provide a guarantee of language use in adolescence or adulthood. During and after the schooling years, Welsh needs to be lived and loved. Living in Welsh is partly about employment and economic benefit, advancement and affluence. Loving a language is about social, cultural and leisure life, and will be separately considered later.

While it is always dangerous to generalize from one minority language situation to another, the case of Ireland signals a warning for Wales. The creation of the Irish Free State made Irish the first official language of the country, and Irish was made compulsory in schools, compulsory to pass as a subject in order to matriculate from school, and compulsory for entrance to much public-sector employment and to university. Despite constant state intervention and schemes to support the Irish language, it has continued to decline in daily usage.

One reason for the decline in the Irish language, despite language rights and language planning, has been a lack of a strong economic dimension to the Irish language. Children leaving school found that the Irish language was of little real value in the employment market. For many jobs, Irish was practically irrelevant. Instead, schoolchildren, their parents and students in Ireland have become increasingly aware of the economic advantages of the European Union languages, particularly French, German and English. The economic value of a language is not the only determinant of its value and usefulness, but it is a crucial factor.

The more the Welsh language can be tied in with employment, promotion in employment and increasing affluence, the greater the perceived value of the Welsh language. The greater the number of jobs that require bilingualism (and often biliteracy), the more importance the Welsh language will have in the curriculum. That is, an economic value to the Welsh language provides needed instrumental motivation for children to become proficient at Welsh in school. The value of competence in Welsh gained at school is advertised among schoolchildren when jobs require Welsh.

The more the Welsh language is aligned with employment and economy, the more parents may become motivated and encouraged to reproduce the Welsh language among their children. A strong economic value to the Welsh language gives added momentum for language reproduction in the family. It also gives momentum to Mudiad Ysgolion Meithrin – that is, learning the language when very young in an informal, subconscious and enjoyable fashion.

The use of Welsh for social, cultural, religious and leisure purposes
The danger of only promoting the economic value of the Welsh language is that it may have short-term monetary associations. There is a possibility of doing the right thing for a temporary reason. Once economic motives are fulfilled, the Welsh language may not be used. For a language to be of increased value and to be used daily, it has to capture particular contexts (domains) where people's non-economic activity occurs. A dominant theme in this chapter is that, for a language to survive and multiply, it has to be used regularly in everyday interaction and relationships. Languages live when they are continually and consistently used in everyday life.

A language also has to be loved. A true story in language planning derives from a leader of the Pennsylvania Amish community who went to see Joshua Fishman, a founding father on the study of language revival and revitalization (Huffines, 1991). Having listened to a long list of all the activities, initiatives and wonderful schemes that were being dreamt up to preserve Pennsylvania German, Fishman asked, 'Ah yes, but do they love the language in their hearts?' The best planning schemes in the world will fail if people do not live in and love their heritage language.

A language thus needs associating with all the positive aspects of cultural, leisure and community life. The widest form of cultural participation needs to be encouraged: from the preparation for eisteddfodau to the dancing of discos: from the rites and rituals of religion to the rhythms of rock music: from quizzes in the pub to quiet group hobbies and pastimes. In such cultural and leisure life, active participation rather than passive experience is needed. Listening to Welsh radio or CDs is doubtless valuable but is a passive, receptive use of the Welsh language. Research suggests that among teenagers, the language is maintained in adolescent years among those who actively participate through Welsh, for example, through Urdd activities (Baker, 1992).

Where there is valued cultural and leisure use of the Welsh language, then language reproduction in the family becomes more encouraged and motivated. In the same way, language production through education becomes more meaningful when it is seen that Welsh has an enjoyable use in cultural and leisure activity.

Language rights, Welsh mass media and Welsh-language institutions

It has been suggested that there are four areas, each directly related to the living use of a language, that are top priority in maintaining and strengthening the Welsh language. Does this mean that other actions and activities are of less value? For example, S4C was once regarded as *yr unig ateb* (the only answer), while bilingual sign-posts and the Welsh Language Act have been major parts of strategies to preserve the Welsh language.

Language rights, mass media in a minority language, signposts and many other strategies, actions and desires may not be of first-order importance in themselves. They are important to the extent to which they contribute to the four priorities listed above. Welsh-language mass media, Welsh-language rights and the many Welsh language institutions which support the language (for example, eisteddfodau, Welsh Books Council, *papurau bro*, Merched y Wawr and Welsh-medium chapels and churches) are essential to the extent to which they give status and prestige to the minority language and thereby encourage parents to reproduce the language in their children, for language production in education to seem worthwhile, and for the cultural and leisure use of Welsh in the community to have stature.

One way of calculating the value of such institutions and influences is to consider the effect on the Welsh language if they were removed. For example, if Welsh-language broadcasting did not exist, then the language would have considerably less status in parents' and teachers' eyes. Parents might be much less likely to bring up their children through the medium of Welsh, and teachers might be less motivated to engage in Welsh-medium education. A language without a strong presence in the mass media would appear as a language of history rather than of a new millennium. Without local eisteddfodau and the National Eisteddfod, the status of the language might decline. Hence parents' willingness to reproduce the language in the family, and schools' enthusiasm to produce children fluent in Welsh could suffer.

Language rights encourage the use of Welsh in the economy, thereby making parents and teachers, pupils and students, more aware of the value of Welsh in employment and affluence. The value of an institution such as the Urdd is particularly in its ability to provide participative situations where children use Welsh in leisure and cultural situations, hopefully attaching positive feelings and value to the language. Any language without a literacy in the next century may be in grave danger of surviving. Literacy in Welsh gives many more uses and functions to that language (for example, in employment and leisure reading). A language without literacy is like a colonized language. When the British colonized areas of Africa and India, they frequently allowed literacy solely in the English language. The indigenous languages were relegated to lower status, non-economic uses; English was the key to educational wisdom, employment and wealth. Thus, a language without literacy has fewer functions and much lower status.

In summary, the relative value of mass media, eisteddfodau, Welsh-language books and Welsh-language institutions is the extent to which they contribute, singly and cumulatively, to the four priorities listed above. Language planning is always going to be a complex equation, a social and linguistic experiment, and endlessly debated. Language planning attempts to do what is most difficult: change people's attitudes and behaviour. Changing minority language attitudes and affecting language behaviour in a democratic society will be an unending challenge.

The relationship between language planning and bilingual education

This chapter now moves onto one specific part of language planning: the part played by bilingual education in Wales in the maintenance of the Welsh language. Current Welsh Office statistics show that 20.9 per cent of pupils are in primary schools where Welsh is the sole, main or part medium of teaching in a class. At Key Stage 1, 19.2 per cent of children are categorized by their schools as 'Welsh first language', and at Key Stage 2 the percentage is very similar, at 19.3 per cent. Such statistics are promising. The figures suggest that the primary schools increase the numbers of fluent Welsh-speakers above the production of first-language Welsh-speakers via the home (see above). Through the National Curriculum second-language Welsh curriculum, all children are taught Welsh as a second language from five to sixteen (as from 1999). This would seem to produce a large population of potential second-language Welsh-speakers, albeit with different levels of fluency.

However, in Year 7 (the first year of secondary schooling), only 12.9 per cent of pupils are taught Welsh as first language. Approximately the same figures occur through the rest of secondary schooling. In Year 9, 12.4 per cent of pupils are taught Welsh as a first language, while in Year 11, 12.0 per cent of pupils are taught Welsh as a first language (Welsh Office, 1997). That is, between primary and secondary schooling, around 7 per cent to 8 per cent of children throughout Wales move from being first-language to second-language Welsh. The WJEC GCSE entries in 1996 confirm this story. Only 11.3 per cent of children were entered for first-language Welsh in GCSE while 23.0 per cent of children were entered for Welsh second-language GCSE.

Overall, primary schools produce more fluent Welsh-speakers than Welsh-speaking homes, and produce sufficient percentages of pupils fluent in Welsh to maintain the language (Welsh Office, 1997). However, some 7 to 8 per cent of all children in Wales move from being first-language Welsh-speakers at primary school to being second-language Welsh-speakers at secondary school. The Welsh language is thus not being sufficiently strengthened and supported by secondary schooling.

It is customary to argue that positive attitudes to the Welsh language decline during the teenage years (Baker, 1992). As the Anglicized mass media, pop culture, peer pressure all become influential, attitudes to the Welsh language tend to become less favourable during these susceptible years. But are secondary schools playing an unwitting part in this deterioration? In these important habit-forming and attitude-forming years, do secondary schools not only fail to support the foundational work of primary schools, but unwittingly provide the occasion for language loss and language attrition? For example, the language of the curriculum in the secondary school often shifts towards English (for example, in maths and science). Given that 19.3 per cent of children leave primary schooling as first-language or fluent Welsh-speakers, it is disconcerting to find that at GCSE, only 5.7 per cent of all examination entries are through the medium of Welsh; 94.3 per cent are through the medium of English.

The language planner's view of bilingual education necessarily focuses on the importance of producing more speakers of the Welsh language than are generated through the home. The evidence presented in this section has suggested that if, as in the inter-war period, there was no bilingual education, then the reproduction of the Welsh language through the family as the main means of language reproduction would lead to decreasing percentages of people speaking the Welsh language. Without bilingual education, it is quite possible that the Welsh language over a century would not survive.

This focus looks to a strengthening of the minority language among first-language speakers, children learning Welsh as a second language as early as possible (*ysgolion meithrin*) and becoming fluent in Welsh through using Welsh in the curriculum of the primary and secondary school. Also, a language planner will regard it as important to have the minority language culture infused throughout the curriculum. Thus the Curriculum Cymreig (a Welsh cultural dimension added to every curriculum area) gives the language rootedness, identity and is connected at a cognitive and affective level with the kaleidoscopic colours of Welsh culture.

However, there are three particular limitations of the language-planning perspective of bilingual education that need to be briefly mentioned. First, there is a danger in the language planner's perspective of regarding bilingual education as for the sake of the language and not necessarily for the sake of the child. Bilingual education can be seen as a salvation for the language, whereas an alternative (but not a contradictory) viewpoint is that the Welsh language is taught for the sake of the child. A humanistic education-alist may argue that bilingual education needs to be defended for its value and contribution to the development of the child rather than the language. Second, the language-planning perspective on bilin-gual education tends to have a limited view of the functions and purposes of education. Among both the supporters and critics of Welsh-medium education, there are occasionally arguments from both sides that separate and artificially disassociate debates about language from debates about effective education. We shall be returning to this theme in the third part of this chapter when the politics of bilingual education are considered.

Third, there is sometimes over-optimism among language plan-ners about what can be expected from and delivered by bilingual education in revitalizing a language. When a language fails to be reproduced in the family, and when there are insufficient support mechanisms (for example, language rights, mass media) outside of schools, too high expectations of language reversal via bilingual education are not uncommon. While bilingual education has an important role in language reproduction, as probably without it a minority language cannot survive except through intense religious usage, bilingual education cannot deliver language maintenance by itself.

Bilingual education as pedagogy

Over the last few decades a growing number of educationalists throughout many countries have supported and promoted bilingual education. While bilingual education has many different forms (see Baker, 1996), the foundational perspective of such people is that bilingual education is typically superior to monolingual education. While one must not underestimate the critics of bilingual education (particularly the anti-Hispanic lobby in the USA and the assimila-tionists in the UK), the philosophy, principles, policies and practices of bilingual education have grown remarkably in recent decades. Educationalists have increasingly considered the value of two or three majority languages in schools, not just taught as languages but used to transmit curriculum content. For example, Scandinavians, the Japanese and inhabitants of other Far Eastern countries are increasingly seeing the importance of languages in the global market, in inter-continental communication and information exchange, while educators interested in minority languages argue for the benefits of bilingual education as standard-raising, child-centred and responsive to parents and pupils as clients.

Among educationalists, arguments for bilingual education vary according to local politics, the status and power of majority and minority languages, but tend to revolve around eight particular advantages of bilingual education.

1. Bilingual education allows both languages (sometimes three languages) to develop fully. Rather than engaging in token second-language learning, two or more languages are well-developed. This allows children to engage in wider communication, having more options in patterns of communication across generations, regions and cultural groups.

2. Bilingual education develops a broader enculturation, a wider and a more sympathetic view of different creeds and cultures. Rather than token multicultural lessons, bilingual education gives deep insights into the cultures associated with the languages, fosters a broader understanding of differences, and at its best, avoids the tight compartmentalization of racism, the stereotyping of different social groups, and fosters a more multiperspective and sensitive-to-difference viewpoint.

3. Bilingual education typically leads to biliteracy. Being able to read and write in two or more languages allows more possibilities in uses of literacy (for example, in employment), widening the choice of literature for pleasure, giving more opportunities for different perspectives and viewpoints and leading to a deeper under-standing of history and heritage, of traditions and territory.

4. Research suggests that when children have two well-developed languages, there are cognitive benefits of being bilingual. Schools are often important in developing a child's two languages to the point where they may be more creative in thinking due to their bilingualism, more sensitive in communication as they may be inter-personally aware, for example, when needing to codeswitch and be able to inspect their languages more (that is, metalinguistic advantages).

5. In heritage language education, for example, when Welsh-speaking children are taught in Welsh rather than English,

children's self-esteem may be raised. When a child's home language is replaced by the majority language, the child, the parents and the child's community may seem to be rejected. When the home language is used in school, then children may feel themselves, their home and community to be accepted, thus maintaining or raising their self-esteem. Positive self-esteem, a confidence in one's own ability and potential, interacts in an important way with achievement and curriculum success.

6. It is not only Canadian immersion studies and studies of heritage language bilingual education that suggest that curriculum achievement is increased through bilingual education. The precise causes of raising standards via bilingual education are neither simple nor straightforward. There is likely to be a complex equation between the support of the home, the enthusiasm and commitment of teachers in school, children feeling accepted and secure and the relationship between language and cognitive development. In Wales, there is a marked lack of research indicating whether bilingual education is more or less successful than monolingual education. While comparisons of designated bilingual schools and monolingual schools are sometimes given (showing favourable results for designated bilingual schools), it is difficult to acquire the data on other variables (for example, social class) to make such comparison fair and to ensure that other explanations have been suitably taken into account.

7. The role of bilingual education in establishing security of identity at a local, regional and national level may be important. As a basic psychological need, security and status in self-identity may be important. Bilingual education has possibly aided the establishment of a Welsh identity in children (although there is little research evidence on this).

8. In Wales, the economic advantages of bilingual education are increasingly being claimed. In Gwynedd, for example, being bilingual is important to secure employment in many public services and sometimes private companies as well. To secure a job as a teacher, to work in the mass media, to work in local government and increasingly in the civil service in Wales, bilingualism has become important. Thus, bilingual education is increasingly seen as delivering relatively more marketable employees than monolingual education.

While bilingual education world-wide has an increasing number of supporters (though it is not without some virulent critics), there are limitations in the pedagogical view of bilingual education. For example, bilingual education is no guarantee of effective schooling. Occasionally, there is a naïvety among those who support bilingual education in assuming that employing two or more languages in the school curriculum automatically leads to a raising of standards, more effective outcomes and a more child-centred education. In reality, the languages of the school are part of a wider matrix of variables that interact in complex ways to make schooling more or less effective. Among bilingual schools in Wales, there appears to be a mixture of the outstanding and the ordinary, those in an upward spiral of enhancing their quality and those which depend on past glories rather than current successes. The school effectiveness research movement has indicated many of the important factors that make schools more or less effective. Bilingual education is only one ingredient among many. Indeed, there is sometimes a lack of clarity of the aims and objectives of Welsh-medium or bilingual education in Wales (plus a variety of different forms of bilingual and Welsh-medium education in Wales). Bilingual schools need to emphasize specifics in the value-addedness of bilingual education. If these valued-added attributes are clearly articulated and monitored with qualitative and quantitative evidence, it can be shown whether the extra aims and objectives of bilingual education are being delivered.

Another limitation of the pedagogical perspective on bilingual education is the type and use of language learnt at school. Canadian research suggests that the language register of formal education does not necessarily prepare children for language use outside the school. The language of the curriculum is often complex and specialized. The vernacular of the street may be different. Canadian children from English-speaking homes who have been to immersion schools and learnt through the medium of French and English sometimes report difficulty in communicating appropriately with French-speakers in local communities. Local French-speakers may find their French too formal, inappropriate, even off-putting.

A further concern about bilingual education is that language learning may stop at the school gates. The minority language may be effectively transmitted and competently learnt in the classroom. Outside school children may switch into the majority language. Thus, the danger of bilingual education in Wales is that Welsh becomes a language of school but not of play; a language of the content delivery of the curriculum but not of peer culture. Even when children are taught through the medium of Welsh at school, the common denominator language of the peer group in the street is often English. When one child turns to English, often so does everybody else. The language of the screen, shop, street may be different from the language of the school. Extending the Welsh language learnt at school to use in the community is something that is difficult to engineer, difficult to plan, but nevertheless vital.

Bilingual education as politics

Wherever bilingual education exists, politics is close by. To assume that bilingual education is educationally justified and, therefore, *ipso facto* must be strongly supported, is naïve. Bilingual education is not simply an educational issue. Behind bilingual education there are always expressions of political ideology, tides of political change and political initiative. To argue for bilingual education solely as a strong plank of language planning and language revitalization is simplistic. Language planning itself is predicated on language politics. What might be posed as pure motives to preserve and conserve the dying languages of the world, hide basic political assumptions and ideologies. The history of education in Wales in the last decade, moving from the secret garden of the curriculum to the motorway of fast political imperatives (for example, in the NC and national assessment, school league tables and teacher training requirements) leaves few in doubt of the powerfulness of political will.

Surrounding bilingual education are usually political debates about national identity, dominance and control by élites in power, power relationships among politicians and civil servants, questions about social order and the perceived potential subversiveness of language minorities. At one level, the expansion of Welsh medium in education in Wales in the last fifty years and the relegation of most immigrant languages in the UK (for example, Punjabi, Gujarati, Greek, Turkish) to Saturday schools and token inclusion at GCSE level, are said to move around the idea that Welsh can claim a territorial principle (it is the heritage language of the territory) while the immigrant languages belong geographically to territories overseas. However, beneath that argument lie debates about English identity, Welsh identity, the movement away from a British identity and the beginning of debates about European identity. Bilingual education for Welsh-speakers has been supported by the strong and well-articulated claims for a Welsh identity separate from an English or a British identity. For immigrants moving into large cities such as London, Birmingham, Coventry, Bradford, Leeds and elsewhere, their request for bilingual education has fallen not only on deaf ears but on antagonistic politicians. One centralized political belief has been that such recent immigrants must take on English identity, even to the point of denying their heritage language and culture.

In an international perspective, bilingual education is rejected when there is a strong assimilationist point of view dominant in politics. For example, in California there has been a strong lobby to ban bilingual education. In the context where Hispanics may be in the majority in the Californian population in a decade, monolingual politicians see bilingual education as being a way of transferring power and control to Hispanics. Bilingual education can thus be allied with the potential subversiveness of minority-language-speakers and be distrusted by majority-language politicians.

The melting-pot philosophy of the United States, with so many immigrant groups, has generally been anti-bilingual education. In comparison, Canadian politicians have generally been more accepting of the Canadian language mosaic (particularly with the long traditions of both English and French in Canada) and relative to the United States and the United Kingdom, Canadians have been more accepting of a culturally pluralist and linguistically diverse political orientation. However strong the educational arguments for bilingual education and for the preservation of dying languages in the world, the politics of power, status, assimilation and social order can deny bilingual education. When there are movements towards national identity – in Wales, Welsh nationalism, devolution and a National Assembly – bilingual education has more of a chance of development and growth.

But what of the future relationship between the politics of Wales and Welsh-medium education? Having achieved a National Assembly and a degree of self-government, the place of the Welsh language in the educational system of Wales is not necessarily clear. One line of argument is that a Welsh Assembly, containing a political pressure group for the expansion of Welsh language in all activities of life, will bring sufficient pressure to bear for a further expansion of Welsh-medium education. Increasing the use of Welsh in the secondary school, moving from second-language Welsh learning to using Welsh to teach parts of the curriculum would seem part of that agenda. For some, therefore, the politics of the new millennium in Wales would seem to lead to a further expansion of bilingual education.

There are other scenarios possible. For example, if the majority of Welsh politicians are monolingual English-speakers, will bilingual education have reached a plateau in its development? If the National Assembly becomes a successful and powerful body, then will issues about national identity decrease? Will foreign trading languages receive more prominence in the curriculum to aid the economic strength of Wales? Given the narrow margin of support for a National Assembly, will there be a strong attempt to unify the peoples of Wales, leaving the Welsh language (sometimes seen as a boundary between English-speaking and Welsh-speaking Wales) to take a lower place in political priorities and initiatives?

Or will the Welsh language and culture be seen as a mark of separateness and distinctiveness within Europe that will enable the expansion of bilingual education? In the move towards a European identity, will there be a counteractive need among people to have a local, regional and national identity? In this case, would the Welsh language and culture become even more important and lead to an expansion in bilingual education?

Conclusions

This chapter has suggested that bilingual education in Wales derives its *raison d'être* not only from a concern for Welsh-language maintenance and revitalization, but also from a variety of educational, economic, social, cultural and political reasons. Thus sources of policy change are not simple or easily defined: parents, pedagogues, politicians are joined in affecting policy-making and policy implementation by the influence of inspectors, advisers and particular LEAs in north and south Wales.

Part of the momentum in policy-making with regard to bilingual schools has come from a grapevine about perceived success in national examinations, the beliefs of some in the extra commitment of teachers and relatively effective ethos of bilingual schools, the utilitarian hopes that Welsh-language skills will enhance job opportunities (a remarkable reversal of nineteenth-century and early twentieth-century beliefs in the lack of economic value of Welsh for employment and mobility), and the concern to preserve a variety of Welsh cultural forms.

Not only at the visible and formal level, but also in an informal manner, OHMCI in Wales supported and influenced the post-war movement from the early primary bilingual education beginnings in Aberystwyth and Llanelli to the compulsory publication of inspections of schools. For example, their publications over three decades have contained implicit assumptions of the cross-curricular validity of the use of the indigenous language, perceptive and considered advice for the progressive evolution of bilingualism throughout the school, not just in the formal curriculum but also in the culture and ethos of the school. It is perhaps easy to underestimate the legitimization process effected by OHMCI on the growth of bilingual education in the last three decades. Such a central government agency has played neither a neutral nor an uninterested role.

Despite such official support, without the pressure, enthusiasm, commitment and interest in bilingual education of groups of parents and teachers, it is unlikely that policies and the provision of bilingual education would have begun or advanced as they have. While local authority officers in Flintshire were of paramount influence in the opening of Ysgol Glan Clwyd in 1956, the growth of *ysgolion Cymraeg* in south Wales owes much to parental endeavour. LEAs responded to the activity of Rhieni Dros Addysg Gymraeg (Parents for Welsh-Medium Education) and the sustained pressure and persuasion of informal networks of local parents and language activists. Such parental groups have naturally contained Welsh-speaking parents who wish the language to be reproduced in their children with the essential help of formal education. However, the pressure for such bilingual schooling has also come from non-Welsh-speaking parents.

Thus bilingual education policy-makers, policy-influencers and policy-implementers in Wales have included professional language planners (for example, the Welsh Language Board) and parents; educationalists who are advisors, inspectors and teachers; and politicians who are local and national; those folk who have manœuvred through affirmative action and central leaders (for example, OHMCI). To what extent do these three groups (planners, pedagogues and politicians) overlap in their agendas, their ideologies and preferred outcomes?

An idealistic conclusion would be to suggest the possibility of integrating the three perspectives. When there can be a wholeness in the three perspectives between language planners, bilingual educationalists and the politicians who influence the growth of bilingual education then a mature, logical, rational and smooth evolution in bilingual education is possible. However, it is apparent in this chapter that, more often than not, there is a separation between the three perspectives. Each is a partial view, a view that could be enlightened and expanded by understanding the perspective of the other. All three perspectives are present in Welsh society. Devolution provides the occasion for a potential meeting of different perspectives and minds.

In particular, educationalists who support bilingual education need to understand the politics behind, and sometimes against, bilingual education for there to be movement forward. The defence and expansion of bilingual education cannot come suddenly from language-planning perspectives (language-planning acquisition) nor through purely stating the many and real advantages of bilingual education. In Wales, bilingual education may flourish or otherwise through the locus of political power, the movement of political ideology and through political influence. This is where language planners and educationalists in support of bilingual education can join forces. The future fortunes of bilingual education in Wales are open to political influence. The benefits of bilingual education are not self-apparent nor intrinsically obvious. Therefore, the notion of bilingual education has to be marketed so that both the public and politicians are persuaded and convinced.

It took less than fifty years to build a strong system of bilingual education in Wales. A movement from the absence of Welsh-medium education to its strength in the primary sector occurred with speed. That speed brings a warning. Unless there is continued support and influence, fast-changing political events could quickly affect the face of bilingual education in Wales, including to its detriment.

Note

1. The analyses of Welsh-language reproduction in the family is based on the author's analysis of the Sample of Anonymized Records from the 1991 census (both the 1% Household data and the 2% Individual data).

References

Baker, C. (1992) *Attitudes and Language*. Clevedon: Multilingual Matters.

Baker, C. (1993) Bilingual education in Wales. In H. Baetens Beardsmore (ed.), *European Typologies of Bilingual Education*. Clevedon: Multilingual Matters.

Baker, C. (1996) *Foundations of Bilingual Education and Bilingualism*. Clevedon: Multilingual Matters.

Baker, C. and Jones, S. P. (1998) *Encyclopedia of Bilingualism and Bilingual Education*. Clevedon: Multilingual Matters.

Huffines, M. L. (1991) Pennsylvania German: 'Do they love it in their hearts?'. In J. R. Dow (ed.), *Language and Ethnicity. Focusschrift in Honor of Joshua Fishman*. Amsterdam and Philadelphia: John Benjamins.

Office of Population Censuses and Surveys (1992) *The 1991 Census of Great Britain*. HMSO: Office of Population Censuses and Surveys.

Stubbs, M. (1991) Educational language planning in England and Wales. In F. Coulmas (ed.), *A Language Policy for the European Community*. Berlin: Mouton de Gruyter.

Welsh Language Board (1995) *A Strategy for the Welsh Language*. Cardiff: Welsh Language Board.

Welsh Office (1997) *Statistics of Education and Training in Wales: Schools 1997*. Cardiff: Welsh Office.

Williams, C. H. and Raybould, W. H. (1991) *Welsh Language Planning: Opportunities and Constraints*. Cardiff: Welsh Language Education Development Committee.

Appendix

The following objectives have been extracted from Welsh Language Board (1995) and reclassified under the four priorities discussed in this chapter.

Language reproduction in the family
Objective 1(ii): To ensure that every child has experience of the language before commencing statutory education.

Objective 4: To increase the number of three year olds who speak Welsh in the family.

Objective 18: To halt and reverse the decline in the number of areas where a significant percentage of residents speak Welsh, or where that was true until relatively recently.

Language production through bilingual education

Objective 1(i): To ensure that Welsh-medium/bilingual nursery education is available within a reasonable distance, and that parents know of the provision before making a decision regarding their children's nursery education, in order to increase the number of parents who choose Welsh-medium education for their children.

Objective 2(i): To enhance and extend the education system so that Welsh-medium education is easily available to anyone who desires it for their children.

Objective 2(ii): To ensure that all pupils are given a fair opportunity to become fluently bilingual by the time they complete their statutory education, and to ensure that appropriate resources are provided in order to achieve this objective.

Objective 3(i): To agree strategic plans with providers for developing Welsh language or bilingual courses throughout Wales.

Objective 3(ii): To ensure that every young person is aware of the Welsh language or bilingual provision and opportunities available within 16+ education.

Objective 5(ii): To ensure that opportunities are available for adults to learn Welsh, and that people are aware of the provision.

Objective 5(iii): To increase the number of adults who succeed in learning Welsh.

Objective 6(i): To ensure that the main participants within the area of Welsh language education collaborate in order to plan the provision of education and training both locally and nationally.

Objective 6(ii): To establish networks between the providers of initial teacher training and in-service training in order to ensure an all-Wales scheme which provided qualified teachers and suitable teaching materials.

Objective 6(iii): To ensure appropriate provision in terms of Welsh-medium books, software and other teaching/learning resources.

Using Welsh in the economy

Objective 8: To increase the opportunities provided by voluntary sector bodies for using the Welsh language.

Objective 9: To increase opportunities to use the Welsh language in dealing with private companies.

Objective 10: To increase opportunities for people to use the Welsh language socially and in the workplace.

The use of Welsh for cultural and leisure purposes
Objective 8: To increase the opportunities provided by voluntary sector bodies for using the Welsh language.

Objective 10: To increase opportunities for people to use the Welsh language socially and in the workplace.

Objective 13: To increase the number of young people who use Welsh naturally as a medium of communication.

Objective 19: Welsh-speakers should be provided with the requisite facilities to support and expand their use of the Welsh language within their communities.

III

Effectiveness and Monitoring

7

A Re-examination of the Effectiveness of Schools in Wales

STEPHEN GORARD

Introduction

This chapter addresses the issue of using raw-score indicators to compare the performance of groups of educational establishments. Despite the growth of sophisticated, some might say over-sophisticated, ways of estimating the value-added to a performance by an institution such as a school, raw-score comparisons continue to be made by researchers, journalists and, most frighteningly, by policy-makers. In Wales, whole programmes of improvement measures and targets have been predicated upon the unproved notion that schools in Wales are underperforming, that students are 'schooled to fail', and that the majority of secondary schools in Wales – English-medium comprehensives – should be looking to English schools and Welsh-medium schools for their models of improvement strategies. Similar forms of comparison have more recently been used to suggest that the compulsory learning of Welsh hinders the learning of other modern languages. In the absence of analyses indicating alternative interpretations of the data, such views have been put forward by the Institute for Welsh Affairs as the basis of an educational policy for the new Welsh National Assembly. The substantive purpose of this chapter is to argue that all such comparisons are rhetorically misleading and to show that under closer analysis the differences and effect-sizes claimed by the advocates of these positions are statistically insignificant. The lack of difference is so easily discernible in the light of background factors that one wonders why politicians, some academics and the media continue to cite the differential effectiveness of schools in Wales in support of their preferred programmes of action.

The supposed Welsh school effect is demonstrated by the fact that schools in Wales generally have lower school outcome measures compared with England, although the growing number of designated Welsh-medium schools (*ysgolion Cymraeg*) in south Wales are doing rather better. It may be that the supporters of this 'effect' represent an alliance between those whose policy presupposed that education in Wales is generally poor (such as previous Secretaries of State for Wales, most notably John Redwood) and those who want to elevate the performance of the *ysgolion Cymraeg*, seeking more general approval for their existence in terms of such schools' relative effectiveness, rather than using the more obvious (but not necessarily straightforward) argument based upon a choice of the medium of instruction. In fact, the evidence for either proposition is very weak, as it is for the proposition that grant-maintained (GM) schools or fee-paying schools *per se* are performing better than their competitors (for example, Gorard, 1998a). This chapter considers some of the weaknesses in the positions and suggests an alternative but, hardly novel, way of analysing school performance data which leads to the opposite conclusion on both propositions. Schools in Wales are doing reasonably well in comparison with equivalent schools in England and there is no evidence of children being disadvantaged by a Welsh education. On the other hand, there is no evidence that Welsh-medium education leads to any general advantage in schooling.

The 'schooled to fail' myth

One outcome of the increasing separation of Welsh educational policy from that of England (Delamont and Rees, 1997) has been the development of school 'improvement' measures and attainment targets specific to Wales, prompted to a large extent by the view that schools in Wales are generally not performing as well as schools in England. It has been shown elsewhere how the notion that schools in England are outperforming those in Wales is seductive (Gorard, 1998b). The Wales 'effect' has been used by school effectiveness researchers to demonstrate the importance of what happens in schools in determining results (Reynolds 1995), and by politicians as a spur for regional school improvement (Welsh Office, 1995a). It is generally based upon raw-score comparisons (Jones, 1996) or raw-score comparisons with some attempt to argue a match between the comparison groups (Reynolds, 1990). This prevailing view is reinforced by memories of the high 'failure rate' in Wales after 1944 (in Istance and Rees, 1995), the findings of the 1981 Loosemore Report, more recent inspection reports (OHCMI, 1993), the relatively low level of qualification among the working population in Wales (Eurostat, 1995), and by the publication of 'league tables' of school examination results (*TES*, 1995). On almost any score of educational achievement that can be devised, it seems that the results in Wales are inferior to those in England (see Table 7.1, for example) and these comparisons have had real implications for local educational policies.

Table 7.1   Relative progress towards Foundation Target 1 (% gaining 5 or more GCSE grade A*–C)

	Spring 1991	*Autumn 1995*
England	53.5	67.4
Wales	51.2	62.2

This negative view of the effectiveness of schools in Wales identified by academics was taken up by policy-makers in the previous government who made it the cornerstone of their improvement strategy and targets (Welsh Office, 1995a, 1995b, 1996a, 1997a). In fact the creation and attempted use of targets for schools started earlier in Wales than in England, prompted, in part at least, by concern over the relatively poor standard of schools in Wales. When alternative evidence contradicting the consensus was presented to them, the Conservatives continued to defend the usefulness of their raw-score comparisons (*Western Mail*, 1997a). Interestingly, the then Labour education spokesman for Wales, Win Griffiths, claimed that he never had and never would make such 'unfavourable' comparisons with England. However, in the new 'New Labour' administration, of which he was a part, raw-score comparisons with England remain the 'research' basis for government policy-making in Wales. They underlie the important message of the White Paper put before parliament called *Building Excellent Schools Together* which states that 'standards of achievement are still far too low, progress in raising them far too slow' (Welsh Office, 1997b: 2). This is justified by statements such as: 'results at GCSE A*–C lag behind those in England ... 11% of pupils leave school without GCSEs, where 8% do so in England' (Welsh Office,

1997b: 3). The new government is supported in this position by the same media who had declared in April 1997 that the 'England–Wales gap does not exist', by saying in December that the gap (presumably rediscovered) is now 'closing' (*Western Mail*, 1997a, 1997b; see also *TES,* 1997a).

The 'schooled-to-fail' argument has also spread to particular concern about performance in modern languages. Using the same logic as the general Welsh school effect, the new Welsh Education Minister has apparently 'ordered his officials to examine the reasons for the under-performance of Welsh schoolchildren in modern foreign languages' (*Western Mail*, 1997c). He has not ordered them to investigate whether there is such underperformance, since the evidence already exists: in 1996 only 26 per cent of children in Wales gained a C in a modern foreign language, compared with 34 per cent in England (in addition, there is a report that one potential investor decided against a site in Wales and reported to the Welsh Office via the telephone that the reason was the poor language skills of people in Wales). One explanation proposed by the Welsh Office for this is language confusion or curricular overcrowding caused by the National Curriculum (NC) order for the Welsh language.

The Welsh-medium myth

A similar logic is used by the Insititute of Welsh Affairs in Jones (1996) with respect to Welsh- and English-medium secondary schools in south Wales. Basing their argument on Reynolds and Bellin (1996), they appear to assume that English-medium schools in Wales are performing worse than their Welsh-medium peers and only consider the possible explanations why. Again, the evidence is taken as being incontrovertible. They present the GCSE results of seven schools in Rhondda Cynon Taff (Jones, 1996) which have undoubted differences in outcome measures (see Table 7.2). The three Welsh-medium schools all have a higher percentage of pupils achieving five or more GCSEs at grade C than the four English-medium schools selected for comparison (but it should be noted that four schools in this unitary authority had better scores than the 'top' Welsh-medium school, and that Ysgol Gyfun Rhydfelen appears only half-way up the raw-score league table of schools in the LEA). The relative position of the schools is similar in terms of other measures such as A level results and the percentage of leavers with no qualifications.

Table 7.2 Comparison of schools in Rhondda Cynon Taff 1996 and 1997 (% gaining 5 or more GCSE grade A*–C)

School	GCSE benchmark 1996	GCSE benchmark 1997
Ysgol Gyfun Cymer	50	64
Ysgol Gyfun Llanhari	49	48
Ysgol Gyfun Rhydfelen	35	46
Porth	31	27
Treorchy	29	34
Tonypandy	26	22
Ferndale	23	27

The possible explanations of these differences given by Reynolds and Bellin include the extra stimulation stemming from a bilingual education, greater clarity of goals in Welsh-medium schools, their range of activities, staff motivation and greater parental involvement, forming an 'interlocking, overlapping community of interest'. The Institute of Welsh Affairs (IWA) comment 'no research has been done to identify factors which account for these differences ... It could prove useful to English Medium schools in Wales' (Jones, 1996: 31). Therefore the raw-scores of Table 7.2, as with the Welsh general school effect, are being used to assemble and promote models of school-improvement, along the lines that all schools should emulate *ysgolion Cymraeg*. The myth is further propagated through the research literature, where there is a widespread belief that Welsh-medium schools are 'better' (for example, Jones, 1997), and through the media where only Welsh-medium schools have been referred to as 'Welsh' schools and the users of English-medium schools in Wales are described as being 'English' (*Western Mail*, 1997d). This is in a similar vein to previous claims by some language activists that the majority of Welsh people are not 'really Welsh' as they are unable to speak Welsh (in Giggs and Pattie, 1994). In effect it has become a key element of the 'official discourse' about schools and schooling in Wales.

The Institute of Welsh Affairs describes itself as an independent think-tank and research institute with core funding from the Welsh Development Agency and Hyder, supplemented by smaller private and business contributions. Its role is 'raise the level of information and debate on Welsh public policy issues'. As part of this role it organized seminars in 1998 to help set a policy agenda for the forthcoming National Assembly. One of these seminars was on education and a draft paper was created for discussion that will become part of the Handbook for the Assembly, an 'authoritative series of papers addressing the key policy issues they will face'. This paper was written by David Reynolds and Eirlys Pritchard Jones (a member of IWA and former head of a Welsh-medium school) and it is therefore no surprise to see that the paper embraces all of the 'schooled to fail' literature and its derivatives such as the claims about the inferiority of English-medium schools in Wales (Jones and Reynolds, 1998). Despite calling for a 'rational, evidence based educational policy' (in contrast to 'ideologically driven' policies, be it noted), the paper cites no actual evidence and clearly takes no account at all of recent education policy research taking place in Wales and about Wales (Jones and Reynolds, 1998: 3).

The importance of intake characteristics

The different types of supposed underperformance described above are surprisingly free from reference to the growing body of work on school effectiveness and models of value-added performance (for example, Gray and Jones, 1986; Mortimore and Mortimore, 1986; Reynolds *et al.*, 1994; Sammons *et al.*, 1994). These show a clear relationship between school outcome measures of the kind used here and the socio-economic status of the students (Willms and Echols, 1992). Unless these characteristics and other significant differences are eliminated between the two groups before comparison, there is no reason to suppose that the effects described by the ensemble of academics and policy-makers above do not arise simply because the students in the comparisons are not matched.

Wales is much smaller than England, with a much lower population density, a smaller choice of schools for parents and generally poorer schools (see Gorard, 1998b, for summary). Wales has traditionally lacked a large middle class and even today the occupational-class profile is clearly flatter than that in England. Wales has an older and ageing population with a high proportion of retired, early retired and long-term sick, while registered unemployment in some parts is still high (Gorard, 1997a). These problems of remoteness, relative poverty and economic inactivity may be sufficient by themselves to explain the lower levels of attainment in schools in Wales compared with England.

In a recent systematic survey of 1,104 residents in industrial south Wales, just over 1 per cent described themselves as speaking Welsh (including both Welsh and English) at home (Gorard *et al.*, 1997). This figure probably gives a more accurate account of Welsh usage than the census figure for the same area of around 8 per cent of the population able to speak some Welsh. For example, an even larger number may be able to speak some French, although the question was not asked in the census, but without using French in the home as a language of communication. In the survey, the Welsh-speakers were significantly older than the average, all described themselves as white – that is, none of the ethnic-minority respondents spoke Welsh – and they are also predominantly male, from a chapel family background. They are generally better educated than average, having remained longer in full-time education than their contemporaries, spent longer in lifetime learning, and gained higher qualifications. The Welsh-speakers are, in general, of much higher occupational and social status and these benefits are also shared by their children. Thus, it might be true that those in south Wales using Welsh-medium schools today are more socially advantaged than those using local comprehensives and this might explain the apparently better performance of the students. It is certainly true that previous analysts have found an over-representation of Welsh-speakers in the highest social classes in south Wales (Giggs and Pattie, 1994). Of course, not all users of *ysgolion Cymraeg* in south Wales are themselves Welsh-speaking (Packer and Campbell, 1994), but given the small proportion of the population speaking Welsh it could not be otherwise (Gorard, 1997b).

This situation has led to a further myth that the English-speaking users of Welsh-medium schools are the same kind of parents as those using English-medium schools (*Western Mail*, 1997d; see also *TES*, 1997b). The 'new survey' data on which this particular report was based in fact dated from 1993 and involved an opportunity 'sample' of twenty-four parents of one class in one Welsh-medium school and a total of nineteen self-selected parents using two English-medium schools. There is therefore no reason to make the bold generalized statements about Welsh-medium schools (note the plural) that the authors do. It is interesting to note that the article nowhere mentions the number of participants or schools, but by use of broadly sweeping statements gives this tiny study a disproportionate grandeur. The authors themselves say at one stage 'it would be unwise to extrapolate findings from such small samples' (*Western Mail*, 1997d: 21), clearly contradicting their somewhat wilder statements in the article. When the authors state that there is 'an absence of a clear division between the two sets of parents', this statement is rather misleading since the numbers involved in each cell of the comparison are so small that any attempt to find significant differences between subgroups is doomed to fail. In addition, when the authors state that 'few' of the parents regard Welsh-medium schools as selective, they are hiding their lack of analysis behind an imprecise term. If eight of their twenty-four parents regard the school as selective, the eight could, in all fairness, be described as few but over 33 per cent is not the impression generally given by the word 'few'. Similarly, the term 'most' can simply mean over half or a majority. Thus, when the authors state that 'most of the parents with children at the Welsh-medium school did not support the idea that Wales might be an independent country', the frequencies in their paper show this actually means fewer than 60 per cent. This is almost exactly the same figure that is described incorrectly as a 'substantial minority' of the users of English-medium schools who agreed with the statement that funding Welsh was a 'waste of money'. To use the same logic as in the previous example, 'most' users of English-medium schools therefore felt that paying for Welsh to be taught was a waste of money. This is hardly the stuff of the headline, 'Even English parents back Welsh taught in classroom'. It is against this background then that the second sustaining myth, that Welsh-medium schools are more effective than their 'English' counterparts, needs to be examined.

One example of this argument is advanced by Jones (1996) but the claim is made without citing substantive evidence. The basis of that argument is that since Welsh- and English-medium schools in Rhondda Cynon Taff, for example, are 'cheek by jowl', taking pupils from overlapping catchments of similar socio-economic characteristics, then the undoubted differences in their outcome measures must be due to something that is happening in the schools concerned. This position may be at least partly based on an earlier study suggesting that Welsh-medium schools perform better even when the type of intake factors described above have been taken into account (Bellin *et al.*, 1996, Higgs *et al.*, 1997). The chief basis for the 'cheek by jowl' argument about equivalent intakes is apparently provided by the principal components analysis in Bellin *et al.*, (1996) and the variant which appears in Higgs *et al.*, (1997). This analysis of the relationship between school intake characteristics and outcome measures produced three factors underlying all of their variables. These factors are unrelated to each other by definition, since orthogonal rotation was used to obtain the solution. One of these factors, the only reliable one on the basis of the number of variables with high loadings according to most sources (for example, Stevens, 1992), is a combined measure of social advantage/disadvantage (such as parental occupational class) and school outcomes (such as GCSE results). The high loadings of several variables (for example, father's unemployment and GCSE results) on this factor suggest that they are alternative 'pure factor' measures (Comrey, 1973) and therefore that both school intake and school performance are in fact measuring the same underlying variable. The fact that scores on this performance factor do not correlate with the scores on the other two – speaking Welsh and ethnic-minority origin – show that speaking Welsh is unrelated to examination performance once other socio-economic differences have been accounted for. Unfortunately, Bellin *et al.* do not draw this conclusion, but try to argue that the independence of Welsh-speaking and social advantage shows that those using Welsh-medium schools are of similar social advantage or disadvantage, and that the market is not 'creaming off' privileged parents for *ysgolion Cymraeg* (1996: 19). They therefore ignore the fact that the independence is a mathematical outcome of their choice of rotation, rather than an empirical finding, and that their Welsh factor only represents that variance attributable to Welsh-speaking after advantage has been isolated.

They also ignore the fact that simple observation of the intake characteristics of pupils in different types of school in Wales shows that the schools in their comparisons are not equivalent (see below), for although both Bellin *et al.* (1996) and Higgs *et al.* (1997) describe the use of multi-level models in their articles, this is not the technique they use because, as they rightly claim, gaining admission to data at the school level is 'very difficult' (Bellin *et al.*, 1996: 6). They therefore chose the alternative of using local census data at the level of enumeration districts in place of school-based data. However, despite discussion of this and the principal components analysis, their most convincing results come from using the school-based indicator of eligibility for free school meals on its own. The principal components analysis may be technically flawed since there are only fifty-one cases assessing twenty-seven variables, far too few according to many accounts (for example, Child, 1970). Some variables mentioned in the text, such as special educational needs, are not described in the factor table, presumably having been omitted from analysis but without explanation or justification. Only fifty-one of the sixty-eight schools in Mid and South Glamorgan were used in the analysis since, in the opinion of the authors, the other seventeen take pupils from an undefined catchment area, although these seventeen include the Welsh-medium schools. Therefore the results do not apply to the Welsh-medium schools and the authors' argument about the existence of separate markets for the different types of schools is hoist by its own petard.

Method

This study uses data from the school-level database created by Gorard and Fitz (1998) for 116 secondary schools over nine years, representing ten LEAs in south Wales. The data for 1995/6 were used to predict outcomes for the seven Welsh-medium schools in the dataset in terms of their background characteristics. The model is created using the equivalent data for all 104 English-medium schools from the same LEAs. The year 1996 was chosen to coincide with the picture presented by the Institute for Welsh Affairs in Jones (1996). Incidentally, it is in order to counter this picture that the seven schools named in Jones (1996) are also named in this paper, with the agreement of Rhondda Cynon Taff LEA. The school performance data come from the *Times Educational Supplement* (1996), while additional local characteristics were obtained from the census 1991 (via National On-line Manpower Information System, NOMIS).

The performance measure chosen was the GCSE benchmark of the percentage of the relevant age cohort gaining five or more grades A–C. This benchmark figure was used for several reasons. It is the most commonly quoted, used in government publications, in league tables, by press and other media, and by many of the articles cited above. Above all, it is the one used in 'home international' publications such as *A Bright Future* (Welsh Office, 1995a). There is an established tradition of LEAs and researchers using public examination results as performance indicators at the school level (for example, Gray and Wilcox, 1995). An analysis leading to a slightly inferior model was also obtained for the schools' overall qualification rate and the reliability of the model was confirmed by analysis of the results for 1997.

The independent variables used to characterize the schools are social class of local householders, qualification of local householders, low income as defined by eligibility for free school meals and population density. These are used for two main reasons. They are conveniently available at this level of disaggregation from census data or Welsh Office STATS1 forms and they have been linked to school performance both by this study and others (Sammons *et al.*, 1994; Gray and Wilcox, 1995). Family social class has been shown to be strongly linked to school performance, while poverty, as assessed by eligibility for free school meals, is an excellent indicator of examination performance (Lake, 1992). Population density is used to distinguish urban, suburban and rural areas, which have been shown to be relevant to educational achievement (Gordon, 1996). Although there are other factors that could be built into the model, some of which were tried and rejected in this study (Gorard, 1998b), many are highly correlated with each other, such as the proportion of lone parents and free school meals. Although it would be ideal to have a larger number of variables available for inclusion at the school level, as argued by Higgs *et al.* (1997), there is an inevitable compromise between depth and breadth in this respect.

The same indicator variables are used for the comparison between the LEAs in Wales and England, but at a higher level of aggregation. This comparison uses data from 1993/4 to predict school outcomes for each LEA in Wales in terms of its background characteristics (Welsh Office, 1995c; census, 1991, via NOMIS). The model used is created using the equivalent data for all 108 England LEAs (DfEE, 1994a, 1994b). The results for 1994 are used since they are from the last complete academic year before the local government reorganization into unitary authorities in Wales (see Welsh Office, 1996b).

All of the independent variables correlate significantly with the

GCSE benchmark at both school and LEA levels, with the percentage taking free school meals accounting for 75 per cent of the variance in results between schools by itself. The relationships between all of the predictors and the dependent variable are approximately linear (Maxwell, 1977). The natural logarithm of the GCSE benchmark figures was also plotted against the independent variables and the relationships were if anything even more clearly linear. Both the log results and the untransformed data were tested using multiple linear regression (Pedhazur, 1982). Multiple regression is a useful analysis since it takes all variables into account simultaneously and partitions the explained variance between them (Achen, 1982). Multiple linear regression analysis was used to answer the question of what can be expected of each school/LEA given its determining characteristics. Diagnostics suggest that the major assumptions underlying regression hold in these two examples, although even where they do not the results can still be used with care (Berry and Feldman, 1985). The variables were added to the model using forward stepwise entry (Norusis, 1994).

The Welsh school effect

The results described here are substantially the same as in Gorard (1998b), and they are presented chiefly to set the scene for a similar analysis at the school level in the next section. The best and most parsimonious model for predicting the 1994 GCSE benchmark figures for each LEA used only three of the potential predictors: the percentage of secondary school children taking free school meals, the percentage of householders in social classes 1 and 2, and the population density. The resulting model was an excellent one with high tolerance for all predictors (R square of 0.852, F of 214, probability of 0.0000). This model is:

GCSE benchmark = 31.52 – 0.59 × meals – 0.06 × density +
0.45 × class.

The predicted results for the eight Welsh LEAs are therefore as in Table 7.3. On this analysis, Wales as a whole is doing as well as equivalent LEAs in England on which the predictions are based.

Table 7.3 Predicted GCSE benchmarks for Welsh LEAs (% gaining 5 or more GCSE grade A*–C)

LEA	Predicted	Observed	Difference
Clwyd	39.08	40.0	+1
Dyfed	39.28	45.0	+6
Gwent	36.47	35.0	−1
Gwynedd	40.78	43.0	+2
Mid Glamorgan	32.78	30.0	−3
Powys	47.51	45.0	−3
South Glamorgan	40.35	40.0	0
West Glamorgan	35.23	38.0	+3

A similar function at an all-Wales level could be imagined which would take the different levels of poverty, education, occupational class and population density in Wales and England and explain the apparent differences in modern language performance (see above) without reference to the problems of monoglots learning Welsh in addition to the subjects learnt by their peers in England. When this factor is taken into account, it may be that schools in Wales are, if anything, more effective with equivalent pupils than schools generally are in England.

The Welsh-medium effect

In the ten LEAs for which data are available at a school level, their stratification index (or meal-ratio based on the proportion of children in each school who are eligible for free school meals) is strongly related to the proportion of the fifteen–year-old cohort gaining five or more GCSEs. The usefulness of this stratification index, devised by Gorard and Fitz (1998), is therefore further validated by its ability to predict GCSE results even more accurately than the simple proportion of pupils eligible for free meals. The correlation at the school level is −0.87 meaning that over 75 per cent of the variance in the GCSE benchmarks could be explained by eligibility for free school meals alone. The relationship is approximately linear, as is the equivalent transformed relationship between the natural logarithm of the GCSE benchmarks and the stratification index (see Figures 7.1 and 7.2). This is especially significant since, although the mean ratio of social disadvantage in the schools of

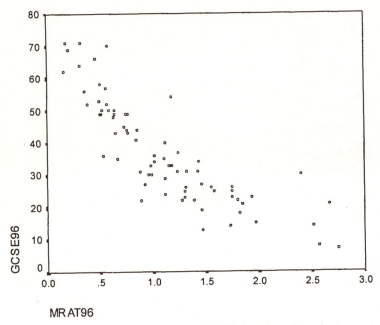

Figure 7.1 Scattergram of school-level GCSE benchmark against poverty

south Wales is 1 (by definition), the mean ratio of disadvantage in English-medium schools is 1.14, while in Welsh-medium schools the ratio is 0.59. Thus, using a model based on social disadvantage, Welsh-medium schools would be expected to gain significantly better results simply to display the same level of performance as the majority of schools in south Wales.

The best and most parsimonious model for predicting the 1996 GCSE benchmark figures for each of the 116 schools used only one of the potential predictors, the stratification index in terms of children eligible for free school meals. The resulting model was an excellent one with high tolerance for all predictors (R square of 0.88, F of 93, probability of 0.0000). Local population density, the size of the school, the percentage of local householders in social classes 1 and 2, the percentage of householders with a qualification from higher education and the number and proportion of children eligible for free school meals were not used by the resulting model, since they contributed nothing further to the accuracy of predictions once the impact of stratification was taken into account (using

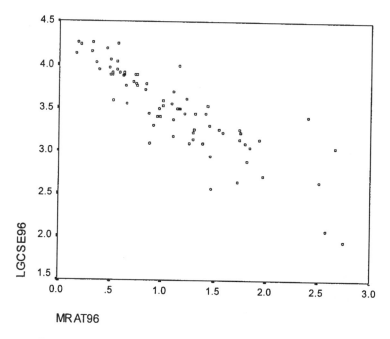

Figure 7.2 Scattergram of log (school-level GCSE benchmark) against poverty

forward stepwise selection). The competing indicators are anyway partially collinear (see Table 7.4) which can cause bias when all are included in the same solution (Menard, 1995).

Table 7.4 Correlations between variables at the school level

	Class	Density	HEqual	NOR	Mratio	GCSE	Qualrate
Class		+0.9	+1.0				
Density	+0.9		+0.9				
HEqual	+1.0	+0.9					
NOR					−0.5	+0.4	+0.3
Mratio				−0.5		−0.9	−0.7
GCSE				+0.4	−0.9		+0.8
Qualrate				+0.3	−0.7	+0.8	

Class = % of local householders in occupational class 1 and 2; Density = local population density; HEqual = % of local householders with qualification higher than A level; NOR = number of pupils in school; Mratio=school's ratio of 'ideal' number of pupils eligible for free meals.

The resulting model is: log(GCSE benchmark) = 4.3 – 0.74 × meal-ratio

The model can be used to predict the expected outcomes from any school in the dataset. Table 7.5 shows this for the same seven schools as in Table 7.2. Interestingly, Ferndale, which had the lowest raw-score on the original table, is the school which appears to have the largest positive school effect (at this level and others). Only one of the Welsh-medium schools has a positive impact, while one of the others is apparently the worst performing school of the seven, using this model. There is no clear evidence here that children are advantaged by attending either type of school in general. There may be individual school effects (the data are neutral on this) but there is certainly no clear school-type effect in Rhondda Cynon Taff. There are *ysgolion Cymraeg* elsewhere in south Wales achieving rather better results than might be expected, such as Ysgol Gyfun Gŵyr, but there are English-medium schools performing just as well, such as Bishopston, and some doing much better, such as Aberdare Girls'. A t-test for independent samples showed no significant difference in the mean residuals between the different types of schools. In south Wales at least there is no difference between the performance of Welsh- and English-medium schools.

Table 7.5 Observed and expected outcomes

School	GCSE benchmark	Expected	Difference
Ysgol Gyfun Cymer	50	48	+2
Ysgol Gyfun Llanhari	49	50	−1
Ysgol Gyfun Rhydfelen	35	46	−9
Porth	31	29	+2
Treorchy	29	33	−4
Tonypandy	26	29	−3
Ferndale	23	18	+5

A similar model for the GCSE benchmark in 1997 was also created but using indicators for 1996. The similarity between this function and that for 1997 is impressive. The function was:

log (GCSE benchmark) = 4.3 − 0.68 × meal-ratio.

The qualification rate is defined here as the percentage of the age cohort in each school obtaining any qualification (such as one GCSE grade G). The best and most parsimonious model for predicting the 1996 qualification rate for each of the eighty-six schools used the same predictors as the benchmark model. The resulting model was a good one with high tolerance for all predictors (R square of 0.76, F of 37, probability of 0.0000). The resulting model is:

$$\text{Qualification rate} = 186.9 - 10.8 \times \text{meal-ratio} + 11.9 \times \text{HE qualification} - 7.2 \times \text{class}$$

Using this model, there is no evidence that *ysgolion Cymraeg* are outperforming other schools in terms of the proportion of children leaving with a recognized qualification at age 16. In fact, there is some evidence of the reverse. Some of the schools with depressed league table positions, such as Ferndale in Rhondda Cynon Taff, have a much higher than expected qualification rate.

Conclusion

How then can we construe the continued use of raw-score data by officials and by academics when in other arenas the latter have been highly critical of analyses which do not feature at least some kind of 'value-added' account? How should we interpret the overly negative assessment of Welsh schools when other measures demonstrate that the Welsh–English gap does not exist to the extent that is claimed in the studies cited above.

A loose alliance of researchers, journalists and policy-makers appear to have established what can only be described as an official discourse about the performance of schools in Wales. The set of public meanings constituting this discourse promotes the idea of underachieving Welsh schools and the relatively greater effectiveness of Welsh-medium schools which might serve as a model for schools in Wales generally. It is both important and dangerous, as it is the foundation of the two sustaining myths identified above, that this discourse involves a disregard of scrupulous and careful analysis of input data which might show that the differences in outcomes are not as great, when social factors are accounted for, as is argued for here.

Discourses are forged and sustained by an ensemble of field positions and field occupants. Clearly the latter may wish to defend the boundaries of the field, the values embedded in their discourse and their own position as judges of what is counted as valid or legitimate knowledge about Welsh schools. According to one account, there may be at heart a community, or 'Welsh class', linking nationalism and language, behaving as a status group in Weberian terms according to Fevre, Denney and Borland, producing changes by agitation which 'have been of most benefit to members of this status group' (1997: 1), and attempting to monopolize resources through social closure (see also Giggs and Pattie, 1994). This community may not wish attention to be drawn to the fact that in general the *ysgolion Cymraeg* have, and always have had, a consistently lower proportion of children with special educational needs, and from families eligible for free school meals, and that when these factors are taken into account, there is an indication that the Welsh-medium schools in south Wales are not especially effective. By remaining vociferous on this issue of effectiveness, the community may also hope to silence questions about language 'apartheid' and racism (Williams, 1997), the difficulties of comparative assessment (Jones, 1997) and lack of choice (Gorard, 1997c). This chapter will be seen as an uncomfortable challenge both to the standard discourse of Welsh-medium superiority and to those who have invested in it politically, academically and administratively. Despite this, the challenge is worth pursuing for two main reasons. One is keeping ourselves intellectually informed, honest and open-minded about what constitutes a key feature of Welsh schooling, since, in the author's opinion, that is the primary business of the educational research community.

The second purpose is to point out the harmful and divisive effects of the discourse for schools, teachers, parents and students. By claiming that most schools in Wales are not doing a good job, the conspirators deny these people the credit that they deserve. Moreover, in a 'market' where student recruitment is vital and loss of students endangers institutional survival, they skew current choices, encouraging the use of Welsh-medium schools by non-Welsh-speaking families – a policy with potentially serious equal-opportunity implications for ethnic minorities in Wales (Gorard, 1997b). They also encourage the use of schools across the border in England and other forms of harmful market migration based upon complacency in schools with high mean SES or unnecessary changes in policy by schools in disadvantaged areas (Willms and Echols, 1992). Finally, their claim may have encouraged the setting of unrealistic performance targets, such as those in the *People and Prosperity*, and the *Bright Future* publications (for example, Welsh Office, 1997a), which have already been 'down-sized' once as the impossibility of their attainment began to dawn on politicians. In the end, then, it has contributed to a situation which evokes from government a concern not with education, education, education, but intervention, intervention, intervention.

Acknowledgements

Thanks go to the ten LEAs providing school-based data for this study, and to John Fitz and Brian Davies for their comments on the draft. Much of the chapter 'A re-examination of the effectiveness of schools in Wales' by Stephen Gorard appeared in the *Oxford Review of Education*, 24(4) (1998), 459–72 under the title 'Four errors and a conspiracy? The effectiveness of schools in Wales'. Relevant sections reprinted with permission.

References

Achen, C. (1982) *Interpreting and Using Regression*. London: Sage.

Bellin, W., Farrell, S., Higgs, G. and White, S. (1996) A strategy for using census information in comparison of school performance. *Welsh Journal of Education*, 5(2), 3–25.

Berry, W. and Feldman, S. (1985) *Multiple Regression in Practice*. London: Sage.

Census (1991) Data available from National On-line Manpower Information System. Durham.

Child, D. (1970) *The Essentials of Factor Analysis*. London: Holt, Rinehart & Winston.

Comrey, A. (1973) *A First Course on Factor Analysis*. London: Academic Press.

Delamont, S. and Rees, G. (1997) *Understanding the Welsh Education System: Does Wales Need a Separate 'Policy Sociology'?* Working Paper 23. Cardiff: School of Education.

DfEE (1994a) *Statistics of Education: Public Examinations GCSE and GCE in England 1994*. London: HMSO.

DfEE (1994b) *Statistics of Education: Schools in England 1994*. London: HMSO.

Eurostat (1995) *Education across the European Union: Statistics and Indicators*. Brussels: Statistical Office of the European Communities.

Fevre, R., Denney, D. and Borland, J. (1997) Class, status and party in the analysis of nationalism: lessons from Max Weber. *Nations and Nationalism*, 3(4), 559.

Giggs, J. and Pattie, C. (1994) Wales as a plural society, *Contemporary Wales*, 5, 25.

Gorard, S. (1997a) *The Region of Study: Patterns of Participation in Adult Education and Training*. Working Paper 1. Cardiff: School of Education.

Gorard, S. (1997b) Paying for a Little England: school choice and the Welsh language. *Welsh Journal of Education*, 6(1), 19–32.

Gorard, S. (1997c) *School Choice in an Established Market: Families and Fee-Paying Schools*. Aldershot: Ashgate.

Gorard, S. (1998a) Whither market forces in education? *International Journal of Education Management*, 12(1), 5–13.

Gorard, S. (1998b) Schooled to fail? Revisiting the Welsh school-effect. *Journal of Education Policy*, 13(1), 115–24.

Gorard, S. and Fitz, J. (1998) The more things change . . . the missing impact of marketisation. *British Journal of Sociology of Education*, 19(3), 365–76.

Gorard, S., Fevre, R., Rees, G. and Furlong, J. (1997) *Space, Mobility and the Education of Minority Groups in Wales: The Survey Results, Patterns of Participation in Adult Education and Training*. Working Paper 10. Cardiff: School of Education.

Gordon, I. (1996) Family structure, educational achievement and the inner city. *Urban Studies*, 33(3), 407–23.

Gray, J. and Jones, B. (1986) Towards a framework for interpreting examination results. In R. Rogers (ed.), *Education and Social Class*. Lewes: Falmer Press.

Gray, J. and Wilcox, B. (1995) *'Good School, Bad School': Evaluating Performance and Encouraging Improvement*. Buckingham: Open University Press.

Higgs, G., Bellin, W., Farrell, S. and White, S. (1997) Educational attainment and social disadvantage: contextualising school league tables. *Regional Studies*, 31, 8.

Istance, D. and Rees, G. (1995) *Lifelong Learning in Wales: A Programme for Prosperity*. A NIACE Cymru policy discussion paper. Leicester: NIACE.

Jones, D. (1997) Bilingual mathematics: development and practice in Wales. *Curriculum Journal*, 8(3), 393.

Jones, E. and Reynolds, D. (1998) *Education policy: An Agenda for the National Assembly*. Cardiff: Institute of Welsh Affairs (mimeo).

Jones, G. (1996) *Wales 2010 Three Years on*. Cardiff: Institute of Welsh Affairs.

Lake, M. (1992) Under the influence. *Managing Schools Today*, 1(9), 12–14.

Maxwell, A. (1977) *Multivariate Analysis in Behavioural Research*. New

York: Chapman & Hall.

Menard, S. (1995) *Applied Logistic Regression Analysis*. London: Sage.

Mortimore, P. and Mortimore, J. (1986) Education and social class. In R. Rogers (ed.), *Education and Social Class*. Lewes: Falmer Press.

Norusis, M. (1994) *SPSS 6.1 Base System Users Manual*. Chicago: SPSS Inc.

OHCMI (1993) *Achievement and Under-Achievement in Secondary Schools in Wales 1991–92*. Occasional Paper 1. Cardiff: OHCMI.

Pedhazur, E. (1982) *Multiple Regression in Behavioural Research*. London: Holt, Rhinehart & Winston.

Reynolds, D. (1990) The great Welsh education debate. *History of Education*, 19(3), 251–7.

Reynolds, D. (1995) Creating an educational system for Wales. *Welsh Journal of Education*, 4(2), 4–21.

Reynolds, D. and Bellin, W. (1996) Welsh-medium schools: why they are better. *Agenda* (Institute of Welsh Affairs, Summer).

Reynolds, D., Creemers, B., Nesselrodt, P., Schaffer, E., Stringfield, S. and Teddlie, C. (1994) *Advances in School Effectiveness Research and Practice*. London: Pergamon Press.

Sammons, P., Thomas, S., Mortimore, P., Owen, C., Pennell, H. and Hillman, J. (1994) *Assessing School Effectiveness: Developing Measures to Put School Performance in Context*. London: OFSTED.

Stevens, J. (1992) *Applied Multivariate Statistics for the Social Sciences*. London: Lawrence Erlbaum.

TES (1995) *Times Educational Supplement School and College Performance Tables 1995*. London: TES.

TES (1996) Times Educational Supplement School and College Performance Tables 1996. London: TES.

TES (1997a) Success as Welsh close on England (12 December), 10.

TES (1997b) Parents opt for medium way (12 December), 11.

Welsh Office (1995a) *A Bright Future: Getting the Best for Every Pupil at School in Wales*, Cardiff: HMSO.

Welsh Office (1995b) *A Bright Future: The Way Forward*. Cardiff: HMSO.

Welsh Office (1995c) *Statistics of Education and Training in Wales: Schools No. 3*. Cardiff: HMSO.

Welsh Office (1996a) *A Bright Future: Statistical Update*. Cardiff: HMSO.

Welsh Office (1996b) *Digest of Welsh Local Area Statistics 1996*. Cardiff: Welsh Office.

Welsh Office (1997a) *A Bright Future: Beating the Previous Best*. Cardiff: Welsh Office.

Welsh Office (1997b) *Building Excellent Schools Together*. Cardiff: HMSO.

Western Mail (1997a) England–Wales gap does not exist (11 April), 8.

Western Mail (1997b) Schools closing gap with England (10 December), 1.

Western Mail (1997c) Languages: inquiry ordered (19 November), 1.

Western Mail (1997d) Even English parents back Welsh taught in classroom (28 November), 2.

Williams, C. (1997) 'Race' and racism: some reflections on the Welsh context. *Contemporary Wales*, 8, 112.

Willms, J. and Echols, F. (1992) Alert and inert clients: the Scottish experience of parental choice of schools. *Economics of Education Review*, 11(4), 339–50.

8

Policies on Schools' Inspection in Wales and England

GERRAN THOMAS AND DAVID EGAN

Introduction

The system of school inspections in Wales has undergone a number of changes since its introduction, perhaps none so fundamental as that brought about by the Education (Schools) Act, 1992 (DES, 1992a). This Act created two new non-ministerial government departments to oversee inspection: the Office for Standards in Education (OFSTED) in England, and the Office of Her Majesty's Chief Inspector (OHMCI) in Wales, which is independent of OFSTED. In 1999 OHMCI changed its name to ESTYN: Her Majesty's Inspectorate for Education and Training in Wales.

In this chapter, it is our aim to review these changes, first, by providing a historical perspective on the evolution of inspection in Wales, and then by looking in more detail at the changes introduced by the 1992 Act. To this end, it has inevitably been necessary to consider the political context in England, since the Act reflected the political imperatives of the New Right, which was so influential on policy-making in Westminster in the 1980s. As so often happens, initiatives taken in England were foisted on Wales, regardless of their appropriateness; however, a degree of difference was allowed for both in the Act itself and in its interpretation. In this sense, the reform of inspection exemplifies the way in which policy-making in Wales in the 1990s continued to be dependent on events in England.

The chapter has been subdivided into six sections. The first deals with the methodologies used to gather information; the second provides an overview of inspection in Wales from its introduction until recent times; the third explains the political pressures which led to the calls for reform in the 1980s; the fourth describes the process by which the policy was converted into an Act of

Parliament; the fifth considers the way in which the Act separated the inspection systems in Wales and England, and thus allowed differences in its implementation; and the sixth and final section discusses the evidence collected and contains our conclusions.

Methodology

The data used as a basis for this chapter have been assembled by the use of two research methods: historical sources and from élite interviews. The historical material was gained from primary and secondary sources including, for the more recent events, contemporary newspaper reports and Hansard. However, since the reform process itself and the final form of the 1992 Act had been controversial, it was felt appropriate to seek further clarification from some of the main participants regarding the thinking which lay behind the process and concerning its nature.

The difficulties connected with élite interviews have been discussed by Walford (1994), and by Phillips (1998), amongst others. Our reasons for carrying out such interviews closely resembled those of Fitz and Halpin (1994: 33):

> interviews with people actively engaged in the policy-making process were intended to provide insights into, and details of, educational policy making not available in documentary form and thus not in the public domain. Secondly, the interviews were intended to clarify, confirm or adjust existing published accounts . . .

One common problem with élite interviews is that of access: policy-makers are busy people and civil servants still in post might fear repercussions if their comments were published. In the event, two informants spoke on the record, two senior civil servants agreed to be interviewed but asked for anonymity (only one is quoted here), three declined to be interviewed (these were still working for government departments) and the minister at the time of the reform, Kenneth Clarke, declared himself too busy. The other major problem is what Kogan (1994: 76, 77) has called:

> the 'Problem of Truth'. We can all try to triangulate accounts from different sources, but in the end we may be able to do no more than

present ... the contrary versions ... we can only do our best; that which we do not know we can hardly disclose, and ethical constraints cannot be overridden.

In our experience, differences usually arose not so much concerning factual matters but rather in the value accorded the events. Thus, when opinions were stated, they did not purport to be statements of fact but could be used to provide useful insights into the tensions at the heart of the reform process. It should also be pointed out that only one interviewee was based in Wales but his comments were mainly factual and do not appear to be contentious.

A brief history of inspection

To be able to understand the recent major changes to the schools' inspection system it is first necessary to consider its history. It is generally accepted that it was with the formation of the Committee of the Council for Education in 1839 that the first two members of Her Majesty's Inspectorate (HMI) were appointed. Organized mainly on denominational lines – and with recruitment from a largely public-school- and Oxbridge-educated clergy – a rapid expansion of HMI took place following the introduction of the Revised Code of 1861 with its 'payment-by-results' system of testing and inspection. The early forays of HMI into Wales had resulted in the notorious Blue Books of 1847, which condemned the state of education in the country in a way that deeply offended Welsh sensibilities (Adams, 1996; Williams, 1990). This resulted in the appointment of the first Welsh-speaking HM Inspector (HMI), the Revd H. Longueville Jones and by 1870, following the Education Act of that year and the introduction of school boards, there were some twenty-one HMIs in Wales, working as part of a Western Division organized from London.

Until 1882 the organization of HMI did not reflect any distinction between England and Wales. In that year, a Welsh Division was created and for the first time a senior inspector, William Williams, was appointed for Wales. The main focus of HMIs' work in Wales, as in England, remained the testing of children under the Revised Code in the elementary schools. A new feature did emerge in Wales with the passing of the Welsh Intermediate Education Act of 1889 that provided Wales with a form of secondary education not adopted in England until 1902. This was to lead in 1891 to the creation of the Central Welsh Board (CWB) as both the examination and inspectorial body for these schools. Thus, from 1897, when Owen Owen was appointed the first chief inspector for the CWB, Wales had two inspection systems. In 1904, when under the terms of the 1902 Education Act the intermediate schools were granted financial support by the Board of Education, matters became even more complicated as these schools were henceforth liable to inspection from both CWB and HMI.

In 1907, as a concession to the growing Welsh national consciousness which had helped to sweep it into power in 1906, the Liberal government granted Wales an important measure of educational devolution through the creation of the Welsh Department of the Board of Education. This significant development was soon followed by another, the appointment of Owen M. Edwards as the first Chief Inspector of Schools in Wales. Edwards was a man of vision and some determination. He created a 'uniquely Welsh organisation of the inspectorate' (Jones, 1982: 24), and even head-hunted able young Welshmen to take up HMI posts for which they 'had not the least desire' (Jones, 1944: 28). It was perhaps inevitable that he would clash with the CWB over their area of joint concern, the intermediate schools. The death of Edwards in 1920 was followed by something of a *rapprochement* between HMI and the CWB, which in 1926 led to a system of joint inspections. In 1947, the life of the CWB came to an end, with its inspectorial work and its inspectors passing to HMI.

HMI numbers continued to grow in Wales with the expansion of Welsh education and the responsibilities of the inspectorate. By 1971, in the year following the transfer of responsibility for all aspects of primary and secondary education in Wales to the Welsh Office (WO) and the creation of the Welsh Office Education Department, HMI in Wales had reached forty-seven in strength.

At the local level, the passing of the 1870 Education Act and the establishment of school boards was to result in urban areas in England and Wales first appointing school inspectors, although they were as likely to be called 'advisers' or 'organizers' as 'inspectors'. The 1902 Education Act and the creation of local education authorities (LEAs) accelerated this trend. However, CWB activities aside, the role of LEAs in school inspection in Wales has been much more limited historically than that of HMI. By 1908 there were 123 local inspectors in England and Wales, with the majority of these employed in large towns and cities. By 1918 Glamorgan, the largest LEA in Wales, had appointed a number of inspectors, whose responsibility was to 'be in touch with the development and organisation of education in each of the districts' (County of Glamorgan, 1920: 116). Across Wales, however, the growth of such LEA services was not always so well developed.

With a further expansion of education services after 1945 this situation was to some extent remedied. By the time that Glamorgan LEA ended its existence in 1974 due to local government reorganization, the advisory service had grown to a strength of twenty-seven (Glamorgan Education Authority, 1974: 18). A further surge of appointments took place from the mid-1980s, due to various initiatives and funding, and virtually all LEAs in Wales had, or were developing, a full advisory service by this time.

The involvement of this greatly expanded LEA advisory force in inspection appears to have been minimal since, in the main, the role of advisers was precisely that implied in their preferred title. A study carried out in 1990–1 (Wilcox, Gray and Tranmer, 1993: 212) found that, prior to the 1988 Education Reform Act (ERA), which placed new responsibilities upon LEAs to inspect their schools, 'few LEAs carried out regular and systematic inspections'. Below 10 per cent of LEA advisory activity was spent on inspection, and in 1986–7 less than 1 per cent of schools in England and Wales were given whole school inspections by LEAs. This study revealed that in essence LEAs did not see inspection as being their role. After 1988 LEAs did begin to respond to the government's desire for them to be more involved in inspection but by 1992 the die was cast and the government was able to characterize LEA arrangements for inspection in some areas as 'shameful' (DES, 1992b: 3).

The political background to the reform of inspection

This government dissatisfaction with the quality and scope of LEA inspections was certainly one factor which drove the reform process. Also, since the war, the esteem felt by teachers and others for HMI had fluctuated, reaching a low point in the 1960s but recovering in the 1970s and 1980s (Lawton and Gordon, 1987: 29; Maw, 1994: 3). However, as early as the 1970s HMI had powerful critics, according to Lawton and Gordon (1987: 141):

> Margaret Thatcher ... had retained firm views about education [from her time as Secretary of State for Education – 1970 to 1974]; she also considered herself to be an expert on educational affairs ... One of the issues on which she felt strongly was HMI. It was rumoured that she considered them to be over-manned, and that they should spend much more time inspecting schools and colleges.

Whatever the truth of this rumour, soon after the election of a Conservative government with Margaret Thatcher as Prime Minister (in 1979), HMI was included in a series of reviews looking at ways of improving government efficiency in England and Wales. This led to the Rayner Report (DES and Welsh Office, 1982). According to Lawton and Gordon (1987: 143), 'the authors of the report seemed to be surprised by the high regard by which HMI were held by teachers, LEAs and professional associations'. The report led to a strengthening rather than a weakening of HMI both in terms of morale and manpower.

Despite the conclusions of the Rayner Report, HMI continued to draw criticism mainly from the political right but also at times from the left. A major factor in changing the relationship between HMI and the government was Sir Keith Joseph's decision in 1983 (when he was Secretary of State for Education) to publish HMI reports. This meant that HMI's views could be used by politicians to support their case in arguments with their opponents.

Another reason for HMI's high profile at this period was that the inspectorate began increasingly to report on the effects of government policies. The Rayner Report had given the following definition of the role of HMI: 'to assess standards and trends throughout the education system and to advise central Government on the state of the system nationally on the basis of its independent professional judgement. This is its first and overriding duty ...' (DES and Welsh Office, 1982: 8). Although Rayner went on to list other duties such as 'maintenance and improvements of standards', 'identification and dissemination of good practice' and 'advice to those with a direct responsibility', it is clear that the focus of the work was to be on providing policy-related advice to ministers. Rayner's view of the role of HMI is echoed by Eric Bolton (senior chief inspector, 1983–91), who explained that: 'By 1989, HMI was publicly and heavily involved in inspecting, reporting and advising on policy and its implementation across the whole of the education service' (Bolton, 1998: 50). Indeed, again according to Bolton (1995: 23–4):

> the Inspectorate's remit left no room for choice about the general direction and focus of its work. If the Government . . . chose to be involved in issues such as the relevance of the content of the curriculum and the quality and standards being achieved, it had a right to expect that the national Inspectorate would be able to provide it with the professional information, advice and judgement necessary for developing, pursuing and evaluating its policies for education.

Thus in the 1980s neither HMI nor the LEA inspectors/advisers saw inspecting schools as being their primary function.

By this time, HMI had negotiated a position whereby the DES could not alter what the inspectors had written without their agreement. It was open to government not to publish HMI reports; however, non-publication could potentially lay the government open to political embarassment and so it was not a favoured option. Eric Bolton explained this point as follows (interview, 7 May 1997):

> The real question was the question of publication . . . the more directly involved government became [in educational policy-making], the more it needed . . . objective informed evidence from HMI about what was going on. What was irritating [to ministers] was . . . it had become assumed that everything HMI did would lead to a published report. And the only people who could stop that were the Secretaries of State themselves, but it was politically impossible for them to do it.

During the 1980s, Conservative MPs and ministers had frequently been hostile to LEAs and their inspectorates and LEAs had come under pressure from the DES on a number of occasions to increase the amount of time spent by advisers on inspection, as opposed to their advisory functions (Wilcox and Gray, 1996: 28–9). Indeed, major changes to LEA inspectorates were due to follow the Audit Commission's report (1989) which was critical of LEA inspection procedures. On the other hand, even as late as 1988 it did not appear that a major reform of HMI was under consideration, despite

Kenneth Baker's hostility. Baker (Secretary of State for Education, 1986–9) has written:

> Of all Whitehall Departments, the DES was among those with the strongest in-house ideology. There was a clear 1960s ethos . . . rooted in progressive orthodoxies . . . It was devoutly anti-excellence, anti-selection and anti-market . . . If civil servants were the guardians of this culture, then Her Majesty's Inspectors of Education were its priesthood. Reports on schools were written with an opaque quality which defied any reader to judge whether the school being inspected was any good or not. (Baker, 1993: 168)

The situation was soon to change, since the fact that the inspectorate had to comment (if only indirectly) on the consequences of government policy led to increasing tensions in England between government and HMI. By 1991, according to Bolton (1998: 45), 'Kenneth Clarke (the Secretary of State for Education) made it abundantly clear that he, and the Government, found it hugely irritating to determine policies for education and then "have HMI running around the country critically commenting on them".' Matters reached such a pitch that in May 1991 several Conservative MPs signed a motion in the House of Commons to abolish HMI (Dunford, 1998: 192). It is worth noting that at this time, the inspectorate in Wales enjoyed a more harmonious relationship with the Welsh Office than that which existed between HMI in England and the government. As Fitz and Lee (1997: 6–7, 11) have pointed out:

> The 'problem' and its solution were . . . construed in entirely English terms by agencies within England . . . The restructuring of inspection . . . was an English solution to an English 'problem'. If there were similar criticisms of HMI in Wales, then these were very muted at the time.

The tensions between HMI and the Secretary of State and other factors (such as the government's wish to monitor the recently introduced National Curriculum) were soon to force matters to a head. When John Major took over from Margaret Thatcher as Prime Minister in 1990, an election was already on the horizon. Major's 'big idea' leading up to that (1992) election was the Citizen's Charter (Cabinet Office, 1991), which was intended to lay down standards in many areas of professional activity. Eric Bolton explained the urgency of the situation as follows (interview, 7 May 1997):

> That Charter thinking was desperately needed by John Major, because he was suddenly facing an election, with no domestic policy ... that was distinctive from his predecessor ... all kinds of people, including initially the big private industries, the big nationalized industries, law, doctors, everybody was to be in this Charter, and all those powerful bodies got out of it one way or other. The teachers, education, HMI, did not have the power to get out of it.

On 8 May 1991, Kenneth Clarke announced to Parliament his decision to review the role of HMI. He explained that 'I will explore all possible options for an Inspectorate capable of delivering an effective system of quality control based on inspection' (DES, 1991a). At that time, there were close links between the government and a number of right-wing think-tanks, including the Centre for Policy Studies. Eric Bolton recalls the situation as follows (interview, 7 May 1997):

> No secret was made of the fact by Sheila Lawlor [of the Centre for Policy Studies] that they really always had a suspicion of HMI. They saw HMI – quite wrongly, I think, given some of the characters I had to deal with within it – as a sort of unified, soft-liberal body ... that had pushed progressive education in every whip-stitch.

In September 1991 John Burchill, who was himself the chief education inspector for Wandsworth, a 'flagship Tory borough', published a paper for the Centre in which he dismissed the then current practices of inspectors with some contempt (Burchill, 1991: 6):

> There is scepticism about the role and influence of HMI and LEA inspectorates in monitoring the work of schools, and concern that they are preoccupied more with imposing recent theories than with reporting on standards in education. Reports are thought to be too vague and often based on personal judgement unsupported by hard evidence.

It is not clear whether Burchill had any specific examples in mind, but HMI had left its flanks unguarded by the publication at around this time of a few ill-judged reports. For example, a critical report was published on King Edward VI School, Stratford-upon-Avon, despite that school's good examination results. According to Senior Civil Servant A (interview, 18 November 1997):

> [Reaction to] that report was a like a mantra. Ministers took it up and ... said, what the devil are you talking about ... and it was taken up very publicly ... [That] report was critical ... in relation to how Ministers felt about HMI, because it gave them [and] the Sheila Lawlors of the world ... the ammunition to say, 'Look, we told you so, didn't we. Look at this garbage they've just produced about this wonderful school'. So that was pretty seminal ... disastrously so in my view, but never mind.

John Burchill's paper (1991) was explicitly written in response to Kenneth Clarke's review of HMI and it is clear that the suggestions made within it are very similar to the Department of Education and Science's original proposals. When one of us questioned John Burchill about the process by which his views influenced government policy in 1991, the conversation went as follows (interview, 18 November 1997):

> GT Can I move on to your own influence upon events in 1991? Did you discuss any of these ideas in person with anyone at the DES, or was any influence purely via the press?
> JB Not directly with ministers ... Wandsworth was influential at the time because of the politics of the Government, and the politics of the borough, so other people [at Wandsworth] had the direct ear [of ministers] ... but I personally was writing as John Burchill ...
> GT So you didn't yourself meet Kenneth Clarke but other people ...
> JB I didn't meet him personally, but I do know the anecdote about him carrying my draft around in his bag for several weeks before making a decision ... I can't disclose my sources! (Laughs)

It is not surprising in these circumstances that the proposals originally put forward by the DES closely resembled John Burchill's suggestions.

To sum up, the background to the reform process seems to have been made up of the following influences. First, the government's wish to monitor the National Curriculum by inspecting all schools on a regular basis. Second, government dissatisfaction with the publication of HMI reports which appeared to be implicitly critical of government actions or policies (or at least, the reports were presented as such by the opposition parties and/or the media). Third, hostility towards LEA inspectorates and HMI from influential right-wing think-tanks and ministers, who regarded the then current inspection procedures as being inadequate and who also suspected HMI and LEA inspectors of subscribing to 'trendy' educational theories. Finally, the Prime Minister's need for a 'big idea' in the run-up to the 1992 general election produced the Citizen's Charter, which was adapted as the Parents' Charter for school matters.

Converting the policy into an Act of Parliament

The review of inspection, including the role of HMI, announced by Kenneth Clarke was the key event which led to the development of a new policy during the following months. The crucial point of the new system was to be that all schools would be inspected within a short time-scale and then at regular intervals thereafter. In private discussions with civil servants, Clarke insisted that the new system should be open to market forces and that inspection teams should be independent of HMI. The process by which the policy was converted into a bill was described as follows by Senior Civil Servant A (interview, 18 September 1997):

> Policy formulation usually is an iterative process. Somebody has an idea, somebody takes the idea and develops it further, another set of people modify that idea and the development of it so consequently it can go to legislation in the final form that ministers are content with. In relation to the 1992 Act there was a very strong ministerial push from [Kenneth Clarke] towards the outline shape of the inspection process ... [He] wanted an inspection system which was strongly market based, which had a contracting element to it and which did not rely solely on HMI to do the work ... [He] also had a strong view about the frequency of inspection. It had to be done reasonably frequently if it was going to cover [all] children during their schooling and a choice of four years was made on [that] basis ... What happens is that the ministers point [out] what they want and ... it's up to civil servants to deliver it. And it was up to HMI to offer ... professional advice to civil servants – to say, 'that won't work, this will work. If your Minister wants X, then he needs to do it in this way.'

The foundations of the new system were spelled out in the Parent's Charter in September 1991, which promised 'regular reports by independent inspectors on the strengths and weaknesses of your school' (DES, 1991b: 2). The Charter also promised annual reports on each child, performance tables for schools, a prospectus for each school and an annual report from the school's governors.

The review of HMI was never published, though extracts from a leaked copy appeared in the *Independent*, which claimed that it presented three options (Hughes, 1991: 19):

> The first is for HMI to carry out the increased number of inspections itself, or to contract for others to do the job . . . The second option is for local education authorities to be obliged to inspect, or to contract the job out. The third is for governors to be obliged to hire an inspection team.

The review rejected the first two options and, according to Hughes, 'concentrates completely on advocating Mr Clarke's preferred approach – so much so, that it seems like a vehicle for confirming and elaborating on a decision which had already been taken'.

The proposals listed in the Parent's Charter formed the basis of the bill presented to Parliament in November 1991. Several of these proposals were highly controversial. Perhaps the idea which caused the government the most embarrassment was that school governors should be allowed to choose their own inspection teams. A powerful lobby headed by former senior chief inspector Sheila Browne drew up a briefing paper for peers, in the hope that the House of Lords would amend the bill. This paper (Hackett, 1992: 4):

> argue[d] that the Bill's fundamental weakness is in allowing schools to pick their own inspectors. As their ability to attract parents will depend in part upon the inspection reports, schools will have no incentive to choose teams which they think might be critical.

When the bill reached the Lords for its second reading on 11 February 1992, it was roundly condemned by peers from various points on the political spectrum; nevertheless, the bill received an unopposed second reading. However, on 2 March 1992, the government was defeated on an amendment proposed by Lord Peston. This amendment gave the responsibility for choosing which inspection team would inspect a particular school to the Chief Inspector for England or for Wales (as appropriate) and removed it from the governors of the school concerned. In order to ensure the passage of the bill before the general election, the government was forced to agree to bring in its own amendment, which had the same effect and also removed some anomalies. Another key amendment restored to LEAs the right to inspect their own schools.

Baroness Blatch (for the government) told peers: 'We regret the fact that a whole new bureaucracy will need to be established to run a centralised system, but we shall make it work' (Hansard, 1992: 1229–30). Thus the powers and responsibilities which were to be given to the new inspectorates were greatly increased.

Ironically, the Act was not welcomed by many of the prime movers for change. Sheila Lawlor (1993: 11, 18) of the Centre for Policy Studies complained that:

> there is every danger that the new arrangements will perpetuate the worst of the old system and undermine the central task of the objective reporting of standards ... The danger now is that future inspection will be undermined by virtue of being run by the same people and inspectorates as managed previous LEA and HMI inspection. This will compound the prospects of perpetuating old attitudes as well as the failed practices of the past.

Lawlor (1993: 11) was also critical of the *Framework for the Inspection of Schools* (OFSTED, 1992), which had been written by HMI and which includes the criteria for inspection, commenting that:

> Much of the Framework is based on a series of principles and preconceptions which will undermine effective inspection ... [the] useful things in the document ... tend to be lost under the welter of inessential, vague or woolly requirements, many of which reflect the progressive educational orthodoxies of recent decades.

Lawlor also wished to remove from OFSTED the power to appoint inspection teams and return this to the schools.

John Burchill was more supportive of local inspection but was no less critical of the Act's outcomes (Burchill, 1993: 3):

> The opportunity was presented by the 1992 Education Act ... to make

local inspections work properly ... under the supervision of a small national regulating body. But the monopoly of HMI has actually been strengthened and the best local arrangements are in danger of being dismantled. Many local inspectors undertaking OFSTED training are dismayed at the lack of rigour and the cumbersome nature of some of the procedures they are learning compared with what they have been used to.

Thus the Act in its final form appeared to please no one – not HMI, not the LEAs, not the politicians on the left and not even the right-wing lobbyists who had brought about the upheaval.

The Education (Schools) Act 1992 in Wales

The degree of autonomy of the inspectorate in Wales following the 1970 Transfer of Functions (Wales) order was explained as follows by Mr Roy James (HM Chief Inspector in Wales 1990–7) (inter-view, 9 May 1997):

> The Welsh inspectorate was placed on permanent loan to the Welsh Office. [Previously] ... in theory the Chief Inspector in Wales might (have been) answerable to the Senior Chief Inspector in England ... but in practice ... the Chief Inspector in Wales had more or less complete autonomy on operational matters ... the work programme in Wales was completely different ... and the organizational set up in Wales was different too, because of differences in scale and scope of the work.

Until the 1992 (Schools) Act, the inspectorate was still constituted as 'Her Majesty's Inspectorate for England and Wales'. The 1992 Act created two non-ministerial departments which became known as OFSTED in England and OHMCI in Wales. Both bodies were given very similar powers and responsibilities, but they are completely separate. In a very real sense, therefore, the 1992 Act gave the Welsh inspectorate independence from its English counter-part.

An early task for the new body in Wales was to publish the *Framework* (OHMCI, 1992a) and the *Handbook for the Inspection of Schools* (OHMCI, 1992b). OHMCI borrowed heavily from the corresponding documents developed by OFSTED for England, so in some ways this new independence was not fully utilized in the short term. However, some differences did appear. The first inspection cycle of all schools in Wales was to be completed in five years, as against four years in England. It appears that there was concern in the Welsh Office about the feasibility of completing a cycle in four years because of the large number of small schools in Wales.

This concern may also explain why, proportionately, the number of HMI was reduced more slowly in Wales. The 400+ HMI in England preceding the 1992 Act were rapidly pruned to around 250. It seems that the 'hidden agenda' was to encourage some of these 'released' HMIs to take up work as OFSTED-registered inspectors, which did transpire to some degree. However, this rapid run-down in numbers left HMI in England unable to make good a shortfall in OFSTED-trained inspectors and the programme in the primary sector suffered severe delays and difficulties at one stage. In Wales, the slower cycle and the retention of a higher proportion of HMI allowed teams of HMI to carry out around 20 per cent of primary inspections, so avoiding similar problems. Thus HMI in Wales continued as a field force in the years immediately following the 1992 Act whereas, in England, the remaining HMI had far fewer opportunities to participate in inspections.

Other differences in working practices arise from the very different scale of the operation in Wales. Whereas HMI in England work in teams, for example, to look at failing schools, HMI in Wales continue to work as a single inspectorate, without the same degree of specialization. Such differences already existed prior to 1992.

Perhaps the most crucial new difference following the 1992 Act concerns the degree of supervision of action plans. These plans must be produced by schools to address the key points for action identified by inspection teams. According to Roy James (interview, 9 May 1997):

we look closely at [and] respond to every action plan, and if there are weaknesses we send them back and ask for them to be changed. If there are serious weaknesses, then HMI will visit that school and try to indicate to the head and the chair of governors what needs to be done ... Additionally we monitor the implementation of the action plans ... I think we have an influence on individual schools and on the system through the work we do on action planning.

In England, where the number of schools inspected is much greater, only a small proportion of action plans can be scrutinized. According to Matthews and Smith (1995: 30), 'OFSTED has monitored a 10% sample of the action plans of schools inspected during the first year'. However, apart from schools in difficulty, there is no process of reading and assessing the quality of all action plans in England, as the number of schools makes this impossible for the reduced HMI force within OFSTED.

It may be that the less radical changes to HMI in Wales resulted from a better relationship between HMI in Wales and the Welsh Office than that which existed between HMI in England and their political masters – or, at least, their right-wing advisers. As Roy James commented (interview, 9 May 1997):

> [I felt] a great deal of disappointment and dismay [at attacks from right-wing commentators], not that HMI shouldn't be subjected to critical scrutiny like every other organization, but because most of the attacks seemed to be ill-founded and not based on factual evidence, based on prejudice and dogma rather than on sound evidence . . . We certainly didn't feel any direct hostility [from government] in Wales. There was a separate review [of the inspectorate] in Wales.

Fitz and Lee (1997: 10) have also pointed out that:

> Wales is different in a number of respects . . . There are no significant pressure groups of the kind, or which could exert the kind of direct pressure, of those found around Whitehall in the period of the Conservative administration. Differences in perspective between OHMCI and the Welsh Office Education Department (WOED) seem to be few.

Discussion and conclusion: diverging systems?

In recent years, there have been a number of major developments which, on the face of it, have increased the differences between the educational systems in England and Wales. Separate National Curriculum orders were produced by the 1988 ERA and Wales has its own standards and curriculum authority. The 1992 (Schools) Act produced an independent inspectorate in Wales. Since 1992, the

Framework and the *Handbook* have been revised several times in England and in Wales, which has increased the degree of divergence between OHMCI and OFSTED – for example, quality is measured against a five-point scale in Wales, whereas this has been replaced by a seven-point scale in England.

The Further and Higher Education (FHE) Act, which passed through parliament at around the same time as the Schools Act, has also introduced some differences. In Wales, the FHE Act gave the responsibility for ensuring quality in further and higher education to the Further and Higher Education Funding Council for Wales; to date, OHMCI has acted as the agent of the council in assessing further education. OFSTED does not oversee inspection in the further education sector in England.

However, views differ on whether this apparent divergence is real or illusory. Jones (1997: 210) has commented that 'One thing has not changed since 1847. The education of the people of Wales has always depended on the actions of Westminster governments.' The difficulty in creating a truly Welsh educational system is explained as follows by Fitz and Lee (1997: 9, 11): 'the convention of cabinet collective responsibility tends to override the powers conferred on the Secretary of State to shape independent policy for Wales ... [this] remains a powerful legitimating practice for the transfer of English focused policies into Wales'. Roy James believes that the differences have increased in recent years, and are likely to go on doing so (interview, 9 May 1997):

> There has been more of a Welsh dimension [in education] in the last five–ten years than ever. I think ... we can respond to Welsh needs, but it is an England and Wales educational system ... It's very difficult on occasions for there be to be a Welsh dimension ... [however] the feeling I have is that [the systems] are diverging. There's a separate office for Her Majesty's Chief Inspector in Wales and in England, and ... the interpretation of their respective roles has diverged considerably ... Welsh Office ministers have been open to divergence where that could be shown to be to the advantage of Wales and the educational system in Wales.

Our conclusions can be summarized as follows. First, the 1992 Act (like the 1988 Act) was an England-based response to the political context in England at that time. Second, policy-making in Wales was reactive, leading to the new system in Wales being broadly similar to the one which had been created for and in England. Third, there is no evidence of policy initiatives, or of political pressure for reform, originating from within Wales. Fourth it does appear, however, that Welsh Office officials and HMI in Wales did try to create a little time and space in which they could amend and modify the policies being developed in England. Finally, the overall experience of change appears to be another example of 'that incremental devolution so characteristic of Welsh education over the past century' (Jones, 1997: 192). Any differences between Wales and England arose as the actors in Wales used what scope they had, on the margins of policy formulation, to reshape what had been designed in and for England.

Acknowledgement

Some of the material used in this chapter appears in Gerran Thomas, 'A brief history of the genesis of the new schools' inspection system', *British Journal of Educational Studies*, 46(4) (1998), 415–27. The material is reproduced by kind permission of the journal's publishers, Blackwell.

References

Adams, S. (1996) The inspection system and inspection in schools in Wales. *Welsh Journal of Education*, 5(2), 105–18

Audit Commission (1989) *Assuring Quality in Education*. London: HMSO.

Baker, K. (1993) *The Turbulent Years*. London: Faber & Faber.

Bolton, E. (1995) HMI 1976 to 1992. In T. Brighouse and B. Moon (eds.), *School Inspection*. London: Pitman.

Bolton, E. (1998) HMI – the Thatcher years. *Oxford Review of Education*, 24(1), 45–55.

Burchill, J. (1991) *Inspecting Schools: Breaking the Monopoly*. London: Centre for Policy Studies.

Burchill, J. (1993) HMI monopoly marches on. *Guardian Education* (26 January), 3.

Cabinet Office (1991) *The Citizen's Charter: Raising the Standard*. London: HMSO.

County of Glamorgan (1920) *Proposals for a Scheme of the County Council*. Cardiff: Western Mail Ltd.

DES (1991a) Press release 146/91, 8 May.

DES (1991b) *The Parent's Charter: You and Your Child's Education.* London: HMSO.

DES (1992a) *Education (Schools) Act.* London: HMSO.

DES (1992b) *Choice and Diversity: A New Framework for Schools.* London: HMSO.

DES and Welsh Office (1982) *Study of HM Inspectorate in England and Wales (Rayner Report).* London: HMSO.

Dunford, J. E. (1998) *Her Majesty's Inspectors of Schools since 1944: Standard Bearers or Turbulent Priests?* London: Woburn Press.

Fitz, J. and Halpin, D. (1994) Ministers and mandarins: educational research in elite settings. In G. Walford (ed.), *Researching the Powerful in Education.* London: University College London Press.

Fitz, J. and Lee, J. (1997) Contrary voices? Education policy and school inspection in England and Wales. Paper presented at the 'Culture, Curriculum and Community: Education Policy in Wales in the late Twentieth Century' Conference, University of Wales, Swansea, 21 November.

Glamorgan Education Authority (1974) *A Record of Progress.* Ystrad Mynach: Glamorgan Education Authority.

Hackett, G. (1992) Private inspectors opposed. *Times Educational Supplement* (24 January).

Hansard (1992) House of Lords, 10 March.

Hughes, C. (1991) A worthless guarantee of quality. *Independent* (14 November).

Jones, A. J. (1944) *From an Inspector's Bag.* Cardiff: Abbrevia.

Jones, G. E. (1982) *Controls and Conflicts in Welsh Secondary Education 1889–1944.* Cardiff: University of Wales Press.

Jones, G. E. (1997) *The Education of a Nation.* Cardiff: University of Wales Press.

Kogan, M. (1994) Researching the powerful in education and elsewhere. In G. Walford (ed.), *Researching the Powerful in Education.* London: University College London Press, pp. 67–80.

Lawlor S. (1993) *Inspecting the School Inspectors: New Plans, Old Ills.* London: Centre for Policy Studies.

Lawton, D. and Gordon, P. (1987) *HMI.* London: Routledge Kegan Paul.

Matthews, P. and Smith, G. (1995) OFSTED: inspecting schools and improvement through inspection. *Cambridge Journal of Education,* 25 (1), 23–34.

Maw, J. (1994) *Calling HMI to Account.* London: Tufnell Press and Institute of Education.

OFSTED (1992) *Framework for the Inspection of Schools.* London: OFSTED.

OHMCI (1992a) *Framework for the Inspection of Schools*. Cardiff: OHMCI.

OHMCI (1992b) *Handbook for the Inspection of Schools*. Cardiff: OHMCI.

Phillips, R. (1998) The politics of history: some methodological and ethical dilemmas in elite-based research. *British Educational Research Journal*, 24(1), 5–19.

Walford, G. (ed.) (1994) *Researching the Powerful in Education*. London: University College London Press.

Wilcox, B. and Gray, J. (1996) *Inspecting Schools*. Buckingham: Open University Press.

Wilcox, B., Gray, J. and Tranmer, M. (1993) LEA frameworks for the assessment of schools: an interrupted picture. *Educational Research*, 35 (3), 211–21.

Williams, E. (1990) HM Inspectorate in Wales. In W. G. Evans (ed.), *Perspectives on a Century of Secondary Education in Wales*. Aberystwyth: Centre for Educational Studies, 127–45.

IV

Post-Compulsory Education

9

From Policy to Practice in Further Education: Patterns of Governance in Wales

MARTIN JEPHCOTE AND JANE SALISBURY

Introduction

In the context of post-16 education, our purpose here is to map and understand better the process of policy-making and implementation in Wales in the period following the incorporation of colleges of further education in 1993. Our focus on Wales is not to suggest that the essential workings of the policy process are different from those in other countries. However, as Wales continues to establish policies and practices which differ from England and other countries, and because of the presence of significantly different institutions and institutional networks (Garmise and Rees, 1997), it is important to offer an insight into the ways in which policies are formulated, the particular arenas in which they are contested and the outcomes to which this gives rise. Moreover, the publication of separate Green Papers on lifelong learning in Wales (Welsh Office, 1998) and in England (DfEE, 1998) and the establishment of a Welsh Assembly provide future contexts for the study of policy-making and implementation. Our intention, therefore, is to begin to offer some theoretical propositions which might have general applicability and, at the same time, to look at the particular conditions for the negotiation of policies and for their outcomes in Wales.

Context

It is something of an understatement to suggest that 'we live in a world where traditional patterns of life and work, old uncertainties and assumptions have all been disrupted' (Cahill, 1994). In the UK, as in many other countries, this has come about as a result of the rethinking and reformulating of the role of the state and the relationship between the private and public sector. It is the public sector which has been the focus for change, with private-sector practices cited often as examples of good practice and as a benchmark for publicly provided goods and services. Deregulation, privatization and so-called marketization have been the hallmarks of one set of changes aimed at bringing about greater choice and efficiency. Another set of changes, including decentralization and devolution, have led to the emergence of new political and power relationships, supposedly to increase involvement in decision-making and bring about greater accountability. Taken together, these changes have created new patterns of interaction between government and society at national, regional and local levels (Kooiman, 1993). Moreover, these changes have called for new ways of conceptualizing how and what part public institutions play in policy-making, implementation and administration. Traditional notions and principles of how public institutions function have, more or less, been abandoned and it remains unclear as to what administrative or management perspective should be applied. According to Lane (1993), the traditional model has variously been criticized because of its normative stance on the conduct and operation of the state, because of its lack of descriptive accuracy and because of its failure to identify mechanisms conducive to effectiveness and efficiency. Overall, it did not properly explain how the public sector actually works. New approaches, he suggested, are based on new principles which involve a different theory about human motivation, efficiency and effectiveness in the public sector. This new thinking, *inter alia*, makes no distinction between politics and administration, recognizes that decision-making in public institutions is irrational, and that administrators are not constrained by procedure but respond to goal achievement and effectiveness, suggesting that public employees act in order to maximize self-interest such as income, prestige and power.

Education has provided an interesting arena in which a number of these changes have been acted out and observed. In compulsory education, paradoxically, the movement has been not towards greater autonomy for teachers, schools and local education authorities (LEAs) but towards greater centralization and control. This is apparent through the increasing marginalization of LEAs and the imposition of a National Curriculum. Contradictions have opened up between the level of political rhetoric which promoted choice and diversity and the practical level. Chitty (1989), for example, identified the tensions between the neo-liberal doctrines of freedom of choice, individualism, the market and the neo-conservative prioritization of social authoritarianism and strong government. In post-compulsory education, the 1992 Further and Higher Education Act (DES, 1992) which, along with the earlier Education Reform Act of 1988 (DES, 1988), brought about the shift from a democratic to a market model of FE, also has a central contradiction at its heart. The 1992 Act, whilst setting up FE colleges as private companies, created a structural framework which ensured their financial dependence upon a governmental quango for funding and planning purposes. The 'system changing legislation' (McDonnell and Elmore, 1991; Elliot, 1996) of the 1988 and 1992 Acts ended somewhat dramatically the incrementalism which had, hitherto, characterized government policy towards the FE sector.

The Further and Higher Education Act (1992) placed a statutory responsibility on separate funding councils in England and Wales to ensure sufficiency and adequacy of provision and, taking effect in 1993, colleges of further education were granted corporate status and removed from the control of their LEAs. However, the incorporation of colleges does not remove them from the public sector since they are still dependent on government for resource allocation and they continue to be regulated through this mechanism, through control over curriculum and examinations and through quality assurance procedures.

Our aim in this chapter is, in the context of post-compulsory further education, to begin to set out new ways of governance by examining the emerging patterns of activity between those social, political and administrative actors who take part in its management and control. We suggest that, since the 1988 Education Reform Act and, in particular, since the incorporation of colleges, further education provides a useful example by which to begin to develop a conceptual framework for describing and analysing the patterns of activity and interactions between the key actors. Moreover, we think that this example could be illuminative of the contemporary process of public policy-making, implementation and management. Because of the variety of actors now involved in policy implementation and mediation, it offers some insight into the complexities of these processes and the consequential conflicts, tensions and competing outcomes. The incorporation of colleges and the apparent devolution of decision-making to the college is in line with that thinking which supposes that a decentralized model is more adaptable to local needs and that implementation, at this level, both allows and encourages a reinterpretation of national policy whilst broadly being in support of it. However, incorporation has led to a host of intended as well as unintended outcomes, including competition between colleges for students, new managerial approaches and, as several writers (Elliott, 1996; Ball *et al.*, 1998) report, a degree of stress and antipathy among those who work in the sector and on whom so much depends for the fulfilment of economic and social policy.

Our previous academic work and day-to-day links with the FE sector, discussions with representatives from key agencies in Wales as well as other published research evidence, all support a perspective which points to the tensions between policy and practice. These tensions, we will argue, are in part a consequence of the often contrasting and contradictory demands on and expectations of those who teach, manage, govern, inspect or work in a complex and changing FE sector. We propose, therefore, to describe briefly the actors and their roles and we provide three illustrations of the impact of policy-making, its mediation and resulting dilemmas. These are (1) the dysfunctions between the labour market and the market for qualifications; (2) regulation and accountability through quality assessment; and (3) the new managerialism. We draw on our own research into the impact of incorporation, including interview data with college principals (Jephcote and Salisbury, 1996), more recent data collected by Rees (1997) and also ethnographic data gathered during the training and first encounters of a group of associate assessors (Salisbury and Jephcote, 1998). We can also corroborate our accounts by reference to recent research publications (Randle and Brady, 1997; James, 1998) and to an avalanche of comment in the pages of the *TES* and even to a regular column in *Private Eye*! At this stage we have to accept that our conceptual framework is incomplete and awaits the outcome of the next stage of our research. In this, we propose to gather data from key actors in Wales to reveal how they react to and perceive the process of policy-making and implementation. In particular, we are interested in the interactions and power relationships between them as revealed in their accounts of recent policy changes and in this way we hope to understand their 'real' and 'assumptive' worlds (McPherson and Raab, 1988).

The administrative and institutional framework

In Wales there are and have been a multiplicity of bodies with potential to influence the FE curriculum. These included the Training Agency (previously the MSC), the Training and Enterprise Councils (TECs), the National Council for Vocational Qualifications (NCVQ), awarding bodies like BTEC, City and Guilds, the Welsh Joint Education Committee (WJEC) which has numerous functions and acted as Wales's Examination Board and, until 1993, LEAs. The Regional Curriculum Base established at the WJEC in 1983 was, for example, involved in curriculum development, research and in-service training for vocational qualifications in conjunction with the Further Education Unit (now the Further Education Development Agency) and the Training Agency.

In Wales the key actors currently shaping the post-16 FE sector include the Further Education Funding Council for Wales (FEFCW: 1994a), which is responsible for funding, the Curriculum and Assessment Authority for Wales (ACCAC) for the curriculum and the Office of Her Majesty's Chief Inspector (OHMCI) which is commissioned by the FEFCW to undertake the assessment of quality on its behalf. In addition, there are a number of other influential bodies including Fforwm, which is an association of college principals, the Further Education Development Association (FEDA) and, of course, the Welsh Office, together with others, such as the TECs and employers and training organizations which have an interest in the work and role of the FE sector. Not least, there are twenty-nine independent colleges which interact with these other actors and whose boards of governors and senior managers are ultimately responsible for the implementation of policy. A particular burden rests on college principals and their boards of governors. As we shall go on to illustrate, it is the interaction of these different players, and particularly at the college level where policy is mediated, which sometimes leads to outcomes that conflict with other policy intentions. In this way, like Kooiman (1993) we recognize the shift away from traditional patterns of governance based on a 'one-way traffic' from those governing to those governed. Instead, we recognize it as a multi-layered, multi-dimensional and evolving process in which we place less emphasis on the boundaries between the social, political and administrative actors and more on the inter-action and on the potential and actual problems, constraints and opportunities.

Williams (1991) provided an authoritative account of the structure of FE in Wales and of the roles and responsibilities of key agencies in the wake of the 1988 ERA. This account highlighted the diversity of the FE sector, the importance of delegated budgets and the func-tions of numerous key players like the inspectorate and the LEA. Although the 1988 ERA focused upon the school and HE sectors, it significantly prepared the ground for the later incorporation of FE colleges. The Act drew upon a 'series of studies and reports reflect-ing a convergence of opinion about the characteristics of a well managed further and higher education system' (Williams, 1991: 1). It not only delegated financial and other managerial powers to governing bodies of colleges but, crucially, determined the compo-sitions of FE college governing bodies, privileging business and industry members (to a minimum 50 per cent of the total) and reducing local authority members (to a maximum 20 per cent of the total). The 1991 White Paper (DES, 1991), along with other subse-quent policy documentation, does not directly criticize the LEA, nor is there any suggestion that they have not carried out their role effectively in the past. Proposed changes were 'constructed in the text' as giving greater freedoms, implying freedom for colleges from the LEA.

Numerous demands and imperatives face the FE sector in the UK and in Wales. Embedded within the discourse of raising stan-dards, these firm demands include: political pressure through the National Targets for Education and Training (NTETs) and lifelong learning objectives; for the sixteen to nineteen age-group partici-pation and achievement rates to match those of other European regions; and calls by the Welsh Office (1995, 1998) and the Funding Council (FEFCW, 1994b, 1997) for increased efficiency and monitoring arrangements designed to give greater account-ability and promote continuous improvement in the quality of further education. Senior college managers are required to intro-duce human resource strategies and to implement and impose the new College Employers' Forum (CEF) 'professional contract' for

FE lecturers. Research in England (Elliott and Hall, 1994; Shain and Gleeson, 1999) and Wales (Jephcote and Salisbury, 1996) has shown how institutional autonomy is challenged through the centralizing tendency of central government policy towards FE and through the increasingly widespread adoption of HRM policies and procedures for lecturing staff which reinterprets their value as resourceful humans (Bottery, 1992: 6).

In Wales, the FE sector has utilized Fforwm, an organization of college principals, to work collaboratively with the Funding Council in the development of a credit accumulation and transfer scheme (CATS) and a unitized curriculum. The resulting CREDIS Framework owes much to the investment of nearly one million pounds by the Welsh Office over a five-year period. The English FE sector was slower to work towards CATS and their implementation in the 430 English FE colleges is still at an early stage of development. The 'policy borrowing' and 'policy following' by the English FEFC, which has clearly learned lessons from Wales, is a reversal of the usual sequence. Furthermore, Fforwm's proactivity in the development of an NVQ level 5 credential in management once again sets Wales as a pioneer. According to Garmise and Rees (1997), Fforwm has become an important regional institution able to voice the concerns of the sector and there is no equivalent in English regions.

In Wales, strategies to promote wider participation and foster social inclusion were pioneered well before the publication of the Kennedy Report (1997). Compared with FEFCE, the resourcing formulae of the Further Education Funding Council for Wales have been more differentiated in their mechanisms to support and fund more generously students recruited from various disadvantaged areas. For the last five years, student addresses and postcodes have been utilized to identify enrolees from those localities deemed to be economically and socially disadvantaged. Acknowledging the strengths of this initiative, England's FEFCE has considered building postcodes into its funding formulae, though the complexities of socio-economic heterogeneity associated with some regions and urban-industrial localities made the scheme unworkable. Provoked, however, into developing an alternative system which accounts for student disadvantage, FEFCE's latest scheme will differentiate funding based on students' prior performance data, for example, GCSE or other qualifications.

A particular priority stressed by FEFCW (1997) is the promotion of continuous improvement in the quality of further education. Thus, apart from using 'recruitment, retention and results' data to inform resource allocation, unlike England, the Funding Council in Wales also provides financial rewards (and incentives) to colleges whose programme areas are awarded a 'grade 1' in quality assessments.

The dysfunctions between the labour market and the market for qualifications

A key role for education in fostering economic growth has become a commonplace policy across Europe, not only at the level of national economies but also in the context of regional development, where examples set by 'successful' European regions have been particularly influential. The latter have been reflected in the policies and strategies adopted by both national governments and the EU, which have emphasized the significance of educational systems as providers not simply of general education but of specific vocational skills, especially at higher and intermediate levels. Many of these policies are based on an assumption that there is a link between, on the one hand, vocational education and training (VET) provision and, on the other, economic failure. In effect, poor standards of VET are seen to be responsible for poor economic performance and, in turn, improving VET as the means to promote economic recovery.

It is implied, therefore, that increasing the output of skills, together with enhancing the skill level and flexibility of workers, will increase productivity and bring about economic growth. It is important to note, however, that this consensus on the role of skills development is widespread but by no means universal. At the specific level, the NIESR studies on which much of this consensus is based have been criticized, *inter alia*, for failing to distinguish adequately the effects on productivity of training as opposed to other factors, such as the quality of physical capital (see, for example, Cutler, 1992). More generally, the implication that an increase in training would in itself benefit economic performance has been questioned. Not only has it been argued that returns to training are in reality extremely difficult to calculate (even at the level of the firm, let alone the national economy, for example, Shackleton, 1992); but also, for some commentators, it is the utilization of skills and managerial product strategy which comprise the crucial constraints on national economic performance, rather than the supply of skills *per se* (for example, Lindley, 1991). Indeed, the *interdependence* of corporate decisions about skills development with other dimensions of managerial strategy (about product quality, production process and skill utilization) has been widely noted.

Despite the familiarity of the link between increased training and improved economic performance, it is actually far more complex than is frequently acknowledged. One implication of this is that strategic intervention in a regional VET system needs to be based upon an explicit model of what is expected to be achieved, rather than depending on the supposedly self-evident benefits of increased training. Moreover, given the interdependence between skills development and managerial strategy more widely, such a model needs to reflect the specificities of the region's industrial structure and patterns of production organization. So that, whereas our point about the dysfunctions between the labour market and the training and qualifications market is a general one, it needs to be looked at in terms of the specific characteristics of a region.

In general terms, the marketization of the further education sector can be regarded as a key strategy for making the sector more responsive and accountable to its client groups, including firms, central government and individuals. Individual colleges have, since 1993, been reconstituted as 'independent' incorporations each with autonomous management structures with governing bodies whose members are drawn mainly from local industry. It should be noted, however, that the representatives from industry were brought in not as a voice representing the local labour market, but for the ways in which their business acumen would, supposedly, benefit the management of the college. Essentially, funding was to follow students, thus creating a competitive market in which colleges were forced to meet students' needs and engage in the marketing of their courses. At the same time, colleges were encouraged to liaise with local industry in order to provide 'tailor-made' courses for employees, not least because this would provide an additional source of income. This obvious lack of articulation between colleges meeting perceived students' needs and meeting employer needs is

symptomatic and, in part, an explanation of the existence and operation in the sector of markets of different kinds. First, there is a
market for qualifications in which students are encouraged to pursue
VET programmes and gain the competencies and qualifications
which they seek. These would include those students who have
recently left school and have not yet entered the labour market, as
well as unemployed persons and those at work looking to upgrade
their own skills. Second, there is a market in which employers
demand labour with particular competencies. Typically, firms
pursue courses of action which seem rational to the individual
employer but which do not necessarily produce the best outcomes
for the economy as a whole. In particular, there is much evidence
to support the view that where a firm experiences a skill shortage it
merely 'poaches' skilled labour from other employers, often with
the consequence of driving up local wage levels and, of course,
without any investment in training. The extent to which employers
have to purchase tailor-made courses partly reflects the inability of
the qualifications market to supply workers with appropriate skills
and the unwillingness or inability of those in work to engage in up-
skilling or the general lack of workers with appropriate skills.

Much of the new VET system in England and Wales functions
principally in terms of objectives which reflect the priorities of
the qualifications market. In some part, the setting up and operation of FE funding councils in England and Wales act to reinforce
this orientation and, moreover, interfere in the operation of the
market in a regulatory capacity. The funding councils have a statutory responsibility (under the 1992 Further and Higher Education
Act) to ensure sufficiency and adequacy of FE provision, broadly
defined in terms of ensuring that individuals have reasonable
access to the course opportunities which they seek in all parts of
the country. Funding is essentially based on the number of enrol-
ments and retention rates, together with adjustments for outcomes
measured in examination success and, in Wales, on the result of
external quality assessment, also in the control of the funding
councils. The ways in which the funding councils regulate and
control the qualifications market is an apparent contradiction in
the marketization of the FE sector and, as our data show, a key
source of tension. It was, for example, a view expressed by a
number of college principals that the setting up and operation of
the funding councils was the manifestation not of their indepen-

dence but, as some stated, the 'nationalization' of the sector (Jephcote and Salisbury, 1996).

The sorts of courses on offer and which students choose also raises questions where, for example, an increase in business and media studies can be discerned. This reveals a particular weakness in the system to deliver appropriate numbers of students with appropriate competencies to the labour market. Clearly, 'choice' as a market principle is exercised but is in no way matched to the needs of the economy or employers and fails to fulfil broader economic policy. Viewed in this light, then, the process of marketization can be seen to be highly complex in its nature and effects, not least because educational institutions are in fact confronted with a diversity of markets. Moreover, the imperatives which derive from these markets are by no means wholly compatible.

Regulation and accountability through quality assessment

Changes in approaches to the assessment of quality in further and higher education are part of a much broader change in the nature of funding, the measurement of performance indicators and the nature of provision. They reflect changes occurring in other public-sector organizations. The aims, structure and processes involved in quality assessment are being redefined and reconstructed in both England and Wales. The Further Education Funding Council for Wales established by the Further and Higher Education Act 1992 has a duty to secure sufficient and adequate provision in the FE sector and to make arrangements for the funding and the assessment of the quality of their provision. The funding council has established a Quality Assessment Committee to advise it on the development of appropriate quality assessment procedures in the FE sector in Wales.

The Quality Assessment Committee (QAC) in its early planning of the assessment regime for the FE sector, advised the funding council 'to move from an inspectorial approach to one where an institution's own evaluation is central to the assessment procedure' (FEFCW, 1993: 19). Though it has a statutory duty to secure assessments of the quality of provision, the Council supports the view that 'ultimate accountability for maintaining and enhancing quality rests with the institutions themselves' (FEFCW, 1995a: 2).

A number of bulletins and consultation papers (for example, FEFCW, 1994a, 1995a, 1995b) circulated to all heads of FE sector institutions in Wales discuss and explain issues such as peer evaluation, colleges' self-evaluation and rewarding high-quality teaching and learning. The Council's avowed aims to liaise with other agencies such as Fforwm and FEDA, the Further Education Development Agency, on quality and other issues are amply demonstrated in their annual reports and corporate plans.

Colleges of FE in Wales experienced a rolling programme of quality assessments. In one of its earlier corporate plans (FEFCW, 1994b) the Funding Council set an annual target which included at least seven institutional reviews and five programme area reviews. *The Framework for the Assessment of Quality* (OHMCI, 1994a), which specified the criteria and evidence by which FE colleges were assessed, has been updated and elaborated at least twice and from 1998 onwards FEFCW expected all colleges to be engaged in self-assessment. The jointly produced *Quality Assessment Handbook* (FEFCW and OHMCI, 1997) sets out the quality assessment arrangements which were introduced in 1997. It was intended that external assessment and institutions' own self-evaluations would be 'built into a more coherent developmental process' (FEFCW, 1994a: 34). Current quality assessment systems in the FE sector in Wales reflect the views of the funding council (which consulted extensively with the sector) that regular self-assessment, in the context of sound quality assurance systems, is essential in enabling all institutions to review critically and improve the quality of their provision (FEFCW and OHMCI, 1997: 1).

Without doubt the Associate Assessor Scheme developed in Wales has a number of positive and anticipated outcomes, though it is a scheme within an imposed model designed to make external assessment more transparent and visible. The recruitment of lecturers from the FE sector as Associate Assessors (AAs) was seen as an important strategy designed to help institutions prepare for peer evaluation and future models of quality assessment, namely self-assessments conducted by colleges themselves. This form of 'peer review' in which AAs work alongside HMI paved the way for the current self-assessment models. Our qualitative ethnographic research into the Associate Assessor Scheme in Wales identified both strengths and tensions. The AAs in our study detailed their wider professional experiences and their daily contact with the classroom, which many felt gave them a more realistic perspective on FE than HMI, and moderation, assessment verifying duties, subject panel groupings along with subject co-ordination were seen as giving them 'credibility'. In turn, their direct first-hand experience of evaluating the standards and quality of work in programme areas was valued by HMI. As one HMI stated: 'AAs are under the skin of their subjects because they deliver daily in their own classrooms . . . that's got to be an asset' (HMI assessor in Salisbury and Jephcote, 1996).

Lecturers who have acted as Associate Assessors are regarded as an asset to their own institutions and as a valuable source of information about the practice of quality assessment. Their familiarity with the *Framework* documents, the numerical scoring and the implications for programmes scored 'below the quality threshhold of grade 3' are important. A recent OHMCI (1994) document specifies clearly a number of ways in which associate assessors can be used by their colleges to promote quality through self evaluation. For example, they might be involved in:

i) staff development on good practice in teaching and learning;
ii) staff development on how to undertake and record classroom observations, and how to evaluate students' work;
iii) staff development on how to report back to teachers, middle and senior management;
iv) briefing senior management about quality assessment;
v) leading an internal programme area review;
vi) evaluating the report of an internal programme area review;
vii) evaluating standards, as a member of a quality assurance committee. (OHMCI, 1994b: 5)

The list presents the ideal usage that senior managers could make of those staff who have been trained as Associate Assessors and it encapsulates the ways in which many of them were made use of following both their initial training and assessment experience. It is clear that AAs were perceived as becoming 'significant others' by the funding council and by the HMI who were now acting on behalf of the FEFCW. Fieldwork and interviews conducted at that time with several key policy actors revealed the presence of major tensions between HMI and senior managers in the funding council's quality division. These are elaborated elsewhere (see Salisbury and Jephcote, 1996), but briefly, a distinct feeling of 'displacement' was

evident on the part of the HMIs who had previously had considerable power and relative autonomy in their former inspection
procedures. As one funding council informant stated: 'They [HMI]
are clearly resisting the way we [FEFCW] need to move . . . it is
obvious that the extensive cohort of assessors we are building up in
Wales is perceived as a threat – and it probably is.' During obser-
vational fieldwork at one institutional quality assessment the
researcher noted how HMI differentiated themselves from their
Associate Assessor colleagues by wearing unofficial HMI identity
badges rather than those provided by the funding council. This was
interpreted by one FEFCW informant as: 'a symbolic, status
enhancing strategy indicating their reluctance to let go'.

Sharing what can only be defined as 'insider knowledge' with
lecturers involved in quality assessment obviously presented HMI
with something of a dilemma: in their successful training and occupational socialization of AAs (which was rated very highly by all of
our AA informants), they were perhaps diluting their own importance and, as one Associate Assessor put it 'doing themselves out of
a job!' Clearly, this has not happened and HMI remain important
players, particularly in the process of the external assessment of
quality and the subsequent monitoring of institution action plans and
target setting resulting from reports. Most importantly, the HMI
who acts as a lead assessor is responsible for writing the final
quality assessment report for publication.

Published reports on the quality of education provide detailed
outcomes on aspects of institutional performance and programme
areas, with each college's statistical profile and examinations data
being presented. The annual publication of examination performance tables for the FE institutions in Wales also renders visible
the contrasts within the sector's provision. Unfortunately, there is a
tendency on the part of the media to reconstruct these sensitive data
in decontextualized ways, for example, as league tables or as sensa-
tional headlines. Our fieldwork in quality assessment settings and
our subsequent analysis of FEFCW quality reports confirmed our
belief that the processes reflect and contribute to the 'discourse of
performativity' (Lyotard, 1984). This discourse privileges instrumental achievement, competition and the functionality of
performance measurement.

The new managerialism

Since the 1980s there has across the public sector been a drive for greater economy, efficiency and effectiveness in the provision of goods and services. The sell-off of state-owned industries is an example of the transfer of ownership and responsibility to the private sector, whereas in other cases, such as local government, limited privatization and competitive tendering became commonplace. In further education, the prevalence of audit and business language – 'units of resource', 'cost effectiveness', 'niche marketing', for example – reflects the changing orientation of the sector, with students recast as 'clients', 'consumers', 'customers' and their importance to the college measured in terms of the income each brings. The marketization of the post-16 sector in Wales and the funding council's position that 'ultimate accountability for maintaining and enhancing quality rests with the institutions themselves' (FEFCW, 1995a) point to an obvious gap between the locus of control and the locus of accountability and has placed great pressure upon the sector. In the section which follows, colleges' resulting managerial strategies are discussed. It should, however, be remembered that college managers are faced with little choice in the ways in which they manage.

At this stage we turn to the findings of our own research to illustrate the impact of the move to marketization and the advent of the new managerialism, characteristic of the reform of the public sector. These reveal and catalogue the tensions apparent in the system since incorporation in 1993, through the narrative accounts gathered from college principals. The tensions are revealed, first, as a set of changing external relationships between colleges, between schools and college and between colleges and state bodies such as the funding councils. Second, there are a set of internal tensions between managers and lecturers, between demands for limited resources such as the need for more teachers, more administrators and more support staff. Both the internal and external tensions are created by, for example, the need to restructure college management, change the college culture and respond to the demands of external quality assessment.

If competition is at the heart of a market model then we should not be surprised that our data suggest this to be a key source of tension and ongoing concern. Successful competition for students is rewarded with funding and increasing student numbers may be taken as, a crude measure of performance and perceived quality. Arguably, the measure provided by the quality assessment process gives a firmer base on which to assess performance and quality, and in a perfect world students and other customers would use this information in making a rational choice about which course to follow or which college to attend. The form and extent of competition reflects local circumstances. For example, it is more serious in urban-industrial areas than in more rural localities, where travel-to-training areas overlap to a far lesser extent (see Foskett and Hesketh, 1996). Moreover, there are instances where institutions have consciously developed, or continued from pre-incorporation days, collaborative arrangements which aim to ameliorate the effects of marketization. One principal articulated the nature of the problem very clearly:

> Well, one of the most difficult dilemmas, I suppose that we have, is that we are – through government policy – we are placed in the market. Not only in relation to other colleges but also in relation to schools as well. And at the same time it is anticipated that there will be co-operation between individual institutions for the greater good. Now that is a real dilemma.

Indeed, in some parts of Wales, most notably the south Wales valleys, mergers between colleges have already occurred and there is a real threat that some colleges may have to close, a possibility which, for example, the creation, prior to incorporation, of a single, multi-campus tertiary college in Gwent sought to avoid. One principal described the situation as a 'free for all' and expected cartels to emerge. Similarly, another thought there would be three or four years of 'trench warfare' with 'our competitors' and blamed the drop in numbers at his own college on increased competition with schools and other colleges. Relationships between colleges and between principals became a casualty of the war. One, for example, spoke of the need to protect 'commercial information', and another described the 'rules of the game' to be to look after the individual corporation first. And another talked at length about the arrangements for networking:

competitiveness, which has always been ruthless in this area of the world, is perhaps becoming even more so. There are certainly some players who have expansionist goals which does mean it limits the areas of collaboration.

A very firm line has to be drawn about some sorts of information sharing because one is always afraid that they might give somebody, who could be seen as a competitor, some sort of commercial edge in a particular situation. So there are some individuals with whom collaboration has become more difficult but I wouldn't say that was generally so.

More recent evidence from England and Wales adds support to our concerns over changing external and internal relationships. A recent study conducted at a college in Wales highlights the deterioration in relationships between senior managers and middle managers and lecturers (James, 1998). The study reports how motivation has suffered because of changing contracts and increased workloads and how anxiety and stress have risen. An in-depth study of a college in England noted the impact on the management style at the college following directives issued by the FEFC and the consequent conflict with lecturers. These changes met with resistance from lecturing staff in the form of non-co-operation, resulting in a clash between 'managerialism' and 'professionalism' (Randle and Brady, 1997), characterized by a dichotomy in goals and values about learning and the curriculum, in key assumptions about the role of lecturers and use of resources and in differences over management ethos, for example, between collegiality and professionalism on the one hand, and control and accountability on the other. A study conducted on behalf of NATFHE (Russell, 1998), also in England, criticized the FEFC's funding mechanism as bureaucratic and wasteful, with an impact on the curriculum such as recruiting students to inappropriate courses, retaining disruptive students who should have been thrown out and the near disappearance of extra-curricular activities.

Concluding remarks

Our three examples illustrate the ways in which the further education sector has been pushed into operating within a reformulated public sector. It has been forced to take on the trappings of the market but in other ways remains highly centralized through the control over funding and regulated through the operation of a number of agencies. Indeed, the existence of a variety of actors in the form of government agencies, professional bodies and independent colleges provides the conditions conducive to contest, conflict and tension. In the words of one of the principals we interviewed: 'The extreme "dog eat dog" competition model is not superior to an agreed framework between institutions . . . The ethics of the market place have dangerous applications to education.'

Our research reveals a substantial disjuncture between the market model underpinning central government strategy and the much more hybrid models, incorporating elements of markets, hierarchies and networks, which characterize the reality of actual educational practice. The impact of these arrangements on the FE sector has been increasingly well documented (Scott, 1996; Shain and Gleeson, 1999). The results of our own research, for example, illustrate all too vividly the intensification of competition between colleges and the ways in which market principles are characteristic of a new college management culture (Jephcote and Salisbury, 1996), the changing relationships between colleges and official bodies (Graham, Jephcote and Salisbury, 1997) and, in the context of quality assessment procedures, how the existence of effective quality management systems is regarded as one indicator of a college's worth as a provider of training and fitness to receive funding (Salisbury and Jephcote, 1998).

Ideas like value for money, efficiency, quality and accountability might appear incontrovertible but, as Ball (1990: 81) pointed out, they provide the mechanisms for both ideological and financial control and are 'indicative of discursive shifts in the meaning and governance of education'. In this shift, education is commodified and legitimized in terms of the ways in which it fulfils the functions of production but, at the same time, differentially impacts on the experience of students and lecturers. For example, as a result of this restructuring of education and the new forms of control over the 'professional', many lecturers are forced to accept part-time, temporary and fractional contracts, often with discriminatory conditions of work and vulnerable to so-called market forces. So, on the one hand, the marketization and commodification of further education can be portrayed as a mechanism to bring about greater efficiency and to increase consumer control. On the other, they have, in fact, led to a series of failures brought about by managers and other key actors who have been coerced into the pursuit of their own purposes, albeit with limited choice, at the expense of students and other consumers of the service. At least some commentators believe that the removal of power from the professionals is unlikely 'to do anything to improve people's dispositional barriers to learning' (Tett, 1999). It has been argued that the incorporation of colleges has led to fewer opportunities for socio-economically excluded communities (Tett and Ducklin, 1995). Rather than empower consumers, a market-driven system perpetuates inequalities and the market confirms and reinforces the existing social class order of wealth and privilege (Ranson, 1994).

As we stated in our introduction, our conceptual framework for describing and analysing new patterns of governance is incomplete and awaits a closer examination of the ways in which actors interact in shaping further education in Wales. We have begun to set out some of the problems and opportunities already evident in this process of negotiation and we have indicated some of its outcomes and contradictions. We are not, however, inclined towards an over-simplistic model, in the sense that we recognize that, once policies are decided, the process of implementation is not automatic and policies do not necessarily achieve their objectives. We are more inclined to an approach which embraces both policy-making and implementation and the ways in which, because of the levels of interaction, policies are negotiated and mediated. This leads us, therefore, towards an actor approach to policy-making and implementation in which we substitute an actors' choice perspective for an ends-means perspective. This is not, however, to exclude or underestimate the importance of structural relationships nor the conditions for action of those involved. We recognize that the control over resources and their distribution is not equal and accept that 'resources must be seen as differently and non-randomly distributed to actors by virtues of their location in various sets of structural social relationships' (Cooper, 1983). To understand the policy process it is necessary, therefore, to examine the structural conditions in which action is formulated, the differential allocation of resources, the conditions for action including social and economic circumstances and the interest-motivated changes legitimized in the policy statements, responses and practices of those actors involved. In our preferred perspective, the notion that bureaucrats and professionals necessarily act in the interest of policy-makers or the public interest is questioned. For us this accommodates the idea that the system can generate both problems and opportunities: on the one hand, there are the problems caused by the interaction of key actors and, on the other, there are ways in which actors can take advantage of situations for the better, which is sometimes cited as a benefit of the 'regional' structure in Wales. However, in an era of competition and survival at the college level, there can be little doubt that decision-makers are driven by self-interest and are tempted to form narrow interest groups and coalitions.

It remains to be seen, therefore, how far the infrastructure for education and training in Wales is able to respond appropriately to the emerging problems and opportunities. If we think of the institutional players in Wales as comprising a system, then the extent to which this will operate effectively is dependent upon the development of a framework of co-operation within which each of these players can fulfil complementary functions efficiently. At one level, of course, this requires the resolution of the essentially *ad hoc* problems which beset any administrative system, such as the micro-politics of organizations and personalities, territorial conflicts and lines of communication. More significantly, however, the development of a coherent operational framework depends upon the definition of objectives for each constituent institution which are mutually consistent and which thereby set the imperatives which drive the different elements of the system in a single direction.

References

Ball, S. J. (1990) *Politics and Policy Making in Education*. London: Routledge.

Ball, S. J. and Bowe, R. (1992) Micropolitics of radical change: budget management and control in British schools. In J. Blase (ed.), *The Politics of Life in Schools*. London: Sage.

Ball, S. J., Macrae, S. and Maguire, M. (1998) Young lives at risk in the 'futures market': some policy concerns from on-going research. Paper presented at the 'Learning Society Seminar', University of Bristol, 27–8 January.

Bottery, M. (1992) *The Ethics of Educational Management: Personal, Social and Political Perspectives on School Organisation*. London: Cassell.

Cahill, M. (1994) *The New Social Policy*. Oxford: Blackwell.

Chitty, C. (1989) *Towards a New Education System: The Victory of the New Right?* London: Falmer Press.

Cooper, B. (1983) On explaining change in school subjects. *British Journal of Sociology of Education*, 4(3), 207–22.

Cutler, T. (1992) Vocational training and British economic performance: a further instalment of the 'British labour problem'. *Work, Employment and Society*, 6, 161–84.

DES (1988) *Education Reform Act*. London: HMSO.

DES (1991) *Education and Training for the Twenty-First Century* (DES/ED/Welsh Office, Cm 1536), vols. 1 and 2. London: HMSO.

DES (1992) *Further and Higher Education Act*. London: HMSO.

DfEE (1988) *The Learning Age*. London: DfEE.

Education and Training Action Group for Wales (ETAG) (1998) *An Education and Training Action Plan for Wales*. Cardiff: Welsh Office.

Elliott, G. (1996) *Crisis and Change in Vocational Education and Training*. London: Jessica Kingsley.

Elliott, G. and Hall, V. (1994) F.E. Inc. – business orientation in Further Education and the introduction of human resource management. *School Organisation*, 1(1), 3–10.

FEFCW (1993) *Annual Review 1992/93*. Cardiff: Further Education Funding Council for Wales.

FEFCW (1994a) *Annual Report 1993/4*. Cardiff: Further Education Funding Council for Wales.

FEFCW (1994b) *Corporate Plan*. Cardiff: Further Education Funding Council for Wales.

FEFCW (1994c) Securing the improvement in the quality of FE in Wales and rewarding high quality teaching and learning. *Bulletin*, (23 September). Cardiff: Further Education Funding Council for Wales.

FEFCW (1995a) Institutional action plans following quality assessments. *Bulletin* (12 January). Cardiff: Further Education Funding Council for Wales.

FEFCW (1995b) Peer evaluation in quality assessment in FE institutions in Wales. *Bulletin* (3 April). Cardiff: Further Education Funding Council for Wales.

FEFCW (1996) *Corporate Plan*. Cardiff: Further Education Funding Council for Wales.

FEFCW and OHMCI (1997) *Quality Assessment Handbook*. Cardiff: Further Education Funding Council for Wales.

Foskett, N. and Hesketh, A. (1996) *Student Decision Making and the Post-16 Market Place*. Southampton: HEIST.

Garmise, S. and Rees, G. (1997) The role of institutional networks in local economic development: a new model of governance? *Local Economy*, 12(2), 104–18.

Gleeson, D. and Shain, F. (1999) Managing ambiguity: between markets and managerialism – a case study of middle managers in further education. *The Sociological Review*, 47(3) (August 1999), 461–90.

Graham, I., Jephcote, M. and Salisbury, J. (1997) Principals' responses to incorporation and the new funding regime. *Journal of Vocational Education and Training*, 49(4), 545–62.

James, J. (1998) The effects of a changing culture on staff attitudes in a further education college post incorporation. Unpublished M.Ed. thesis, University of Wales, Cardiff.

Jephcote, M. and Salisbury, J. (1996) Principals' responses to incorporation: a window on their culture. *Journal of Further and Higher Education*, 20(2), 33–48.

Kennedy, H. (1997) *Learning Works: Widening Participation in Further Education.* Coventry: FEFC.

Kooiman, J. (ed.) (1993) *Modern Governance: New Government–Society Interactions.* London: Sage.

Lane, J. (1993) *The Public Sector: Concepts, Models and Approaches.* London: Sage.

Lindley, R. (1991) Interactions in the markets for education, training and labour: a European perspective on intermediate skills. In P. Ryan (ed.), *International Comparisons of Vocational Education and Training for Intermediate Skills.* London: Falmer.

Lyotard, J. F. (1984) *The Post Modern Condition: A Report on Knowledge.* Manchester: Manchester University Press.

McDonnell, L. and Elmore, R. (1991) Getting the job done: alternative policy instruments. In A. Odden (ed.), *Education Policy Implementation.* New York: SUNY Press.

McPherson, A. and Raab, C. D. (1988) *Governing Education: A Sociology of Policy since 1945.* Edinburgh: Edinburgh University Press.

OHMCI (1994a) *The Framework for the Assessment of Quality.* Cardiff: Office of Her Majesty's Chief Inspector.

OHMCI (1994b) *Guidelines for Self Evaluation in FE Colleges in Wales, 1994–95.* Cardiff: Office of Her Majesty's Chief Inspector.

Randle, K. and Brady, N. (1997) Managerialism and professionalism in the Cinderella service. *Journal of Vocational Education and Training*, 49(1), 121–40.

Ranson, S. (1994) *Towards the Learning Society.* London: Cassell.

Rees, G. (1997) Vocational education and training regional development: an analytical framework. *Journal of Work and Education*, 10(2), 141–9.

Russell, B. (1998) Wasteful cash system blamed, *TES* (30 January), 33.

Salisbury, J. and Jephcote, M. (1996) *Quality Assessment in Further Education Colleges: The Associate Assessor Scheme in Wales.* Cardiff: School of Education (Mimeo).

Salisbury, J. and Jephcote, M. (1998) *From Principal to Chief Executive: Incorporation and the Occupational Re-socialisation of FE College*

Principals. Cardiff: School of Education (Mimeo).

Scott, P. (1996) Markets in post compulsory education: rhetoric policy and structure. In N. Foskett (ed.), *Markets in Education: Policy Process and Practice.* Southampton: CREM.

Shackleton, J. (1992) Training too much? A sceptical look at the economics of skill provision in the UK. *Hobart Paper, 118.* London: IEA.

Tett, L. (1999) Gender equality, the learning society policies and community education. In J. Salisbury and S. Riddell (eds.), *Gender Policy and Educational Change.* London: Routledge.

Tett, L. and Ducklin, A. (1995) Further education colleges and educationally disadvantaged adults. *Scottish Educational Review,* 27(2), 154–64.

Welsh Office (1995) *People and Prosperity: An Agenda of Action for Wales.* Cardiff: Welsh Office.

Welsh Office (1998) *Learning is for Everyone.* Cardiff: Welsh Office.

Williams, G. (1991) *A Handbook for College Governors in Gwent.* Newport: Gwent LEA.

10

Changes in Government Policy and the Development of Higher Education in Wales, 1975–1996

GETHIN WILLIAMS

Introduction

What follows is an account of an ongoing study, which addresses a perceived gap in our knowledge and understanding of the development of higher education in Wales over the past twenty-five years or so. These are acknowledged to be years of rapid change and great turbulence for higher education in the UK and have generated a substantial body of literature tracking and analysing change, including changes in government policy.

The distinctive experience of Wales, within the wider context of the UK, has not, however, been fully charted and analysed. This, it may be argued, is not entirely surprising, since for most of the period the university and public sectors of higher education in Wales functioned as integral parts of wider UK systems and were barely distinguishable, in particular, from the English university and public sectors in whose slip-streams they followed. Such a view needs to be tested, as does the contrary perception that Wales, by definition, provides an unique and distinctive context for the operation of government policy. And the testing will need to extend beyond 1 April 1993, when the Higher Education Funding Council for Wales (HEFCW) assumed responsibility for the funding of both the university and public sectors in Wales, unified by the Further and Higher Education Act 1992.

One of HEFCW's strategic objectives is the creation of 'an identifiable and coherent Welsh Higher Education Sector' (Andrews, 1996). The creation of a separate funding council for Wales could be seen, in itself, as establishing a distinctive Welsh higher education sector. But the concept of 'an identifiable and coherent sector' implies a belief in an identity and coherence which extends beyond funding (Rees and Istance, 1997). This merits close examination, as does the influence of the concept on HEFCW's interpretation of its own role, in particular the extent to which it has chosen to create and exploit opportunities to migrate from the Higher Education Funding Council for England (HEFCE) in major policy areas. Of necessity, HEFCW will need to take account of the forces presently at work making for a much stronger regional or subnational dimension in the organization of higher education in the UK (Scott, 1993), among which devolution and the arrival of the Assembly are particularly significant for Wales.

Of potentially greater significance for individual higher education institutions is their positioning within the UK and internationally. There can be little doubt, for example, over where the University of Wales, Cardiff, as recently admitted to the Russell Group, wishes to position itself. By the same token, however, such positioning raises doubts over its perceived long-term future within the University of Wales and thereby over the future of the federation itself. But these tensions are not new. Within the University of Wales there have been periodic attempts since the early 1960s to uncouple constituent institutions, and pressures remain, bolstered by growth in size, the new funding arrangements and the presence of the University of Glamorgan.

While it is not thought necessary to go as far back as the early 1960s to establish a meaningful historical context, the choice of 1975 as a starting-point for the study is largely self-selecting. This was the year in which HE was significantly expanded on the public-sector side of the binary line, in the wake of the 1972 White Paper and DES Circular 7/73. In Wales the Polytechnic of Wales was to be joined by four Colleges/Institutes of Higher Education (Gwent, North East Wales, South Glamorgan and West Glamorgan) which together with two Training Colleges (Bangor Normal and Trinity College, Carmarthen) and three Monotechnics (the Welsh Colleges of Agriculture, Librarianship and Music and Drama) created a new presence in advanced further education (AFE), identifiable as a distinct higher education sector which would merit its own advisory body in 1982. This was also the time when the financial climate changed dramatically for the university sector as the halcyon days enjoyed post-Robbins gave way to increasingly hard times, to which the constituent colleges of the University of Wales were not immune (Morgan, 1997). The remaining sections provide a synoptic view of the study period, describing how the project is being tackled and offering some reflections on the extent to which the original research strategy appears to be achieving its intended purposes.

Synoptic view

Before proceeding to describe the study and offering reflections on work in progress, I will provide a brief synoptic view, focusing attention primarily at the sectoral level. For this purpose the study period is divided into four parts.

1975–1980

This is the period when the macro-economic climate and the climate of public opinion changed (Halsey, 1995) to the detriment of both the university and public sectors. It was also the period when projected student numbers for 1981 in Great Britain had to be revised downwards. Official projections for full-time and sandwich students which had been 750,000 in December 1972 were progressively revised downwards from 640,00 in November 1974 to 544,000 in March 1979 (Open University, 1984).

In the university sector the 1972–7 quinquennium was suspended midway to be replaced by annual funding. The capital spending tap was 'turned off viciously', removing one of the University Grant Committee's most powerful weapons for shaping university development, which was now to be achieved through its handling of the recurrent grant (Moore, 1987). One of the victims of the fall in capital spending was the University of Wales Institute of Science and Technology (UWIST) whose plans for a transfer to a new site at Llantarnam had to be abandoned following an announcement by the government in June 1976.

In the public sector the new higher education colleges and institutes (HEIs), hoping for generous support to get them off to a good start, fell victim to the same harsh economic climate. Cuts were imposed on local government expenditure and appropriate contributions were expected by local education authorities from their HEIs. This was at a time when the majority were coping with the consequences of merger, facing strict controls on course approval by the

Regional Staff Inspector and Regional Advisory Council, and seeking to match the exacting standards of validating bodies, most notably the Council for National Academic Awards (CNAA) (Silver, 1990). There was also another phase in the rationalization of initial teacher training to contend with in 1977, which Swansea Institute escaped after a successful campaign by West Glamorgan LEA, led by Lord Heycock. The Polytechnic of Wales (PoW), formed in 1975 following the merger between Glamorgan Polytechnic and Barry Training College, failed in its attempt to retain teacher training.

Prior to its removal from office in 1979, the Labour government had sought to find ways of exercising more effective control over the funding and management of AFE but ran out of time to implement the recommendations of the Oakes Working Group (1978). The same problems remained, however, when the Conservative government came to power and these were tackled early. The AFE 'open-ended' pool was capped in 1980 and the search for new management arrangements continued.

Although AFE in Wales transferred from the DES to the Welsh Office in 1978, both the public and university sectors during this period functioned essentially as parts of England and Wales systems. Indeed, during the debate on devolution the University of Wales indicated that it wished to remain part of a UK-wide system funded by the UGC (Morgan, 1997).

1981–1988

This was the crucial period when the adjustments necessary for the transition from an élite to a mass higher education system were made. In the university sector, the UGC lies at the centre of the action and will, therefore, command particular attention. Attention will need to be given to the change in its role from 'buffer to strategist' (Shattock, 1994) and the way its strategic planning role developed under successive chairmen: Sir Edward Parkes, 1978–83, and Sir Peter Swinnerton-Dyer, 1983–8. In Sir Peter's view the UGC became, over the years, 'a body of experts addicted to planning' (Swinnerton-Dyer: 1991).

The UGC was notably, through cuts in funding estimated at 13–15 per cent over the period 1981/2–1983/4, to play a more proactive role and chose to do so by defending the unit of resource, which required a 5 per cent cut in student numbers, and by adopting a selective approach (rather than 'equal misery') for the allocation of grant in 1981. Both had dramatic consequences and needed to be defended in some detail before the Select Committee for Education and Science (University Grants Committee, 1982). The University of Wales suffered an average outcome in terms of the reduction in grant allocation of 17 per cent from 1980/1 to 1983/4, while maintaining the same numbers of home and EC students as in 1979/80, which was better than the average fall of 4 per cent (Shattock, 1996). In this it fared better on the basis of the 'informed prejudice' (a term used by Sir Edward Parkes to describe the approach, defended in University Grants Committee, 1982), employed for the 1981 allocation, than it did in 1986, when a more transparent formulaic approach, incorporating research selectivity, was applied (Moore, 1987).

By the mid-1980s the UGC had become the kind of pragmatic planning body acceptable to early Thatcherism (Swinnerton-Dyer, 1991). As a consequence, universities were faced with increased demands for information, involving the presentation of academic and financial plans. In addition, improvements were expected in management and governance in accordance with the recommendations of the Jarratt Report (1985). Increasingly, periodic follow-up reports were required on actions taken to implement a selective approach to research, rationalize subject provision and related staffing, adopt Jarratt, and other areas where a strong steer had been given. For the most part, if with varying degrees of enthusiasm, the UGC received the kind of co-operation it expected.

In one conspicuous case, however, and that in Wales, relations broke down with the UGC. In 1986 it became necessary for Sir David Hancock, Permanent Secretary at the DES, to intervene, on the advice of the UGC, in the affairs of University College, Cardiff (UCC) and thereby set in motion a series of events which became a *cause célèbre* and sent shock waves throughout the university sector. This had major repercussions for the UGC itself and the University of Wales which led to the merger of UCC and UWIST in 1988, after sharing the same principal from 1987 (Shattock, 1994).

While *de jure* the UGC remained at arms length from the government, until replaced by the UFC in 1989, *de facto* the relationship changed in important ways during the period 1980–8. In the early 1980s, for example, there was a public exchange of correspondence between Sir Keith Joseph and Sir Edward Parkes which aimed to clarify the legitimate role of government in shaping the strategic development of the university sector (University Grants Committee, 1983, 1984a). Apart from serving the interests of ministers and civil servants at the DES, the exchange had the great merit for the UGC in providing much needed cover in its relations with the heads of institutions, whose interests it was expected to defend.

Included in the correspondence was a request from Sir Keith for a view of the higher education provision needed in the 1990s. This request gave rise to further correspondence on the consultation process to be adopted to complete the exercise. It was left to Sir Peter Swinnerton-Dyer, when taking over as chairman, to conduct a major consultation exercise by questionnaire which provided the basis for a report published in September 1984 (University Grants Committee, 1984b). A response was also prepared in 1984 by the National Advisory Board (NAB) (involving the Welsh Advisory Board, WAB) to a similar request from the Secretary of State and the two reports shared a joint introductory statement which presented the view that the Robbins axiom should be restated as: 'Courses of higher education should be available for all those who are able to benefit from them and who wish to do so.'

The Green Paper (DES, 1985) which followed, and which was expected to be informed and influenced by the responses, proved a great disappointment to the UGC, NAB and their constituents. A major disappointment was the failure of the government to commit itself to a stable medium-term planning horizon, also called for in the Jarratt Report (1985).

The NAB, like the UGC, had been asked by the Secretary of State to look at the management and governance of its sector. A study group was established, on which WAB was represented, and a series of studies conducted, with the aid of consultants and secondees, which provided the basis for a report published just before the appearance in April 1987 of the White Paper (DES, 1987), by which it was largely overtaken. In particular the government rejected the form of incorporation proposed by the NAB (1987) which left the HEIs under local government administration. They were to be incorporated, taken out of local government and funded by a Polytechnics and Colleges Funding Council (PCFC) which would operate in parallel with the UGC's successor, the UFC.

A similar solution had been one of two main options considered in 1981 when the local authorities fought successfully for the other option, which allowed them to retain ownership and also gave them appropriate representation on the new National Advisory Bodies for Local Government Higher Education, one for England and another for Wales, set up in 1982. Both had three tiers consisting of a committee, chaired by a minister, a board chaired by an independent chairman and working groups/panels chaired by members of the board.

In Wales, where the Welsh Joint Education Committee (WJEC) argued strongly that it should perform the WAB role, the expedient was adopted of having equal representation on the WAB Committee from the WJEC (representing the educational interest) and the Welsh Counties Committee (representing the financial interest). Accordingly, eight county councillors were appointed, with each of the county councils represented, although only seven had responsibility for a HEI. The expedient worked well if judged by patterns of attendance, which in the majority of cases were exemplary, and the generally good relations developed with ministers, notably Sir Wyn Roberts who was chairman of the WAB Committee from 1985 to 1992. There were some early territorial problems over the respective roles of the committee and the board and adequacy of representation on the third-tier panels but these were largely resolved.

While the WAB in this and other respects displayed distinctively Welsh characteristics, it operated for the most part in the shadow of the NAB which, in scale of operation and organizational capability, necessarily dwarfed the WAB. Even so, the opportunity was taken, as appropriate, to make adaptations to the Welsh context, for example, as occurred with the funding methodology. Also there were issues, like the rationalization of initial teacher training (ITT) across the binary line, which had a unique Welsh setting.

The primary function of the WAB was to advise the Secretary of State for Wales each year on the allocation of funds for the provision of higher education in Wales, based on the size of the quantum, agreed by the Welsh Office and local authority representative bodies, and the distribution of target student numbers by programme, mode and level. A transparent funding methodology was developed and refined over the years which sought to reconcile the need to maintain a satisfactory unit of resource with ambitious plans from the colleges to expand and thereby increase access. The balance achieved was largely acceptable to the HEIs and their LEAs.

One institution, the PoW, however, was deeply dissatisfied with the funding it received compared with its counterparts in England and took the opportunity at regular intervals to press its case with its own LEA (Mid Glamorgan CC), the WAB and the Welsh Office and to mobilize support from the CNAA and the Committee of Directors of Polytechnics (CDP). As a member of the CDP, the director of the PoW had argued from the early 1980s for corporate status and was greatly disappointed by the exclusion of Wales from the provisions for incorporation and independence made for England in the 1988 Education Reform Act (ERA). Following the publication of the NAB's Report and the government's White Paper in 1987, corporate status became a hotly discussed issue in Wales. The Welsh Office, in a Consultative Paper issued in August 1987, made no secret of the fact that it favoured incorporation for the major HEIs in Wales but also made it clear that it was a matter to be settled by the institutions and their LEAs, by whom they would continue to be administered. Provision was made, however, in section 227(4) of the 1988 ERA, for the Secretary of State for Wales to bring the arrangements more in line with England if the need arose.

As it transpired, the status quo was maintained as none of the Welsh LEAs were disposed to grant corporate status. The persistent claims for incorporation made by the PoW, supported by its board of governors, strained relations with Mid Glamorgan County Council, which up to that point had generally been good, despite the constraints on the financial support it was able to provide as a poor, overstretched authority with a large stock of old school buildings to replace. The primary cause of the deterioration in relations, which began in 1987, was a critical report from the district auditor in 1986 exposing deficiencies in financial control procedures applied to the regional management centre at the PoW. Matters went from bad to worse as the issue dragged on without satisfactory resolution and drew the attention of the media. It became another Welsh *cause célèbre*, this time in the public sector, also having sector-wide implications and requiring intervention from the Welsh Office (described below).

As far as relations between the university and public sectors during this period are concerned, there were important differences between England and Wales. In Wales there was very little co-operation at sectoral level, although at institutional level there were good working relationships with the University's validating board and Faculty of Education. The University of Wales was represented on the WAB Board by the vice-chancellor, with patterns of attendance varying with the holder of the office. But the WAB struggled to establish a joint liaison panel with the university, which when eventually established met on only two occasions.

In England the UGC and NAB were required by government to collaborate and consult, with the chairmen of the two bodies being in regular formal (through reciprocal observer status) and informal contact. The chairman of the WAB Board also attended the NAB Board as an observer and joined with the chairmen of the UGC and NAB for periodic meetings. The public sector represented a much greater challenge to the university sector in England than it did in Wales, where it was comparatively underdeveloped. Even so, the opportunity for expansion, provided by the decision of the UGC to protect the unit of resource by restricting access, was not missed.

1989–1992
This was the period in which the transition from an élite to a mass system gathered momentum, as the government created the conditions and provided the encouragement for an expansion whose success was so great that by November 1992 it was having to apply the brakes and call for a period of consolidation. The encouragement was unmistakable in the public utterances of Secretaries of State for Education, Kenneth Baker at the University of Lancaster on 5 January 1989 and John MacGregor at Portsmouth Polytechnic on 6 June 1990. The conditions necessary for achieving expansion were to be the release of market forces, increased competition, improved efficiency and productivity, all driving down the unit of resource as 'fees only' students were recruited in large numbers.

In the university sector the UFC took over from the UGC and brought a number of significant changes in its wake which were less to the liking of the chief executive, Sir Peter Swinnerton-Dyer, than the chairman, Lord Chilver. These have been described in graphic terms (Swinnerton-Dyer, 1991, 1996) with a trenchant critique of quasi-markets and an account of the unsuccessful competitive bidding exercise, insisted upon by Lord Chilver but considered doomed to failure by his chief executive, as part of the 1991–5 Planning Exercise.

Although the universities operated as a cartel to subvert competitive bidding, they nevertheless competed strongly for students and recruited 'fees only' students in large numbers for which recognition was received, in due course, by the funding mechanism. With the separation of the funding of teaching and research by the UFC, the outcomes of the research assessment exercises (RAEs) became even more obtrusive. The performances of the colleges of the University of Wales in the 1989 and 1992 RAEs were considered disappointing, though improving.

The improvement of the research performance of the University of Wales through collaboration was an ambition of Sir John Meurig Thomas, appointed to a new part-time post of Deputy Pro-Chancellor, as a result of the adoption by the university of the recommendation of the Daniel Working Group on Powers and Functions (Daniel, 1989). With the benefit of hindsight it can be seen that the Daniel Report was quickly overtaken by events. Had the UGC mode of operation prevailed, then the attempt by the federal university to obtain a stronger purchase on the strategic development and effective management of its constituent institutions, in the wake of Jarratt (1985) and the UC Cardiff crisis, might have been appropriate. In the circumstances which prevailed as the UFC took over, when planning was seen as a 'Socialist heresy' (Swinnerton-Dyer, 1991), the balance of power shifted decisively to the institutions as the battle between the 'centripetalists' and the 'centrifugalists' (Morgan, 1997) was fought again. Early experience of operating the Daniel reforms and the appearance of the 1991 White Paper prompted a further review, this time by the Rosser Working Party (Rosser, 1993), which displayed a realism which had the necessary calming influence.

An apparent tendency to swim against the tide by displaying strong *dirigiste* tendencies was also observable in the WAB. Like the Daniel Working Group, the WAB's impulse to plan derived from anxieties over the competitive weaknesses of Welsh institutions as compared with their English counterparts. By the time the Programme Review Working Group had completed its assessment of the strengths and weaknesses, by programme and institution, of public-sector provision in Wales (WAB, 1990), its fears were being realized as the PCFC sector in England appeared to be steaming speedily away. This success was considered by the HEIs in Wales to derive from the new-found freedoms enjoyed by PCFC institutions in England, which they envied.

They were, therefore, highly critical of the Programme Review which proposed the use of remits and appeared to strongly favour the PoW while imposing a strait-jacket on developments elsewhere. A modified remit system was adopted, however, and incorporated into a new planning framework which required the submission of institutional plans. In recognition of the way the general tide was running, the framework became increasingly flexible as controls on course approval were eased and greater freedom was given to exercise virement within more broadly defined programme areas. In Wales, as elsewhere, market forces were to be harnessed rather than resisted.

Similarly, the time for incorporation had arrived. The serious breakdown in relations between the PoW and Mid Glamorgan CC reported by Price Waterhouse to the Welsh Office (which had commissioned the investigation) in May 1990 made inevitable the incorporation of the major HEIs in Wales and their removal from local control. An announcement was made by the Secretary of State on 30 January, 1991, of his intention to use the powers available to him under section 227(4) of the 1988 ERA to achieve this reform, with the Welsh Office taking over responsibility for funding. The WAB, whose board had been slimmed down, reconstituted and renamed the Standing Working Group, reflecting its changed status, in 1989, came to an end in December 1991. By that time it was known from the White Paper (DES, 1991), published in the May, that further reforms were to be introduced, involving the removal of the binary line and the creation of separate Higher Education Funding Councils for England, Wales and Scotland.

1993–1996

Among the most striking features of this period is the contractual basis developed for the relationship between HEFCW and the Welsh Office (codified in a Management Statement and Financial Memorandum) and HEFCW and Welsh HEIs (codified in Financial Memoranda). This was a feature introduced by government in the 1988 ERA to define more clearly its relations with the UFC and PCFC and increase its control over the development of both sectors (Swinnerton-Dyer, 1991). The degree of control has significantly increased since, as may be seen from the guidance from government which now accompanies the annual announcement of the allocation to HEFCW. Such guidance, which may incorporate targets and deadlines for achieving them, is reflected in the contents of the strategic plans, operational plans and annual reports which HEFCW is required to submit annually to the Welsh Office. This high degree of transparency and public accountability may also be seen in the use made of circulars for official communication with HEIs. These are public documents widely circulated and easily accessed. In all, a substantial archive is being created which will greatly assist the work of present and future researchers.

The key transaction between HEFCW and HEIs in Wales is the annual allocation of funds for teaching and research. The former is distributed using a methodology involving 'core' and 'margin' elements, with a provision for 'clawback' from HEIs who under- or over-recruit. For research three elements have been distinguished: QR and CR (formula-driven) and initiatives (proposal-based). QR is the allocation based on quality as adjudged by the RAE and represents the bulk of funding for research, distributed selectively. CR is given to institutions in proportion to their income from contract research. A number of initiatives have been taken designed to strengthen research in Wales (a priority identified for the Council by the Secretary of State in his initial letter issued in May 1992), two of which, QW and DevR, merit attention. QW funding, amounting to a total of £7.1 million over the period 1993/4 to 1995/6, was distributed to particular departments identified as having potential, on the basis of their 1992 RAE performance, for improving their ratings in the 1996 RAE. DevR funding, amounting to a total of £3.8 million over the period 1993/4 to 1996/7, was provided to support the development of a limited research base in the former public sector on a highly selective basis. The outcomes of the 1996 RAE were seen by HEFCW as an encouraging vindication of its research policy (HEFCW, 1997).

While funding dominates the year's business, the Council has wider responsibilites, among which quality assurance is probably the most important. This is an area in which HEFCW, operating within a national statutory framework, chose to develop a distinctly Welsh approach to Teaching Quality Assessment (TQA) based on the cultivation of a meaningful partnership with institutions and an increasing emphasis on institutional critical self-evaluation (Williams, 1996). It is hoped that with the absorption, post-Dearing, of the QA division of HEFCW by the Quality Assurance Agency (QAA), which has been given responsibility for TQA as well as institutional Academic Audit, the distinctive developmental and collaborative approach nurtured in Wales will not be replaced by the harsher, inspectorial approach identified with HEFCE. In this and other matters there will be great interest in the scope afforded to and the inclination shown by HEFCW for establishing an identifiable and coherent Welsh dimension in higher education in the UK.

The study

The primary aim of the study is to identify and analyse the major changes in government policy during the study period and to assess their impact on the development of HE in Wales at the subnational, sectoral and institutional levels. A comparison will be made of developments on both sides of the binary line before and after its removal and the opportunity will be taken to place the development of higher education in Wales within the general context of policy formulation and implementation in the UK.

Particular attention is being given to three sets of policy issues considered to have greatest salience for the emerging 'public shape' (Halsey, 1995) of HE. The first relates to the *changing character of higher education* in terms of *size* (notably patterns of growth and the transition from and élite to a mass system), *configuration* (notably the binary line, the postitioning of institutions, and the place of teaching and research), and the *curriculum* (notably the range of undergraduate and postgraduate programmes and changes in their design and delivery).

The second relates to the *management of higher education*, with particular reference to the *rise of managerialism* in its several forms (hard, soft, new public management), the *marketization of transactions* (competition, contracts, quasi-markets) and the *encouragement of consumerism* (HE Charter, stakeholder interests, transparency), each having implications for *staff* (tenure, appraisal, productivity) and *financial* (solvency, unit of resource, income generation, value for money) *management*.

The third relates to the *enhancement and sharpening of accountability* at the *macro* (government and funding councils), *meso* (funding councils and HE institutions) and *micro* (governing bodies, chief executives, staff, students and other stakeholders) *levels*. While the major preoccupation of policy has been with financial stewardship, increasing importance has been given to *quality assurance and academic standards*, with an elaborate framework of accountability put in place. Audit features prominently in both. Of particular interest at the institutional level is the potential discrepancy between *de jure* arrangements and *de facto* practice in terms of *governance, executive authority* and the place of the *collegium*.

Two main theoretical perspectives are being employed which are considered to have correspondences likely to produce valuable synergy. The first is identified with Ball (1994: 14) who takes the view that 'the *complexity* and *scope* of policy analysis precludes the possibility of successful single theory explanations' and creates the need for 'a toolbox of diverse concepts and theories'. Further elaboration is given to this approach and the issues surrounding its use in Walford (1994) and Halpin and Troyna (1994) which have also informed the theoretical underpinning of the study. Attention is drawn, in particular to the work of Fitz and Halpin (1994: 32–50). This approach is considered particularly appropriate to the tracing and analysis of policy trajectories between levels and the iteration between them as policy is constituted and reconstituted, interpreted, mediated and implemented over time.

Viewed from an institutional perspective, the changes in policy represent challenges of strategic importance which have to be well managed. It is considered appropriate, therefore, to draw on a second perspective associated with the work of Pettigrew (1987; and Whipp, 1991; *et al.*, 1992) on the management of strategic change, which highlights the iterations between the content, process and contexts (inner and outer) of strategic change. This work has been further developed to explore the process of transformational change (Ferlie *et al.*, 1996), which requires simultaneous strategic change at all, or most, levels within a system. The focus of attention has been the public services, most notably the health service. Attention has also been given to education and the impact of the new public management upon the schools and higher education sectors.

The two perspectives are considered to have correspondences which increase their power in application when brought together. Both acknowledge complexity and the importance of understanding the processual and longitudinal dimensions of change. Both explore the iterations between organization levels through time and the significance of emergent as well as intended outcomes. Both take on board the contributions of serendipity, opportunism and negotiation and address the micro-political and cultural dimensions of context, with their associated vocabularies and discourses. It is hoped that the bringing together of these perspectives will make a valuable contribution to education policy studies.

Three main sources of data are being employed. First is the significant body of literature which tackles the major policy issues to be addressed (Bargh, Scott and Smith, 1996; Bird, 1994; Cuthbert, 1996; Halsey, 1995; Middlehurst, 1993; Salter and Tapper, 1994; Scott, 1993, 1995; Shattock, 1994, 1996; Tapper and Palfreyman, 1998; Trow, 1994 and 1998). This output is valued for the insights provided into developments at the UK level, with the English experience predominating. Only Morgan (1997) directs his attention specifically to Wales, in the third volume of the commissioned centenary history of the University of Wales. The final chapter, which is devoted to the period from the 1970s to the 1990s, has particular relevance and value, although it does not, of necessity, tackle the public sector, share the same preoccupations or employ a similar analytical framework.

The second source is the familiar range of primary documents, most of them in the public domain, originating at the UK, Wales, sectoral and institutional levels, encompassing legislation, Green and White Papers, circulars, reports, policy statements, minutes, press releases, speeches, correspondence, newsletters, etc. Many of these, notably at the sectoral and institutional levels, are being closely examined by a researcher for the first time (for example, the Welsh Advisory Body for Local Government Higher Education papers held at the National Library of Wales). Others, such as the annual surveys of the University Grants Committee and the reports of the Public Accounts Committee and Select Committees, although already well picked over, have proved worth revisiting.

The third source consists of transcriptions of exploratory conversations held with a representative cross-section of key players who were invited to provide personal recollections and perceptions of past events from the vantage points which they occupied. The insights gathered from these conversations are being used as aids and prompts to map the territory revealed by documentary sources and to set against the range of perspectives found in the literature.

On the basis of the information gleaned from the above, it is intended to produce a narrative considered to represent an accurate and verifiable 'thin description' (Geertz, 1973) of the period. This will then be subject to analysis employing the chosen theoretical perspectives and taking account of the evaluations of the expert authorites (derived from the literature search) and the selective perceptions of key players (derived from the exploratory conversations) to produce a 'thick description' (Geertz, 1973). The thick description will provide, in turn, the basis for a single, 'all things considered', inter-subjective version of reality, accompanied by variants capable of producing alternative versions expected to derive from the vantage points of the key players, the evaluations of the expert authorites and the 'assumptive worlds' (McPherson and Raab, 1988) or 'appreciative settings' (Vickers, 1965) of both.

It is intended that appropriate sections of this version, with variants, will be presented for comment to a wider group of key players, but including those with whom exploratory conversations have been held. For practical reasons it is anticipated that these will be written responses to sets of standard questions, rather than taped interviews, as originally anticipated. The final report will take account of the feedback received.

Reflections on work in progress

The study is more concerned with how policy is interpreted, mediated and implemented than with how it is formulated. Even so, the prior step of defining and characterizing policy in terms of identifiable ends and means cannot be avoided. This is not an easy task, particularly for the period up to the 1988 ERA if what is being sought is a consistent, carefully formulated set of policies with clear objectives and a strong political will to see them achieved in the medium and long term. Certainly this is the view of two notable insiders. Lord Crowther Hunt's experience as a new Labour minister of education, who drew a blank with the Prime Minister and his Secretary of State, is frequently quoted (Crowther Hunt, 1983). Richard Bird, Deputy Secretary at the DES from 1980–90, reflecting on his experience from a unique vantage point, concludes: 'The general message that I offer is that most of the significant developments of the decade happened in piecemeal and pragmatic fashion. There were certainly some overall trends of policy, though these could by no means be assembled into any kind of grand strategy'

(Bird, 1994). This emphasis on piecemeal, pragmatic improvisation in response to changing circumstances is one made, without exception, by the insiders consulted. It is striking how frequently the phrase 'overtaken by events' appears. According to this view we are led to consider the political model of policy- making suggested by Gareth Williams (Oxtoby, 1981), seen as 'a series of tactical decisions that emerge from the interplay of pressure and interest groups'.

Salter and Tapper see things happening more by intention and design and draw attention to the long-standing bureaucratic drive of the central state to secure control over higher education. They acknowledge, however, the major shift brought about by the 1988 ERA and the 1992 FE and HE Act in the power of the state to orchestrate change in HE: 'After decades of incremental progress, of prod and nudge politics, of wait and see, the state has acquired powers which make a qualitative shift in its relations with the institutions of higher education' (Salter and Tapper, 1994: 1). It is evident that account will need to be taken, when tracking policy changes, of a host of factors including secular international trends, domestic economic and social imperatives and the emergence of a new dominant discourse. In accordance with the kind of contextualist analysis being employed, particular attention will need to be given to the currency of ideas and climate of opinion informing and informed by the Thatcher government. For this purpose the insights provided by studies of the new public management (Ferlie *et al.*, 1996) are considered particularly valuable.

It is against this wider background that an attempt will be made to identify a distinctive Welsh dimension in the evolution of policy, of which there is limited evidence, so far, at the macro and meso levels. A rich picture is emerging from the combined sources described in the previous sections, although there are obvious limitations which are acknowledged. There is the general point that the study relies on documentary sources in the public domain and is preoccupied with the 'public shape' of higher education as opposed to its 'private life' (Halsey, 1995). It follows that the study is deficient to the extent that it casts its net at the surface (Trowler, 1997), thereby neglecting deeper structures. Even so, experience shows that sources like formal minutes and reports, tracked over an extended period of time, can be revealing, despite the fact that they generally provide filtered accounts addressed to particular audiences and possess a micro-political dimension. The conventions of good reporting and the checks and balances of formal approval tend, however, to sustain their value for building up a useful thin description. This has been the experience, for example, with the minutes of the WAB Committee and WAB Board/Standing Working Group, supplemented by exploratory conversations with a representative group of 'key players'.

In all, exploratory conversations have been held to date with forty key players drawn from agencies operating at the macro and meso levels and including academics holding senior positions at institutional level. There has been less of a concern with accurate and detailed recall (the task of producing a verifiable factual account resting primarily with the researcher) than with broad general perceptions of situations, events and features of the unfolding drama which have the greatest salience and significance in personal recollection. The problems with recollections, inevitably selective and variously coloured, are readily acknowledged, particularly when they stretch back twenty years or more. The selective perceptions, deriving as they do from the occupation of different vantage points, have the great merit, however, of providing valuable prompts and insights when tackling documentary sources. With the aid of familiar devices such as sampling, audit trailing and triangulation, it is proving possible to produce the kind of intersubjective versions of reality, and variants upon them, described in the previous sections.

There are encouraging signs that the conceptual framework chosen will provide valuable insights. Here again, however, limitations and potential problems need to be acknowledged. Attention will be confined, for the present purpose, to two features.

First, there is the fact that the two theoretical perspectives chosen, despite the correspondences identified in the previous sections, derive from different traditions and discourses which might be considered incompatible. One of the objectives of the study is to test how far discourses grounded in different academic traditions can be brought together to produce new insights, notably for practitioners. This is a problem that was addressed at the annual meeting of the Association for the Study of Higher Education held in Florida in November 1998 (Cuthbert and Thorne, 1998), with the needs of the practitioner at the soft end of managerialism in mind. The present study is similarly positioned for the purposes of relating theory to practice and draws on earlier research conducted by the author (Williams, 1989).

Second, the comprehensive contextualist framework which informs the analysis (represented in Figure 10.1) is easier to map than to navigate. There is an abundance of landmark events whose reverberations within and between levels may be trailed and evaluated. But there are practical limits to the number of interfaces which can be explored as policy iterates and are subject to interaction. It is proving necessary, therefore, to select trajectories carefully with the aid of sampling and audit trailing. Use is being made, in accordance with contextualist practice, of dramatic events capable of throwing into high relief the tensions and conflicts surrounding policy and the means adopted for their resolution.

The opportunity will be taken, therefore, to consider the following:

(a) University College Cardiff funding crisis 1986–7;
(b) the Daniel (1989) and Rosser (1993) Reports;
(c) the Polytechnic of Wales, District Auditor's Report 1986;
(d) the Polytechnic of Wales, Price Waterhouse Report 1990; and
(e) the conferment of University College status on the Cardiff Institute of HE and the Gwent College of HE in 1996 following their earlier achievement of degree-awarding powers.

Readers may wish to test for themselves the power in application of the contextualist frameworks represented in Figures 10.1 and 10.2 by selecting landmark events, associated with changes in HE policy, with which they are familiar and on which they might like to reflect, taking into account trajectories between levels and the vantage points which they occupied. When so doing consideration might be given, for example, to (i) changes in the climate of opinion and currency of ideas associated with changes in policy and reflected in policy discourses and their associated vocabularies; (ii) the part played by identifiable 'key players' in the mediation of policy; (iii) discrepancies between *de jure* and *de facto* structures and processes for the management and governance of institutions as they affect, in particular, patterns of accountability and the operation of effective checks and balances; and (iv) the attention and time given to strategic planning, financial management and quality assurance structures, processes and standard operating procedures.

Figure 10.1 University sector: organizational contexts for the formulation, mediation, interpretation and implementation of government policy on higher education in Wales

POLICY CONTEXTS	GLOBAL NATIONAL	Economic Political Social Cultural	
POLICY SOURCES	FUNDING: EDUCATION: RESEARCH:	Treasury DES/DfE/DfEE, Welsh Office DES, DTI	
KEY EXECUTIVE MEDIATING AND INFLUENCING AGENCIES	FUNDING: QUALITY ASSURANCE: RESEARCH: VALIDATION & ACCREDITATION: ASSOCIATION, REPRESENTATION & NEGOTIATION:	UGC/UFC, HEFCW AAU/HEQC/QAA, HEFCW (TQA), SPBs Research Councils, Sponsors, Clients Validating Agencies and SPBs Fraternities, Associations, SPBs, TUs	
UNIVERSITY OF WALES	ACADEMIC BOARD & USPs SVC's COMMITTEE	COUNCIL & COURT	THE REGISTRY
INSTITUTIONS	VICE CHANCELLOR SENATE FACULTIES SCHOOLS/DEPTS	COUNCIL & COURT VICE CHANCELLOR PRO VCs DEANS HEADS OF SCHOOL/DEPTS	CENTRAL ADMIN REGISTRY ADMIN SUPPORT STAFF
	Academic Policy	*Management & Governance*	*Administration*

Figure 10.2 Public sector: organizational contexts for the formulation, mediation, interpretation and implementation of government policy on higher education in Wales prior to incorporation

POLICY CONTEXTS	GLOBAL NATIONAL	Economic Political Social Cultural	
POLICY SOURCES	FUNDING: EDUCATION: RESEARCH:	Treasury DES/DfE/DfEE, Welsh Office DES, DTI	
KEY EXECUTIVE MEDIATING AND INFLUENCING AGENCIES	FUNDING:	AFE Pool/WAB/Welsh Office	
	QUALITY ASSURANCE: CNAA, UWVB, BTEC, HMI		
	RESEARCH:	Research Councils, Sponsors, Clients	
	VALIDATION & ACCREDITATION:	CNAA, UWVB & USPs, BTEC, SPBs	
	COURSE APPROVAL:	RSI, WJEC, WAB	
	ASSOCIATION, REPRESENTATION & NEGOTIATION:	Fraternities, Associations, SPBs, TUs	
LOCAL AUTHORITY		COUNTY COUNCIL	
		EDUCATION COMMITTEE	PERSONNEL COMMITTEE
INSTITUTIONS	PRINCIPAL ACADEMIC BOARD FACULTY SCHOOL/DEPT	GOVERNING BODY PRINCIPAL VICE-PRINCIPAL(S) DEANS HEADS OF SCHOOL/DEPTS	CLERK/CAO REGISTRY ADMIN SUPPORT STAFF
	Academic Policy	*Management & Governance*	*Administration*

Conclusions

As the study has just reached the half-way stage, there is a natural reluctance to draw anything approaching firm conclusions. Reliance has been placed, therefore, on sharing early impressions. Even so, two conclusions can be reached with some degree of confidence and they relate to the importance and potential value of the study and the need for future studies.

The work completed so far has confirmed, if confirmation were needed, that a serious gap exists in our knowledge and understanding of the development of HE in Wales over the past twenty-five years. It is hoped that, once completed, the study will go some way to closing the gap, identify areas warranting further detailed scrutiny and provide a platform for continuing research. The situation post-1993 is much less problematic for researchers in terms of the information put in the public domain by HEFCW (see earlier) and the range, quality and continuity of statistical information published by the Higher Education Statistical Agency (HESA). There will be less justification, therefore, for a repeat of past neglect, particularly as expectations grow of a significant improvement in public discussion of all aspects of education policy with the coming of the Assembly. Looming on the horizon, for example, is the relationship of HEFCW to the Assembly. The Committee of Scottish Higher Education Principals (COSHEP) has been quick off the mark in exploring the prospects for Scottish Higher Education with the arrival of the Scottish Parliament (COSHEP, 1998). Nothing has yet surfaced from similar concerns which must be exercising the heads of higher education in Wales. It is hoped that by tracking and evaluating the experience of negotiating a turbulent past, this and similar studies will help inform the shaping of a dynamic future.

References

Andrews, J. (1996) Present and future policies of the Higher Education Funding Council for Wales. Paper presented at a conference of HE Funding Councils held at Belfast in April. Cardiff: HEFCW.

Ball, S. J. (1994) *Education Reform: A Critical and Post Structural Approach*. Buckingham: Open University Press.

Bargh, C., Scott, P. and Smith, D. (1996) *Governing Universities in a Changing Culture?* Buckingham: SRHE and Open University Press.

Bird, R. (1994) Reflections on the British government and higher education. *Higher Education Quarterly,* 48(2), 74–85.

Committee of Scottish Higher Education Principals (1998) The Scottish Parliament: the prospects for Scottish higher education. Discussion Paper prepared for the 4th COSHEP Forum, 30 October. Edinburgh: Napier University.

Crowther Hunt, Lord (1983) Policy making and accountability in higher education. In M. Shattock (ed.), *The Structure and Governance of Higher Education.* Guildford: SRHE, pp. 46–66.

Cuthbert, R. (ed.) (1996) *Working in Higher Education.* Buckingham: SRHE and OU Press.

Cuthbert, R. and Thorne, M. L. (1998) Higher education management: discourse and discord. Paper presented at the 23rd Annual Meeting of the Association for the Study of Higher Education, held in Miami, FL, November.

Daniel, G. (1989) *Report of the Working Group on Powers and Functions.* Cardiff: University of Wales.

DES (1985) *The Development of Higher Education into the 1990s* (Cmnd 9524). London: HMSO.

DES (1987) *Higher Education: Meeting the Challenge* (Cmnd 114). London: HMSO.

DES (1991) *Higher Education: A New Framework* (Cmnd 1541). London: HMSO.

Ferlie, E. *et al,* (1996) *The New Public Management in Action.* Oxford: Oxford University Press.

Fitz, J. and Halpin, D. (1994) Ministers and mandarins: educational research in elite settings. In G. Walford (ed.), *Researching the Powerful in Education.* London: University College Press.

Geertz, C. (1973) *The Interpretation of Cultures.* New York: Basic Books.

Halpin, D. and Troyna, B. (1994) *Researching Education Policy.* London: Falmer Press.

Halsey, A. H. (1995) *Decline of Donnish Dominion.* Oxford: Clarendon Press.

Higher Education Funding Council for Wales (1997) *Circular W97/12HE.* Cardiff: HEFCW, March.

Jarratt, A. (1985) *Report of the Steering Committee on Efficiency Studies in Universities.* London: CVCP.

McPherson, A. and Raab, C. D. (1988) *Governing Education.* Edinburgh: Edinburgh University Press.

Middlehurst, R. (1993) *Leading Academics.* Buckingham: SRHE and Open University Press.

Moore, P. G. (1987) University financing 1979–86. *Higher Education Quarterly*, 41(1), 25–42.

Morgan, P. (1997) *The University of Wales 1939–1993*. Cardiff: University of Wales Press.

National Advisory Body (1984) *A Strategy for Higher Education in the Late 1980s and Beyond*. London: NAB.

National Advisory Body (1987) *Management for a Purpose*, Report of the Good Management Practice Working Group. London: NAB.

Oakes, G. (1978) *Report of the Working Group on the Management of Higher Education in the Maintained Sector*. London: HMSO.

Open University (1984) *E324: Management of Post-Compulsory Education, Block 1, Part 4*. Milton Keynes: Open University Press.

Oxtoby, R. (ed.) (1981) *Higher Education at the Crossroads*. Guildford: SRHE.

Pettigrew, A. (ed.) (1987) *The Management of Strategic Change*. Oxford: Blackwell.

Pettigrew, A. and Whipp, R. (1991) *Managing Change for Competitive Success*. Oxford: ESRC and Blackwell.

Pettigrew, A., Ferlie, E. and McKee, L. (1992) *Shaping Strategic Change*. London: Sage.

Price Waterhouse (1990) *Review of the Management Structure and Financial Control Systems within the Polytechnic of Wales*. Cardiff: Price Waterhouse and Welsh Office.

Rees, G. and Istance, D. (1997) Higher Education in Wales: the (re-) emergence of a national system? *Higher Education Quarterly*, 51(1), 49–67.

Rosser, M. (1993) *Report of the Rosser Working Party*. Cardiff: University of Wales.

Salter, B. and Tapper, T. (1994) *The State of Higher Education*. Ilford: Woburn Press.

Scott, P. (1993) The idea of the university in the twenty-first century: a British perspective. *British Journal of Educational Studies*, 41(1), 4–25.

Scott, P. (1995) *The Meanings of Mass Higher Education*. Buckingham: SRHE and Open University Press.

Shattock, M. (1994) *The UGC and the Management of British Universities*. Buckingham: SRHE and Open Univesity Press.

Shattock, M. (ed.) (1996) *The Creation of a University System*. Oxford: Blackwell.

Silver, H. (1990) *A Higher Education: The CNAA and British Higher Education 1964–89*. London: Falmer Press.

Swinnerton-Dyer, P. (1991) Policy on higher education and research. *Higher Education Quarterly*, 45(3), 204–18.

Swinnerton-Dyer, P. (1996) The management and funding of higher education and research, *The Thirtieth Anniversary Seminars*. London: SRHE.

Tapper, T. and Palfreyman, D. (1998) Continuity and change in the collegial tradition. *Higher Education Quarterly*, 52(2), 142–61.

Trow, M. (1994) Managerialism and the academic profession: the case of England. *Higher Education Policy*, 7(2), 11–18.

Trow, M. (1998) American perspectives on British higher education under Thatcher and Major. *Oxford Review of Education*, 24(1), 111–29.

Trowler, P. (1997) *Academics Responding to Change: New Higher Education Frameworks and Academic Cultures*. Buckingham: SRHE amd Open University Press.

University Grants Committee (1982) *Annual Survey: Academic Year 1980–81* (Cmnd 8863). London: HMSO.

University Grants Committee (1983) *Annual Survey: Academic Year 1981–82* (Cmnd 8965). London: HMSO.

University Grants Committee (1984a) *Annual Survey: Academic Year 1982–83* (Cmnd 9234). London: HMSO.

University Grants Committee (1984b) *A Strategy for Higher Education into the 1990s*. London: HMSO.

Vickers, G. (1965) *The Art of Judgement*. London: Methuen.

Wales Advisory Body (1990) *Review of WAB Programme Areas, a Report Prepared by the Programme Review Working Group*. Cardiff: WAB.

Walford, G. (ed.) (1994) *Researching the Powerful in Education*. London: UCL Press.

Welsh Office (1987) *Consultative Paper, Maintained Further and Higher Education in Wales: Reform of Finance, Governance and Law*. Cardiff: Welsh Office Education Department.

Williams, G. (1989) Experimentation in reflective practice: a conceptual framework for managers in highly professionalised organisations. In R. Mansfield (ed.), *Frontiers of Management*. London: Routledge and BAM.

Williams, G. (1996) Taking up the HEFCW challenge. In R. T. P. Aylett and K. J. Gregory (eds.), *Proceedings of a Conference held by Goldsmiths College and IBM*. London: Goldsmiths College.

11

From Adult Education to Lifelong Learning: Policy, Process and Institutional Change

ROB HUMPHREYS AND DANNY SAUNDERS

Introduction

This chapter is written at a time of considerable flux for the fields of adult education and continuing education in Wales and the UK, particularly as they are constituted within the higher education sector. Higher education as a whole has undergone rapid and far-reaching change in the past decade and this looks set to continue, following the publication of the report of the National Committee of Inquiry into Higher Education (the 'Dearing Report') (NCIHE, 1997) – which was itself completed in an astonishingly short space of time, given its wide-ranging brief and the complexity of the issues under investigation. The election of the Labour government in 1997 and the foregrounding of the concept of 'lifelong learning' within education policy as a whole have, together with Dearing, created a whole new policy context for adult and continuing education within the UK.

The foundations of this new context were further laid by the publication of the Kennedy Report on further education (Kennedy, 1997) and the report of the National Advisory Group for Continuing Education and Lifelong Learning (NAGCELL, 1997). The new context was then made manifest with the publication of separate Green Papers on lifelong learning for England, Wales and Scotland (DfEE, 1998; Welsh Office, 1998; Scottish Office, 1998) and by a series of government initiatives, such as the University for Industry, the New Deal, and the National Grid for Learning, which sought to place 'learning' at the heart of economic, and – to some extent – social policy.

In this chapter we seek to explore this new terrain for the field of adult education in Wales, particularly adult education as it exists in the higher education sector. Furthermore, we seek to question the prevailing discourse of 'adult education', given the emerging discourse of 'lifelong learning' which has become a *leitmotif* of the 'joined up' policy, which the Blair government promotes. The focus is on the policy process, rather than outcomes, and by exploring as a case study the Community University of the Valleys scheme, which is located in south Wales, we draw some provisional conclusions regarding the distinctiveness or otherwise of policy formation in Wales in this area of higher education. We emphasize that an understanding of the historical development and trajectory of educational provision for adults by higher education institutions is essential in understanding the contemporary policy context.

Higher education and change

The moves towards mass higher education in the UK in recent years have led to sustained debate about the very nature, distinctiveness and purpose of the sector (Barnett, 1990; Duke, 1992; Scott, 1995; Barnett, 1997; Coffield and Williamson, 1997; Smith and Webster, 1997; Watson and Taylor, 1998). The pre-existing nature of the sector, as both a set of institutions and as an academy of scholars, has in fact come under criticism from two directions. The first was (and continues to be) that of policy-makers who wish to see the sector as a whole play a more direct and measurable part in benefiting the national economy. The second was (and continues to be) that of an intellectual challenge to the nature of knowledge and truth itself, which we might loosely place under the heading of postmodernism (Barnett and Griffin, 1997). How far the latter development has shaped government policy in recent years is perhaps open to question, but the far-reaching changes to the sector must be seen as part of deep-rooted shifts in Western societies as whole. As Scott suggests, these changes 'must be interpreted in the context of the restless synergy between plural modernisations – of the academy, polity, economy, society and culture' (Scott, 1995: 10).

This is not the occasion to rehearse these debates. We introduce them in order to contextualize changes in higher education in the UK (and therefore Wales), and also because these same pressures inevitably affect university adult education provision, in terms of its existence (or otherwise) being justified in both economic or socially beneficial outcomes and its distinctiveness as a discipline or field of study.

One of the difficulties of defining 'adult education' as a distinct field is that the exercise has a tendency to be tautological. Adult education is identified as being what distinct adult education providers or institutions 'do'. Thus, such a circular definition encompasses the provision of university adult education departments and an organization such as the Workers' Educational Association (WEA) but it often fails to include mature students following orthodox undergraduate or postgraduate courses, still less those adults who are in further education or studying on a part-time basis or following some kind of education in the workplace. This latter provision is, of course, subsumed under the heading of 'training'. Bell (1996) has argued that the dichotomy between education and training which exists in both academic and policy-making discourses has served to exclude the majority of adult learners. This applies too, we suggest, to the history of adult education. Lewis's (1993) definitive history of adult education in Wales in the first half of the twentieth century makes the distinction between workers' education and liberal forms of education for adults, but makes little mention of workplace training (see also Rees, 1997).

The above points are made only to highlight the limitations of our own discussion. For it is with the field of university adult education in Wales, as traditionally understood, that we are concerned. We make no apology for this. The very challenge to a body of provision which is to a large extent bounded and distinct in institutional terms – a challenge from both without and within – can serve to illuminate complex policy processes.

University adult education provision in Wales

It has recently been argued that the higher education system in Wales constitutes a distinct administrative system yet, in terms of patterns of recruitment and as a 'social system', Welsh higher education institutions are integrated into an 'English and Welsh' system (Rees and Istance, 1997). A more convincing argument can perhaps be made that there has been a historic distinctiveness about higher education provision specifically aimed at adults, particularly that provided by the constituent colleges of University of Wales. At Cardiff, Bangor, Aberystwyth and Swansea, this was delivered via 'extra-mural' departments which contained full-time academic members of staff from different disciplines (the college at Swansea was the last of these four to create a separate department of this type, in 1960). Given that this provision – in the main short courses of a liberal adult education nature – was inevitably aimed at students resident locally, it was inevitable that local patterns of provision developed. Partnerships distinguished such provision in south Wales, with local trade unions, co-operative societies and Nonconformist chapels being involved. To this must be added the origins and distinct configuration of the University of Wales itself, which was created by the 'Liberal Wales' of the second half of the nineteenth century and 'created for, and to some extent by, the common people' (Morgan, 1996: 1).

Understanding the historical roots of university adult education in Wales is essential in understanding the present provision and set of institutional practices and in understanding the pressures exerted by, and responses to, new policy initiatives in the 1990s. It might be added, however, that the power of popular memory and even myth in this area can serve to cloud accounts of that history. The very social purpose ethic which has underpinned much (liberal) adult education in Wales (and England) historically can lead to the normative features of that provision distorting the historical actuality. Rees *et al.* (1997) point out that similar processes operate in contemporary debates around the concept of the 'learning society'. We would add that this is particularly complicated in south Wales, as the notion of a 'tradition' of adult education in the region (itself derived in part from previous normative conceptions of adult education) is invoked in debates about the nature and purpose of contemporary policy (Francis and Humphreys, 1996).

In a somewhat similar manner, there is a danger of selectivity in considering the history and contemporary nature of the higher education sector as a whole in Wales. The sector now comprises more than the original constituent colleges of the University of Wales, for example, Trinity College Carmarthen and the various institutes of higher education. To this social and educational cocktail must be added the University of Glamorgan, formerly the Polytechnic of Wales, which, having its origins as a local authority institution, had somewhat different patterns of full-time student recruitment which included more locally based and mature students. For this institution, therefore, the notion of the 'extra-mural' had less relevance.

Nonetheless, as indicated earlier, we are primarily concerned with what might be termed 'traditional' adult education provision in Wales (and south Wales in particular) and the challenges posed to it by shifts in policy and the policy process. We cannot chart its history. It was, clearly, shaped in part by UK-wide policy initiatives (such as the 1919 Report and the Russell Report of 1970) but our central point is that the nature of Welsh society, politics and culture, and the nature of the University of Wales, meant that a pattern of (mainly extra-mural) university adult education was provided within the region which had differences from, as well as similarities to, patterns elsewhere in the UK.

The contemporary context: dimensions of change

Higher education institutions were faced with a series of challenges in the area of educational provision for adults in the 1980s and 1990s. First amongst these were the rapid, far-reaching and at times dislocating changes to the local economy and society. The most notable in south Wales were the run-down and eventual near-disappearance of the deep mining industry and substantial job losses in the steel industry and manufacturing more generally. At least as significant was a longer-term development which saw the entry into the regional labour force of women, with the result that gender relations underwent substantial change. These changes, accompanied by high levels of unemployment and social deprivation (particularly in valley areas) meant that the social and cultural landscape of the 1990s was very different from that of the 1970s and completely transformed from that of the 1940s.

Second, an emerging feature of the new social landscape was the growth of what is now termed the voluntary or 'third' sector, representing new patterns of social organization, often at community level rather than at the workplace and with women often occupying leadership positions.

Third, there was a change in the governance of higher education in Wales and changes to the regime of funding of adult education. The 'Responsible Body' system was abolished and, in 1993, the newly created Higher Education Funding Council for Wales (HEFCW) followed its larger counterpart in England in conducting a review of university continuing education. The result of this exercise was that the vast majority of CE provision was now to carry credit which would enable it to be 'mainstreamed' into the emerging credit transfer and modular higher education curriculum. This development was not without its critics who argued that this was an abandonment of the valuable liberal tradition within adult education in Wales (Gruffudd, 1994; Jones, 1994–5).

Fourth, the European state became a key component of funding of some adult education provision, particularly in south Wales. As Field (1996) has suggested (writing in the context of EU funding for the UK as a whole), this occurred in a rather piecemeal fashion but, nonetheless, given that the valley areas of south Wales were designated an Objective 2 area for funding purposes, EU monies became increasingly important in underwriting adult education provision. European funding was looked upon from within the south Wales adult education world as being relatively benign (Francis, 1994).

Finally, the very definition of adult education (already alluded to) was challenged conceptually and in terms of policy development. In the same way that ideas of the postmodern challenged the nature of knowledge and its production in universities as a whole, they also posed a challenge to the idea of liberal adult education in particular, based as it was on Enlightenment values (Usher and Edwards, 1996; Usher, Bryant and Johnston, 1997), although, not surprisingly, liberal and socialist values in this context found their defenders too (Wallis and Allman, 1996). In addition, the emerging policy and theoretical discourse of 'lifelong learning' has served to create opportunities for new thinking and new practice in educational provision. It has also served to erode the notion of adult education as a tightly bounded field, discipline, set of professional practices or, indeed, provision. As Edwards has characterized it, lifelong learning is a 'moorland' with permeable boundaries, whereas adult education is (or was) a field which was bounded by fences and barriers (Edwards, 1997; see also Matheson and Matheson, 1996; Longworth and Davies, 1996; Sand, 1998; Smith and Spurling, 1999). But it should be noted also that 'lifelong learning' and the closely related concept of the 'learning society' have been criticized for being too vague and flexible; they are attractive to politicians at the level of rhetoric, but often mask ideological differences and are insufficiently informed by empirical analysis or historical understanding (Hughes and Tight, 1995; Strain and Field, 1997; Macrae, Maguire and Ball, 1997; Keep, 1997; Rees *et al.*, 1997; Tight, 1998a, 1998b; Gorard et al., 1998; Gorard, Rees and Feure, 1999; Field and Schuller, 1999).

These conceptual challenges have been matched by a 'not unconnected' practical challenge to preconceived notions of 'adult education'. In terms of educational provision, the moves to a modular degree structure, with the accreditation and 'mainsteaming' of adult education provision within higher education, has led to a blurring of boundaries between full-time and part-time study. Similarly, the increase in mature age learners within higher education has led to a questioning of the idea of 'mature student' as a distinct minority and of 'extra-mural' as a distinct strategy or set of practices (see Duke, 1992, for an early discussion of these developments in the UK as a whole).

These changes in context and policy, not all specific to the region of south Wales, constituted both challenge and opportunity to adult education as a discrete institutional set of practices and provision. In what follows, we seek to illuminate the policy process in this field via an exploration of a case study of what might be termed the modernization of one part of adult education in south Wales.

A case study: the Community University of the Valleys

It is a common perception that adult education, conceived of as a separate practice and provision, has often been relatively marginal in institutions of higher education, particularly the so-called 'old' (that is, pre-1992) universities. What is less remarked upon is how adult education (or continuing education) practitioners, as individuals or more often as departments, have utilized that marginality to prosper and to gain influence. Duke and Taylor (1993), in the context of the 1992 Review of Continuing Education, have described this as working in the 'interstices' of the higher education system. Scott (1996) has used a similar formulation, arguing that adult education practitioners have worked in the 'creative spaces' of institutions and, in so doing, have increased their influence.

The Community University of the Valleys (CUV) scheme, which began in 1993 at the University of Wales Swansea (UWS), is an example, we suggest, of adult education practitioners working within the 'interstices' of changing institutions, changing funding regimes and a changing regional society and economy. The CUV has its roots in the changing economy of the west of the south Wales coalfield, in particular the Dulais Valley, following the 1984–5 miners' strike and the subsequent collapse of the deep-mining industry. There follows a very brief résumé of these origins.

In the Dulais Valley, the women's Miners' Support Group continued to exist after the strike and sought to play a role in the future of the valley. This led to the setting up of the DOVE Workshop, a small voluntary training organization for women, which was funded initially by the Urban Aid scheme. After gaining a premises for its activities in the form of the Community Centre at Banwen (the village at the top of the valley), DOVE began to seek out educational providers, such as the WEA, Neath College and the Department of Adult Continuing Education of UWS, in order to enhance its portfolio of provision.

After initially providing short liberal adult education classes and information technology classes (the latter funded by the European Social Fund), DACE set up a community-based Access course at the Banwen Centre in 1989, the first of its kind in Wales. Once the case had been made for community-based Access provision, on the grounds that it targeted students who could not otherwise avail themselves of similar provision on the main Swansea Campus, a key and pressing question was inevitably posed: *access to what?* The barriers which had prevented potential Access students from taking up opportunities on the Swansea Campus would still exist after completing an Access course. The need for continued educational progression routes became clear and consultation began with existing and former Access students at the Banwen Centre as part of a one-year project funded by the Universities Funding Council (UFC). Local organizations such as the DOVE workshop and Onllwyn Community Council were also involved in this process. The result of the consultation exercise was the identification of a need for a *community-based* undergraduate curriculum. The eventual development of such a curriculum, in the form of the CUV, requires an understanding of the new set of institutional and funding relationships for higher education in Wales and the wider UK which pertained in the 1990s, together with an understanding of institutional and other *constraints* which were equally influential in shaping the project.

Funding, governance and institutions: opportunities and constraints

The CUV was, in part, the product of a changing system of governance of higher education in Wales, and of a plurality of funding regimes for infrastructural developments. The creation of HEFCW in 1993 meant that there was a potential degree of flexibility in the funding of higher education in Wales which did not exist previously (though the degree of divergence should not be exaggerated). A concern of HEFCW, since its creation, has been that continuing education opportunities should be provided in all parts of Wales. This criterion applies to the funding of some continuing education provision and would appear to mark out the Welsh Funding Council from its counterpart in England. In addition, strategic goals of further and higher education funding in Wales were shaped by, and increasingly linked to, Welsh Office policy on economic development. The fact that an area like the Dulais Valley was an area which was targeted by a number of Welsh Office initiatives – most notably the 'Valleys Initiative', launched by the then Secretary of State for Wales, Peter Walker, in 1988 – meant that the proposal for the CUV fitted into wider strategies for economic regeneration. The 1995 Welsh Office document *People and Prosperity* identified education and training as central in the development of the Welsh economy, and used a discourse of 'lifelong learning' in this context (Welsh Office, 1995). It would appear that such a discourse, which as we noted is now a *leitmotif* of government policy and is utilized across the political spectrum, was sufficiently broad and flexible to enable a then essentially free-market-orientated Welsh Office and a more centrist or left-leaning adult education profession to share objectives in a project such as the CUV (see Coffield, 1997, for a discussion of this kind of policy-making at a UK level).

The CUV proposal was approved by HEFCW on a recurrent funding basis, calculated on an orthodox full-time student equivalent (FTE) basis. The first cohort of students enrolled in October 1993. But the project benefited also from the availability of European funding. UWS was successful in bidding for money from the European Regional Development Fund (ERDF), in order substantially to enlarge the Centre at Banwen. Other funds at the 'start-up' stage were forthcoming from Neath Borough Council, British Coal, the Coal Industry Social Welfare Organisation (CISWO) and

Onllwyn Community Council. These various funding bodies and agencies, together with the DOVE Workshop and the other educational providers which utilize the Centre at Banwen, might be seen as a coalition of interests which temporarily came together under the overarching theme of economic and social regeneration. Inevitably, there were – and continue to be – differing nuances and emphases within this coalition, not least, tensions between community development and individual student achievement and between those outcomes measured in terms of employment for students and those measured – more intangibly – in terms of individual and social well-being. There are, of course, occasions when these issues are not in any way oppositional but there are also occasions when they can appear to be contradictory, and, as is to be expected, the various providers and funders have differing views as to the priorities of this kind of provision, in terms of outcomes. In addition, it cannot be assumed that the students of the CUV will articulate such matters in the same manner (Humphreys and McGoldrick, 1998).

There is certainly nothing new about a university department of adult education organizing courses through the use of 'outreach' centres. What is striking about the CUV is the new kind of community and institutional partnerships involved in the scheme. Drawing on the success of Swansea, the University of Glamorgan and the Open University in Wales joined the CUV to create a tripartite partnership and to support one another in the organization and teaching of adult education programmes. The focus has been predominantly on the valleys populations and those communities which exhibit the highest levels of social deprivation. The widening of the scheme to include the University of Glamorgan has also extended the range of community-based partners, which now include the BELL Centre at Blaenllechau in the Rhondda Fach and the community education centre at Abercynon.

Although the initial base was at Banwen, the provision has developed to include the whole range of short courses (both carrying credit and the specially funded 'non award-bearing' provision) under the umbrella of the CUV. The scheme also enables students to transfer to courses which are offered by the Open University or the University of Glamorgan, which widens the curriculum considerably.

At times the provision involves adult learning in its traditional face-to-face mode of delivery, and at others new distance learning technologies have been deployed through Internet applications and videoconferencing. Furthermore, new learner friendly assessment methods associated with portfolios and the use of learning outcomes (thereby allowing for the accreditation of prior experience through Credit Accumulation and Transfer (CAT) frameworks) have encouraged learning within the workplaces of local communities. It should be emphasized that the CUV has also recognized the importance of local schools and compact initiatives have led to close contact with pupils' parents in order to raise educational aspirations and widen access.

It is important to note at this point that a development such as the CUV is not solely a response to shifts in higher education policy nor is it a straightforward implementation of a proposal contained in the parent institutions' mission statements. Those statements themselves are the product of pressures and politics within the institutions. Whilst a new emphasis on home-based students and the local and regional role of the university has been a product of government moves towards a mass higher education system in the UK as a whole, the shaping of this policy and to some extent the speed of its implementation at a local level, will be a product of the politics and organizational culture of the institutions themselves. In the case of UWS, DACE has been a key player in developing the CUV and then seeking to broaden the mission statement subsequently. In the case of the University of Glamorgan it is the Educational Development Unit (a co-ordinating centre, rather than a 'traditional' adult education department) which acts in a not dissimilar way. In other words, the development of the CUV has been largely an incremental one in which it has to some extent been a response to events and changed circumstances, as much as it has been a worked out strategy from the start. And in the case of both UWS and the University of Glamorgan, the CUV has become a symbol and a mechanism through which the parent institutions are themselves undergoing change.

The policy process: five dimensions

Our initial discussion, the outline sketch above of the development of the CUV and indeed our experience as practitioners working on the CUV scheme, suggests an analytical framework which may assist in making sense of the policy process in this area of higher education and, to a large extent, within higher education as a whole. Although the framework has its limitations, not least because of the definitional problems which we discussed earlier, nevertheless, it does, we suggest, begin to move the more abstract debates around such concepts of lifelong learning onto the firmer ground of actual policy in operation. The framework has five dimensions, each of which is interrelated but which can be separated out for analytical purposes:

First, policy-making in this area (as in other aspects of higher education policy) in Wales is conducted to a large extent within the broad framework of UK policy. For example, the funding regime for students in higher education and the research assessment exercises are UK-wide policy matters. Scott was quick to identify that the creation of separate funding councils for higher education had the potential to create national (or 'subnational') systems of higher education within the UK (1995: 21). Coupled with the probable impetus which will be given to a distinct Welsh policy-making agenda by the National Assembly, there is undoubtedly greater 'space' for divergences within the UK than ever before and we return to this below. We contend, however, that this space is not unlimited: the UK-wide framework remains important and will continue to be so for the foreseeable future.

Second, the European sources of funding were integral to the development of the CUV and remain so in the context of lifelong learning policy generally. Thus the European state acts as a shaper or filter in the policy-making process. The availability of Objective 1 EU funding for large parts of Wales from the year 2000 will, at least in the short to medium term, serve to increase the role of the European state in this area, given particularly that education and training initiatives will be among the main recipients of these funds.

Third, the local and regional economic and social context is centrally important, in particular the growth of new forms of organization in the voluntary sector and, of course, the wider context of social and economic decline and deindustrialization. In addition, greater participation in higher education and a new student funding regime which will mean more locally based students and policies designed to attract more students from 'under-represented groups', are likely to lead to higher education institutions which are more responsive to their locality and region than has been the case in the post-1945 period.

Fourth, the internal politics and organizational cultures of higher education institutions were important. The flexibility and ability of leading individuals to take risks (Saunders, 1998) cannot be underestimated in the sphere of working in the 'interstices' of educational policy and politics, as we have attempted to demonstrate with the development of the CUV. Furthermore, there is some evidence to suggest that the success of the CUV initiative has been a *shaper of* policy, as well as being *shaped by* policy. Other community-orientated initiatives have emerged in its wake, notably the 'Community University of North Wales' (there are examples, too, in England). More importantly, perhaps, a Welsh Office letter to the HEFCW in 1997, giving 'guidance' on priorities, states that the Secretary of State wishes 'to promote access, and to develop 'community universities' as part of his lifelong learning agenda' (Welsh Office, 1997b: para. 24) This new initiative is in the context of increasing links between higher and further education. The attractiveness and flexibility of the term 'community' notwithstanding, we would suggest that there has been some 'bottom–up' influence here.

The above factors each shape the policy process in the area of adult education and within higher education as a whole in Wales. They must be seen 'in the round' and as interactive. However, it is the rapid institutional development within Wales which is probably now the most significant element in the new policy context and it is to these very recent, ongoing developments that we now turn.

The growth of specifically Welsh institutions has undoubtedly led to a specifically Welsh policy agenda in a number of areas. Most notable is that of schools education since the late nineteenth century. Interestingly, this had less effect on adult education than the political and social factors which we drew attention to earlier. The development of newer Welsh institutions, particularly since the creation of the Welsh Office in 1964, has been more significant in a number of ways.

First, there has been an increasing emphasis on policy-making for a 'Welsh' economy. There are obvious empirical problems in identifying a discrete Welsh economic sphere but the accruing of powers at the Welsh Office has led to a discourse of this kind and policy-making which applies to Wales, especially in the field of economic development. Given the emphasis on skills enhancement and education and training in recent policy-making – now largely subsumed under the new discourse of 'lifelong learning' – these areas of policy have also taken on a specifically Welsh focus.

The notion of *lifelong* learning has led to a development in which Welsh Office policies for schools in Wales, contained in the 'BEST' White Paper, are followed by a similar initiative for lifelong learning in the shape of the Green Paper *Learning is for Everyone* (Welsh Office, 1997a, 1998). Although there is a considerable way to go before there is a seamless structure between pre-16 and post-16 education in Wales, it would have been illogical not to have produced a separate Green Paper in Wales. It might be added that, given the Labour government's commitment to devolution, there has been a growing political emphasis on separate policy initiatives for Wales, even when the overarching policy framework has a UK-wide basis.

Underlying individual policy initiatives in adult education, lifelong learning and in other aspects of higher education policy in Wales is the continuing evolution of a distinct Welsh institutional structure. We have referred earlier to the importance of a separate funding council for higher education in Wales. Another significant factor here is that there is also a separate funding council for further education in Wales and, furthermore, the two bodies share a common administration and executive, unlike those in England. Given the relatively small number of higher and further education institutions in Wales, the potential for collaboration between the sectors is, at least in theory, increased, leading to what Scott (1995: 21) has described as 'vertical integration', as opposed to 'nationwide [that is, UK] horizontal integration', in which the two sectors remain largely sealed off from one another.

In 1998, the first report of the Education and Training Action Group for Wales (ETAGW), charged with addressing the problems of skills shortages in the Welsh economy, recommended a new institutional structure for further education in which an enlarged funding council would absorb some of the responsibilities of the Training and Enterprise Councils and which would have greater powers of co-ordination of sixteen to eighteen and adult education provision (ETAGW, 1998). The final report, published the following year, did not diverge significantly from these proposals for a new funding structure (ETAGW, 1999).

The recommendations of the ETAGW were drawn up specifically to enable the National Assembly for Wales to take decisions and make policy early in its first term. The Assembly will, obviously, constitute a new policy-making forum and it is difficult to see how the development of a separate policy-making agenda for lifelong learning and for higher and further education as a whole will not be enhanced. This is particularly so in the case of further education, as this funding council comes directly under the remit of the Assembly. Even in the case of higher education, whose funding council will remain at arm's length, with powers which cannot be reduced by the Assembly, Welsh distinctiveness will surely increase.

The creation of the Assembly will also create a policy-process for further and higher education which is more transparent and far more openly subject to political pressure and debate. In response to both the Green Paper on lifelong learning, and the reports of ETAGW, there have been criticisms that each takes an over-economistic and utilitarian view of education and learning. Critics have sought to use notions of citizenship and social capital in order to develop what they see as a more rounded vision of lifelong learning (Humphreys and Francis, 1998, 1999). To some extent the final ETAGW report did address such issues, though how far they will be incorporated into actual policy, as opposed to merely being used at the level of rhetoric, remains to be seen. Prior to the creation of the National Assembly, such debates were played out in rather muted form in the shadows of non-elected bodies. Whilst lobbying on all policy areas will no doubt continue – and, indeed, may increase – the Assembly will alter the policy process simply due to its democratic nature. The fact that no political party has a majority in the first four-year term of the Assembly will surely also have a bearing on the policy process. Whatever the outcome in terms of *process*, education and training are likely to remain central in terms of actual policy *content*, not least because they remain at the heart of policies for economic development (Hill, Roberts and Miller, 1998).

But ambiguities remain, too, when one considers the prospects for policy being made which has a genuinely *lifelong* approach. One of the first acts of Alun Michael as the First Secretary of the newly elected National Assembly, was to create separate secretariats for pre-16 and post-16 education in his new 'cabinet'. This, in turn, led to the creation of separate Assembly committees for these areas. Given this structural dichotomy, it would appear that considerable political and policy-making energy may have to be expended if 'joined-up' policies are to be developed and put into effect in the area of lifelong learning.

Conclusions

In this chapter we have sought to make some general points about the shifting nature of what was once termed 'adult education' within higher education in Wales, both at a conceptual level and in terms of practice. Using the case study of the Community University of the Valleys, we have sought to develop a framework of analysis which takes into account the various dimensions of the rapidly changing policy process in this area and in higher education as a whole.

University adult education has changed beyond recognition. It has, in certain institutions, been developed within the 'interstices' of shifting policy in the rapidly changing context of institutions, the locality and region. It has been 're-invented' as continuing education, more latterly, as lifelong learning, and has taken new forms, such as the CUV.

We would suggest that what we have shown, above all, is the dearth of research on the policy process itself in Wales and on outcomes. We have been necessarily descriptive and speculative. But it is clear that empirical work is needed on such matters as the impact of European funding on adult education provision; the changing organization and funding of continuing education, following the review in 1992; the exact way in which the various policy processes interact in practice; comparative studies which would include mature age students both within the 'adult education' provision and on 'orthodox' schemes of study; and the efficacy or otherwise of progression routes. Not least, research is required into the relationship between the changing institutional patterns within Wales, their associated political influences and the process of policy formulation and implementation. We have sketched out a framework which perhaps points in the right direction, and the results of the ESRC 'Learning Society' research in Wales will be an important step in providing empirical data, but neither will exhaust the research agenda in this key and, perhaps, neglected area of educational policy.

References

Barnett, R. (1990) *The Idea of Higher Education*. Buckingham: SRHE and Open University Press.

Barnett, R. (1997) *Higher Education: A Critical Business*. Buckingham: SRHE and Open University Press.

Barnett, R. and Griffin, A (eds.) (1997) *The End of Knowledge in Higher Education*. London: Cassell.

Bell, B. (1996) The British adult education tradition: a reappraisal. In R. Edwards, A. Hanson and P. Raggatt (eds.), *Boundaries of Adult Learning*. London: Routledge.

Coffield, F. (1997) Introduction and overview: attempts to reclaim the concept of the learning society. *Journal of Education Policy*, 12(6), 449–55.

Coffield, F. and Williamson, B. (eds.) (1997) *Repositioning Higher Education*. Buckingham: SRHE and Open University Press.

DfEE (1998) *The Learning Age: A Renaissance for a New Britain*. London: HMSO.

Duke, C. (1992) *The Learning University*. Buckingham: SRHE and Open University Press.

Duke, C. and Taylor, R. (1993) The HEFCE review and the funding of continuing education. *Studies in the Education of Adults*, 26(1), 86–94.

Edwards, R. (1997) *Changing Places: Flexibility, Lifelong Learning and a Learning Society*. London: Routledge.

ETAGW (1998) *An Education and Training Action Plan for Wales: A Draft for Consultation*. Cardiff: Education and Training Action Group for Wales.

ETAGW (1999) *An Education and Training Action Plan for Wales*. Cardiff: Education and Training Action Group for Wales.

Field, J. (1996) Towards a Europeanisation of adult education. *Studies in the Education of Adults*, 28(1), 14–28.

Field, J. and Schuller, T. (1999) Investigating the learning society. *Studies in the Education of Adults*, 31(1), 1–9.

Francis, H. (1994) A Welsh response to European Union education and training initiatives. *Adults Learning*, 6, 26–30.

Francis, H. and Humphreys, R. (1996) Communities, valleys and universities. In J. Elliott, H. Francis, R. Humphrey and D. Istance (eds.), *Communities and their Universities: The Challenge of Lifelong Learning*. London: Lawrence & Wishart.

Gorard, S., Rees, G., Fevre, R. and Furlong, J. (1998) Society is not built by education alone: alternative routes to a learning society. *Research in Post-Compulsory Education*, 3(1), 25–35.

Gorard, S., Rees, G. and Fevre, R. (1999) Two dimensions of time: the changing social context of lifelong learning. *Studies in the Education of Adults*, 31(1), 35–48.

Gruffudd, H. (1994) Achredu echrydus – diwedd diwylliant y dosbarth allanol. *Barn*, 377 (Mehefin), 16–17.

Hill, S., Roberts, A. and Miller, N. (1998) The Welsh workforce. In J. Osmond (ed.), *The National Assembly Agenda: A Handbook for the First Four Years*. Cardiff: Institute for Welsh Affairs.

Hughes, C. and Tight, M. (1995) The myth of the learning society. *British Journal of Educational Studies*, 43(3), 290–304.

Humphreys, R. and Francis, H. (1998) Breathing new *LIFE* into Wales. *Adults Learning*, 9(10) (June 1998), 6–8.

Humphreys, R. and Francis, H. (1999) *The Learning Country: Citizenship and the New Democracy in Wales*. Cardiff: NIACE Cymru.

Humphreys, R. and McGoldrick, T. (1998) Widening access in a former coalfield region: institutional and student perspectives on community based higher education. In P. Alheit and E. Kammler (eds.), *Lifelong Learning and its Impact on Social and Regional Development*. Bremen: Donat Verlag.

Jones, A. G. (1994–5) The future of university extra-mural studies: a north Wales perspective. *Planet*, 108 (December/January).

Keep, E. (1997) There's no such thing as society . . . : some problems with an individual approach to creating a Learning Society. *Journal of Education Policy*, 12(6), 457–71.

Kennedy, H (1997) *Learning Works: Widening Participation in Further Education*. Coventry: Further Education Funding Council.

Lewis, R. (1993) *Leaders and Teachers: Adult Education and the Challenge of Labour in South Wales, 1906–1940*. Cardiff: University of Wales Press.

Longworth, N. and Davies, W. K. (1996) *Lifelong Learning*. London: Kogan Page.

Macrae, S., Maguire, M. and Ball, S. (1997) Whose 'learning society'? A tentative deconstruction. *Journal of Education Policy*, 12(6), 499–509.

Matheson, D. and Matheson, C. (1996) Lifelong learning and lifelong education: a critique. *Research in Post-Compulsory Education*, 1(2), 219–36.

Morgan, K. O. (1996) Y Brifysgol a'r werin: the People's University. In J. Elliott, H. Francis, R. Humphreys and D. Istance (eds.), *Communities and their Universities: The Challenge of Lifelong Learning*. London: Lawrence & Wishart.

NAGCELL (1997) *Learning for the Twenty-First Century: First Report of the National Advisory Group for Continuing Education and Lifelong Learning*. London: National Advisory Group for Continuing Education and Lifelong Learning.

NCIHE (1997) *Higher Education in the Learning Society: Report of the National Committee of Inquiry into Higher Education*. London: National Committee of Inquiry into Higher Education.

Rees, G. (1997) Making a learning society: education and work in industrial south Wales. *Welsh Journal of Education*, 6(2), 4–16.

Rees, G. and Istance, D. (1997) Higher education in Wales: the (re-)emergence of a national system? *Higher Education Quarterly*, 51(1), 49–67.

Rees, G., Fevre, R., Furlong, J. and Gorard, S. (1997) History, place and the learning society: towards a sociology of lifelong learning. *Journal of Education Policy*, 12(6), 485–97.

Sand, B. (1998) Lifelong learning: vision, policy and practice. *Journal of Access and Credit Studies*, 1(1), 17–39.

Saunders, D. (1998) *Old and New Learning: Risk and Uncertainty in Higher Education*. Pontypridd: University of Glamorgan.

Scott, P. (1995) *The Meanings of Mass Higher Education*. Buckingham: SRHE and Open University Press.

Scott, P. (1996) The future of continuing education. Paper presented at the UACE Annual Conference, Leeds, March.

Scottish Office (1998) *Opportunity Scotland: A Paper on Lifelong Learning*. Edinburgh: HMSO.

Smith, A. and Webster, F. (eds.) (1997) *The Postmodern University? Contested Visions of Higher Education in Society*. Buckingham: SRHE and Open University Press.

Smith, J. and Spurling, A. (1999) *Lifelong Learning: Riding the Tiger*. London: Cassell.

Strain, M. and Field, J. (1997) On 'The myth of the Learning Society'. *British Journal of Educational Studies*, 45(2), 141–55.

Tight, M. (1998a) Education, education, education! The vision of lifelong learning in the Kennedy, Dearing and Fryer reports. *Oxford Review of Education*, 24, 473–85.

Tight, M. (1998b) Lifelong learning: opportunity or compulsion. *British Journal of Educational Studies*, 46(3), 251–63.

Usher, R. and Edwards, R. (1996) Liberal adult education and the postmodern moment. In J. Wallis (ed.), *Liberal Adult Education: The End of an Era?* Nottingham: University of Nottingham.

Usher, R., Bryant, I. and Johnston, R. (1997) *Adult Education and the Postmodern Challenge*. London: Routledge.

Wallis, J. and Allman, P. (1996) Adult education, the 'critical citizen' and social change. In J. Wallis (ed.), *Liberal Adult Education: The End of an Era?* Nottingham: University of Nottingham.

Watson, D. and Taylor, R. (1998) *Lifelong Learning and the University: A Post-Dearing Agenda*. London: Falmer Press.

Welsh Office (1995) *People and Prosperity: An Agenda of Action for*

Wales. Cardiff: HMSO.

Welsh Office (1997a) *Building Excellent Schools Together*. Cardiff: HMSO.

Welsh Office (1997b) Higher Education Funding for 1998–9. Letter to HEFCW, 18 December.

Welsh Office (1998) *Learning is for Everyone: The BEST for Lifelong Learning*. Cardiff: HMSO.

12

Welsh for Adults: A Policy for a Bilingual Wales?

STEVE MORRIS

Introduction

The Welsh for Adults provision within the further education and higher education sectors in Wales is a unique element of continuing education within this country and it arises from a society and a linguistic background unique in the UK. Courtney (1992: 15) has observed:

> adult learning is as much a phenomenon of a society and how it defines itself and its destiny as it is a function of individual men and women and their efforts to interpret that destiny in their own terms. Adult learning rests on individual interest and initiative. It also emerges from a particular kind of society at a particular moment in its history.

This can certainly be applied to the field of Welsh for Adults as an important part of continuing education and lifelong learning within the context of a bilingual society and communities seeking to define Welshness in Wales.

The current framework and organization of this provision has developed at an impressive rate during the last quarter of a century and this chapter will initially map this development and examine recent organizational and funding changes which have impacted upon it during the last decade. It will be argued that this sector of continuing education has a growing policy role and contribution in the context of realizing the aims of the 1993 Welsh Language Act and providing a means of increasing bilingualism/reversing language shift in Wales. To this end, research into the motivations of students attending these courses will be discussed and how the students' aspirations can be tied into the institutional and political aspirations prevalent today in Wales. The chapter suggests that the development of this provision needs to be actively encouraged and recognized as a distinctive part of continuing education/lifelong learning in Wales in order to realize and promote policy for a truly bilingual country in the future.

A historical overview

Of course, there existed a tradition of provision for adults to learn Welsh throughout the twentieth century. This provision has included night classes, early radio and television courses (the first radio language course for adults was broadcast in 1948) and numerous self-tuition textbooks. It was, however, during that particularly vital period in the language's development when the disappointing returns of the 1961 and 1971 censuses were being digested, and activity to revive and regenerate the language became focused, that serious consideration was given as to how this provision could be developed and expanded in order to harness the growing desire of non-Welsh-speaking adults to gain knowledge and proficiency in the Welsh language.

There were a number of developments during the 1960s and 1970s which prompted a greater demand and a consequential need for revision of Welsh for Adults provision in Wales. First, by 1964, there were 3,634 primary school pupils and 1,192 secondary school pupils in Welsh-medium schools, with a large number of these coming from non-Welsh-speaking homes. Many of the parents of these pupils wished to acquire the language to complement their children's education (a motivation which has been seen to be more and more influential in the increase in the number of adults learning Welsh as this sector has expanded in Anglicized areas). The establishment of Mudiad Ysgolion Meithrin – the Welsh-medium nursery schools movement – in 1971 intensified the need for revised provision for parents wishing to learn Welsh.

Second, a growing awareness of the possible demise of the language (epitomized in the warning given by Saunders Lewis in his radio lecture 'Tynged yr Iaith') which resulted in the public campaigns and demonstrations organized by Cymdeithas yr Iaith Gymraeg and others throughout the 1960s and onwards, increased the desire of some members of the community who felt that speaking Welsh was an integral part of being Welsh and endeavoured to become fluent in the language. Recent research has indicated that this motivation is a strong factor in many adults attending courses (Davies, 1986; Morris, 1996). Third, as a consequence of the success of the campaigns referred to above, the need for bilingual staff in public bodies and local government has further stimulated the call for greater Welsh for Adults provision in more recent times and increased the number of those adults who attend courses for motivations of a more 'instrumental' or 'utilitarian' nature.

Inevitably, many learners desired a 'quick route' to fluency and this gave rise to a fundamental shift in the field of teaching Welsh to adults during the early 1970s. It was during this period that an expanded network of Welsh for Adults classes was developed through the extra-mural departments of the University of Wales as well as colleges of further education, the Workers' Educational Association (WEA), local authorities' community provision and several voluntary movements. One of the most significant developments was the holding of the first 'Wlpan' courses in the early 1970s in Cardiff, Pontypridd and Aberystwyth (Rees, 1974; James, 1974). This system had been developed from intensive teaching which originated in Israel where the main aim had been to linguistically – and culturally – assimilate non-Hebrew-speaking Jewish incomers and to ensure that Hebrew would be the main language of the new state (Crowe, 1988). The intensive methods of the 'Wlpan' were adapted for the purpose of Welsh and principles were introduced such as intensive, functional-structural drilling, emphasis on oral skills, emphasis on Welsh as the principal teaching and class language and attending classes five times a week for a period of three to four months at a time. This development was a very important step forward in the organization of Welsh for Adults in Wales, giving a better opportunity for students to succeed in learning to speak basic Welsh in a comparatively short period – even though the length of the Wlpan courses in Wales is still less ambitious than the original Hebrew model or the 400 hours minimum in the Basque Country.

As a result of the development of the Wlpan courses in Wales, provision for Welsh for Adults during the 1980s developed along the lines of intensive courses (and higher level courses) generally being provided by the former extra-mural departments of the University of Wales and the former Polytechnic of Wales and non-intensive provision being located either in colleges of further education, within the community education service or the WEA. Funding for the intensive sector (under section 21 of the Education Act 1980) was targeted from the Welsh Office via the University of Wales Registry (apart from the Polytechnic of Wales) to the individual institutions and included support for posts within each of the extra-mural departments to develop, promote and co-ordinate the provision. Occasionally, extra funds were made available for further developments, such as the establishment of 'super-Wlpan' courses of 300 hours (or more) in areas where these had not hitherto been available. The Further and Higher Education Act of 1992 brought about the establishment of Further Education and Higher Education Councils for Wales and with it a requirement for the Councils to make adequate provision for promoting proficiency in Welsh.

As a result, a Joint Review Group (JRG) was established by the Councils in February 1993 with the following terms of reference:

> In the light of the new funding arrangements for further and higher education in Wales, to review the provision of Welsh for adults and the supporting activity designed to sustain and develop this provision and, as a result, to prepare recommendations to the Further and Higher Education Funding Councils for Wales on:
>
> i) the activity needed to ensure the maintenance and development of Welsh for adults;
> ii) the way in which this activity might be funded; and
> iii) how the funding of Welsh for adults might be channelled in future. (Welsh Funding Councils, 1994b: 11)

The Joint Review Group's final report was published in spring 1994, following wide consultation with providers and a variety of other interested parties, including, by that time, the newly established Welsh Language Board (WLB). Many of the recommendations of the JRG were accepted by the Funding Councils (Welsh Funding Councils: Circular W94/48HE) and have resulted in numerous changes in the way that Welsh for Adults is both funded and organized during the last few years. Amongst the major changes/recommendations were:

1. Acknowledgement that the Councils do not see themselves as having a strategic planning remit in the field of Welsh for Adults. This was perceived to be the role of the WLB.

2. Rejection of the call to establish a committee to advise the Councils on funding matters for Welsh for Adults which the JRG had proposed. The majority of the submissions to the JRG had emphasized the need for Welsh for Adults to be seen as a distinct curriculum area with a unique role to play within Wales in fostering and promoting the Welsh language. To this end it had been hoped that the proposed committee would be able to make recommendations about strategic developments in the field and funding allocations.

3. The establishment of a development fund, in addition to recurrent funding, commencing in 1995/6 at £300,000 and decreasing to £100,000 by 1997/8. The rationale behind the decrease in the development fund over the three years was that any new provision or growth in student numbers generated from development activities would, by 1998, be supported by recurrent funding.

4. Providers were to be encouraged to form local consortia which would jointly plan for integrated provision and clear progression routes for students, initiate developmental activities and undertake joint training and marketing initiatives. These consortia were to be established by October 1994.

5. It was agreed that all future funding for sub-higher education Welsh for Adults provision (that is, the bulk of the provision) would be made by the Further Education Funding Council for Wales (FEFCW) through the recurrent funding methodology (RFM), arguing that this 'will guarantee all providers access to funds based on the same criteria and from a single source' (Welsh Funding Councils, 1994a: para. 32). The programme area weight would increase from 1.0 to 1.2 in order to provide additional funding to maintain the tutor-organizer functions previously supported by section 21 funding (although institutions were not compelled to do so). The FEFCW would review the use made of this additional weighting annually. The funding councils rejected the recommendation that funding should be linked to consortia membership, whilst acknowledging that the majority of respondents to the consultation paper had been in favour of this.

6. Future funding was to be linked with outcomes and consequently required the introduction of an appropriate system of accreditation for Welsh for Adults.

7. The FEFCW agreed to continue to fund the post of the national Welsh for Adults officer (located at the WJEC) who has a pivotal role in securing planning and strategy at a national level.

Prior to the publication of Circular W94/48HE, a national committee consisting mainly of practitioners in the field of Welsh for Adults – the WJEC Welsh for Adults Panel – had published its own report (WJEC, 1992) in response to the continued expansion of the sector and the Further and Higher Education Act. This report looked at the work undertaken in the field in its entirety and proposed a holistic strategy for advancing the sector, thereby placing it firmly in the wider ambit of 'Reversing Language Shift' (for a definition see Fishman, 1991) in Wales. The idea of 'Reversing Language Shift' is one which has been gaining currency amongst those concerned with language planning in Wales, implying as it does here action to bring about a change and an increase in the use of Welsh within a bilingual context where the main movement has been towards greater use of the other language (here, English). Organization of provision was addressed as also, crucially, were other areas which uniquely affect any successful Welsh for Adults delivery, for example, social opportunities, teaching materials, counselling, marketing, co-ordination and research. Much of this was ignored in the funding councils' reorganization, which was primarily concerned with funding and failed on the whole to accept the specific role of Welsh for Adults as part of a wider strategy to revive the Welsh language in Wales.

It fell to the WLB, whose role and remit had been formalized in the Welsh Language Act 1993, to attempt to work with the Welsh for Adults Panel and the eight local consortia and formulate a comprehensive strategy for this area of provision. In their submission to the JRG, the WLB argued for a national strategy for Welsh for Adults which should be seen against the broader national strategy to promote the Welsh language. It proposed a national forum to include the funding councils, the Curriculum and Assessment Authority for Wales (ACCAC), the Welsh Office and any other interested bodies. Although this went beyond the remit of the JRG, it did nevertheless recognize and recommend that the Councils give consideration to this 'new national context'. The Councils acknowledged in Circular W94/48HE:

> although [they] do not have a strategic planning remit, which is the role of the WLB as the lead agency for overall development of Welsh language usage, there is merit in reaching a shared understanding of respective roles and responsibilities in relation to issues which are the concern of both bodies . . . (1994a: para. 9)

The changes to be implemented by the funding councils, together with the recommendations for one body to be responsible for funding the provision and another (the WLB) having responsibility for the formulation of strategy, inevitably provoked concern and criticism from those involved in the everyday delivery of the Welsh for Adults programme. Four points in particular gave cause for concern. First, as the WLB, at that time, had no national strategy for the Welsh language, it was felt that it was premature for it to be involved in formulating a strategy for Welsh for Adults when this should, properly, be seen as part of a wider strategy for promotion of the Welsh language in Wales. Second, it was felt that the continuation of a strong, central unit (such as that provided at the time by the National Welsh for Adults Officer in the WJEC) was vital to co-ordinate and steer any strategy or future policy in the field. Funding for the unit had only been guaranteed for one academic year. Third, the linking of funding with accreditation was not felt to be entirely appropriate to the ethos of Welsh for Adults, as the primary goal for the majority of the students following courses was not to attain qualifications *per se* but to become fluent in Welsh. Finally, the programme weighting of 1.2 was – and continues to be – a particular bone of contention as English as a second language (ESOL) attracts a weighting of 1.5. ESOL had also been dropped from the ten-hour rule for the enrolment unit. This, in particular, was seen as an important point of principle.

Another cause for concern was the apparent impotence of local consortia to deal with institutions which chose to ignore local agreements and deliver provision contrary to the consortia's strategic plans. This problem remained unresolved until March 1998 when the funding councils issued Circular FE/CL/98/38. In this, the FEFCW emphasized that all funding to institutions for Welsh for Adults provision would be conditional on them participating and adhering to the relevant consortium strategic plan. The same circular also announced that the programme area weighting would be increased by 0.05 and that this additional weighting would be conditional on the contribution of receiving institutions to certain areas of consortia activities. Further to this, the FEFCW has insisted that institution heads must sign a note of intention that, in order to receive Welsh for Adults funding, they name the consortium/consortia of which they are a member, state that the institution will keep to the strategic plan, confirm that 0.2 of the Welsh for Adults funding will be earmarked for development of the field and that the other 0.05 will be earmarked for specific consortium activities. In many respects, the functioning of the eight local consortia has been able to offer an example of good practice for co-operation between different further education institutions and also institutions of higher education in integrated programme planning, joint marketing and tutor-training and the identification of clear progression routes for students. The FEFCW makes specific mention of this in the above circular: 'The Council wishes to support consortia working as a model of the kind of strategic partnership and collaboration at a local level which is currently being encouraged by the Government'.

Agreement was reached between the FEFCW and the WLB over what their respective roles should be and this was presented to a meeting of the chairpersons of the eight consortia in May 1995. One of the main roles of the WLB was to develop a strategic overview of the Welsh for Adults provision in Wales and in doing so, maintain a close working relationship with the FEFCW in order to develop and agree upon an all-Wales strategy for Welsh for Adults. Another important aspect of the WLB's role would be to raise the profile of Welsh for Adults in Wales – in other words, to help market the provision. During the next two years, the old Welsh for Adults Panel was to all intents and purposes supplanted by the WLB's Welsh for Adults Strategy group which focused all its efforts on producing an all-encompassing strategy for the field which would also, it was hoped, complement the Board's own developing policies and strategies for promoting the Welsh language in all walks of Welsh life. A final version was presented to the members of the board in November 1997. Significantly, many of the main recommendations within it mirror those suggested in the earlier document (WJEC, 1992) and it takes a holistic view of the field in general, placing it firmly in the area of language planning rather than viewing Welsh for Adults as just another subject on the curriculum (which has tended to be the attitude of the FEFCW). In particular, it argues for a strengthening of the consortia network, a raising of the programme area weight to 1.5, the retention of the central co-ordinating unit and an accreditation framework which would be sensitive to and meet the needs of adult learners of Welsh. At least the first two of these points have now been partially addressed.

Welsh for Adults provision as a component of holistic language policy

The potential for the WLB's new Welsh for Adults National Strategy to enhance and impact upon Welsh language policy in the future is considerable. If it is fully implemented and accepted not only by the funding councils but also, and just as crucially, by other public bodies whose co-operation in promoting the spirit of the 1993 Welsh Language Act within the communities of Wales is paramount, then it could have a significant impact. It is encouraging that this strategy document formed part of the agenda for the WLB's first ever public meeting held at Bridgend in December 1997. The cornerstone for the strategy is the aim of ensuring that anybody who wishes to learn to speak Welsh will receive as much support as possible to do so and that the provision will be actively marketed throughout the country. A recent edition of *Y Tiwtor* (the journal for tutors who teach Welsh for Adults) highlighted that the strategy will enable the field to make a significant contribution towards increasing the number of people able to speak the language, in addition to safeguarding and developing Welsh as a living national language in the future.

It is this potential to be able to play a key role in any attempts to reverse language shift in Wales which marks out the Welsh for Adults provision within continuing education as having a unique contribution to make in the national life of the country. Jones (1993: 10) has been a long-time advocate of this role and has stated categorically: 'I certainly believe that in the restoration of the language, the determining factor is and must be the adult-learning movement.' The Welsh Office initiative on lifelong learning in Wales accepts this point stating that:

Welsh provision for adults will become an integral part of the lifelong learning philosophy. It will provide adults with the opportunities to learn the language alongside their children. It will inspire them to retrain to develop their language skills. It will provide a route back into education for those adults who have had little or no further education or training since school and new opportunities for those who want to extend their knowledge and skills. (Welsh Office, 1998: 28)

This recognizes the specific role that Welsh for Adults has not only within a strategy for lifelong learning in Wales, but also as a means of tilting the linguistic balance in Wales back in favour of the Welsh language by coupling adult learning with the growth of Welsh-medium education in schools. Attention has been drawn to the fact (Tomos, 1992) that success in learning Welsh often convinces students who previously had negative attitudes towards education that they do indeed have an ability to study and many subsequently progress onto other fields of study, having been encouraged and given confidence in their abilities. It is, however, helpful in critically assessing the validity of these claims to consider briefly the demography of Welsh-speakers and the motivations of those adults who have already attended courses from the standpoint of any indications they may give regarding implications for future successful language and educational policy directions.

The past twenty years have seen great changes in *who* speaks Welsh, *where* it is spoken and the *domains* in which it is used. The 1992 *Welsh Social Survey: Report on the Welsh Language* (Welsh Office, 1995) gives an interesting insight into many of these changes, some of which were not clearly revealed by the 1991 census figures. For example, 66.1 per cent of the population of Wales is unable to speak Welsh. Of the remaining 33.9 per cent, 16.9 per cent were either fluent Welsh-speakers or able to speak a fair amount. An additional 17 per cent claimed to be able to speak 'a little Welsh' and obviously a number of these had failed to record themselves as Welsh-speakers in the 1991 census (See Table 12.1).

There obviously exists, therefore, a substantial pool of potentially linguistically competent people within Wales (17 per cent) for whom it would require a comparatively small effort to raise confidence in the language and bring them to a higher degree of fluency. These Welsh-speakers very often form the major cohort of continuing education courses (*cyrsiau gloywi*) designed to build confidence in spoken and written Welsh and hone linguistic skills which are frequently under-estimated and undervalued by those possessing them.

The effects of Welsh-medium education at the school level are clearly visible in the number of children aged three to fifteen who are able to speak at least a little Welsh: 53 per cent (of which 18.9 per cent claim to be fluent or to speak a fair amount of Welsh). Although the high percentage (34.4) in this age group who are able to speak only a little Welsh should perhaps be treated with some caution, the figures nevertheless provide optimism for the future

Table 12.1 Ability in Welsh

Fluent	13.4%
Able to speak a fair amount	3.5%
Able to speak a little	17.0%
Total	33.9%
Unable to speak any	66.1%

Source:Welsh Social Survey: Report on the Welsh Language (1992)

potential pool of Welsh-speakers growing up in Wales and point to a reversal in the previous trend of top-heavy Welsh-speaking figures concentrated in the older age groups.

Section 2.8 of the 1992 Social Survey is of particular interest in the context of this chapter as it deals with learning the language. Almost 8 per cent of fluent adult speakers of Welsh only started to learn the language when they were at school (a figure likely to increase in the future) with a further 1 per cent starting to learn after completing their full-time education. This means that approximately 26,300 adult fluent speakers of Welsh successfully acquired the language by means other than home transmission. The Survey also provided important information on the learning intentions and reasons for not learning of non-Welsh-speakers and non-fluent speakers. Over one in ten (209,700) stated that they were likely to learn or improve their ability in Welsh at some stage in the future, of which 43.9 per cent could not speak Welsh and have never been able to speak the language. Even more revealing in the light of the stated aims of the most recent Welsh for Adults Strategy is that, of those not expecting to learn or improve their Welsh, 26,000 gave as their reason that they knew of no opportunity to learn. These figures present a great challenge for the provision of Welsh for Adults and national strategy/language policy in the future, for if this demand could be successfully met, the situation of the Welsh language could be greatly changed within a very short period of time.

One other important aspect of Welsh for Adults as a component of any comprehensive language policy in Wales is that it primarily addresses the majority of the population who are unable to speak the language. Attitudes amongst this section of the population towards the Welsh language are therefore a prime consideration. A survey conducted by NOP for the WLB in 1996 (Iorwerth, 1996) revealed some favourable general attitudes towards the language, with 71 per cent of those asked saying that they were in favour of using the Welsh language and 88 per cent believing that we should be proud of it. Three-quarters agreed that Welsh and English should have equal status in Wales and 83 per cent thought that public bodies should be able to deal with the public in both languages. Only 12 per cent were of the opinion that Welsh speakers have too much opportunity in employment prospects. There is always a problem in translating positive attitudes into positive action! However, what the survey does illustrate clearly is that there is a new consensus in Wales regarding the language, a consensus which it could be argued did not exist to the same degree even twenty years ago. As Baker (1992: 97) has stated, 'Where a language is fighting for survival, encouraging positive attitudes becomes crucial'.

It is revealing, in the light of the encouraging findings of both the Welsh Social Survey 1992 and the 1996 NOP poll, to find that the motivations of students attending Welsh for Adults intensive provision mirror in many respects recent developments in the use of the language in Wales. Research (see Morris, 1996, 1997a, 1997b) carried out by the department of continuing education at University of Wales Swansea between 1992 and 1995 of all students (608) attending Wlpan intensive courses in the geographical area served by the department has shown that the main motivation given by a majority of respondents was: I live in Wales and feel I should speak the language. This integrative motivation noted by 39 to 48 per cent over the three years of the study confirms the positive attitude noted in the NOP survey and underlines the feelings of many non-Welsh-speakers that the language belongs to them as well. The second most frequent motivation was having children in a Welsh-medium school. Once again, this is extremely important from the point of view of holistic language policy, as many parents desire to complement the newly acquired linguistic skills of their children by developing their own linguistic ability. There are obvious implications here for increased successful intergenerational language transmission when this occurs at an early enough stage in the children's linguistic development.

The third most common motivation was that learning Welsh would be of advantage in the student's workplace, the only example of an instrumental motivation (see Gardner, 1985, for a discussion of these concepts of motivation). The link between gaining the necessary linguistic skills to be able to use Welsh competently in the workplace and the increased demand for employees with these skills following the 1993 Welsh Language Act is one which is likely to accelerate in importance in the future and provides yet another example of the interface between Welsh for Adults provision and language planning policy. Similar motivations have been noted in HMI reports (Welsh Office, 1991). An additional factor has been the use of this provision by many incomers into Welsh-speaking areas within Wales to assimilate into those communities where they have chosen to settle (Morris, 1997a). The research also highlighted an interesting age profile with the largest group of students falling in the twenty-five to thirty-four age group. These figures are encouraging when viewing this aspect of continuing education as a way of facilitating language revival in Wales as this is the age group most likely to be bringing up young children. The potential impact on the development of the language with young adults learning the language and, at the same time, sending their children to receive Welsh-medium school education has been recognized in the 1998 Green Paper on lifelong learning. Of those students in the sample who had children, nearly 70 per cent of these were attending Welsh-medium schools. In addition, of those parents whose children attended English-medium schools, nearly half felt that the inclusion of Welsh as a compulsory subject within the National Curriculum had influenced their decision to learn Welsh. All of these motivations illustrate and reinforce the need for Welsh for Adults provision to be viewed as being more than just a field of continuing education curriculum. It has to be seen as a vital component of language policy and planning within Wales, with the potential to contribute positively and practically to a reversal of language shift in the country.

Given the changing political landscape in Wales with the establishment of a National Assembly, it is useful to cast our eyes to countries or regions with similar linguistic and political developments to our own in order to assess how best the Welsh for Adults provision can contribute to the creation of a more bilingual Wales. A number of the bilingual autonomous regions of Spain provide constructive comparison in the search for an appropriate model. Both the Basque Country and Catalonia have within their autonomous governments specific language planning departments and have long accepted the importance of training adults in appropriate language skills – either as a second language or in retraining for those who lack the necessary confidence in the indigenous language – and have located this provision within the remit of these departments. Much emphasis and considerable resources are directed to the co-ordination and development of this aspect of language planning and the interface between community, education and policy is clearly beneficial and constructive. It is common in these communities of Spain to refer to the 'normalization' of the Catalan and Basque languages, a process which obviously cannot be achieved without the co-operation and active participation of those members of the community who are not fluent in these languages but whose attitudes are favourably disposed towards the 'normalization' process.

The Basque situation is perhaps more similar to that of Wales than the situation in Catalonia. The Basque language bears no similarity to Castilian (Spanish) the two languages being as different from each other as are Welsh and English. The percentages speaking Basque and Welsh are broadly the same, approximately 20 per cent of the respective populations. The Basque language was forbidden during the Franco regime but public support for the language in post-Franco Spain has been considerable. Adult Basque courses are mostly provided through HABE, a governmental organization, and AEK, which also receives support through HABE. In the Basque- Autonomous Community, there are a large number of centres which teach Basque to adults and literacy skills to Basque speakers. This sector of the population is considered very important in making up the shortfall of competent Basque speakers required to implement bilingual policies within the Community and the government has established a national system of accreditation and certification which clearly makes evident the level of ability of an individual in the language. The use of the *euskaltegi*, a special school to teach Basque to teachers, could be of particular interest to us in Wales as we struggle in a similar way to find sufficient numbers of teachers able to teach Welsh in schools at different levels. Again, in the Basque Country, the emphasis is on holistic language planning within the autonomous government and teaching Basque to adults plays a big role in this process. A policy of language normalization exists which in the context of both the Basque Country and Catalonia means helping to restore the language to those domains where it would have been used and its use developed had it not been for the interference of the Franco regime. Any programme of language normalization in Wales would obviously arise from a different historical perspective. However, the Catalan model of enacting normalization through a consortium between the autonomous government's language department and the various local authorities with a primary aim of jointly planning and presenting linguistic policies at a local level (including the Catalan for Adults provision) could well be emulated in a Welsh context.

So far in Wales, the main policy-makers – primarily the Welsh Office and in the most recent reorganization of Welsh for Adults provision, the FEFCW – have failed to realize the uniqueness and potential of this sector of continuing education as part of the language planning process. One example of this is the funding mechanism currently in place which treats this provision like any other academic subject, fails to reward or positively encourage cohesive planning and thereby militates against holistic language policy-making. The drawing up of a comprehensive national strategy by the WLB and practitioners in the field could be an important step towards the fusing of language policy with the kind of provision being delivered. However, in order to realize the full potential of this field as an integral part of future language planning policy and any Welsh attempt at language 'normalization', both the national co-ordination function and the resourcing role will need to be located at the heart of a possible language directorate within the new democratically elected National Assembly rather than an unaccountable quango. By this means it will start to become possible to address and face the challenge of channelling the well-disposed attitudes and aspirations of those who wish to be a part of the efforts to reverse language shift in Wales into an effective policy for re-creating a bilingual Wales in the new millennium.

References

Baker, C. (1992) *Attitudes and Language.* Clevedon: Multilingual Matters.
Courtney, S. (1992) *Why Adults Learn: Towards a Theory of Participation in Adult Education.* London and New York: Routledge.

Crowe, R. (1988) *Yr Wlpan yn Israel*. Aberystwyth: Canolfan Ymchwil Cymraeg i Oedolion.

Davies, J. P. (1986) Dadansoddiad o nodau graddedig ar gyfer oedolion sy'n dysgu'r Gymraeg fel ail iaith. Unpublished Ph.D. thesis, UCNW Bangor.

Fishman, J. A. (1991) *Reversing Language Shift*. Clevedon: Multilingual Matters.

Gardner, R. C. (1985) *Social Psychology and Second Language Learning: The Role of Attitudes and Motivation*. London: Edward Arnold.

Iorwerth, D. (1996) Cymru tros yr Iaith. *Golwg*, 8(18), 7.

James, D. L. (1974) Wlpan Cymraeg Aberystwyth (1). *Yr Athro*, 26 (December), 106–16.

Jones, B. (1993) *Language Regained*. Llandysul: Gwasg Gomer.

Morris, S. (1996) The Welsh language and its restoration: New perspectives on motivation, lifelong learning and the university. In J. Elliott, H. Francis, R. Humphreys and D. Istance (eds.), *Communities and their Universities: The Challenge of Lifelong Learning*. London: Lawrence & Wishart.

Morris, S. (1997a) Ethnicity and motivation amongst adult learners of Welsh. In B. Synak and T. Wicherkiewicz (eds.), *Language Minorities and Minority Languages*. Gdansk: Wydawnictwo Uniwersytetu Gdanskiego.

Morris, S. (1997b) Adult education, language revival and language planning. In *Actes del Congrés Europeu sobre Planificació Lingüística/ Proceedings of the European Conference on Language Planning, Barcelona 9–10 de novembre de 1995*. Barcelona: Department de Cultura, Generalitat de Catalunya.

Rees, C. (1974) Wlpan. *Barn*, 145 (November/December), 563–5.

Tomos, R. (1992) Diwydiant dysgu Cymraeg. *Golwg*, 5/7 (15 October), 10–11.

Welsh Funding Councils (1994a) *Circular W94/48HE: Welsh for Adults*. Cardiff: WFC.

Welsh Funding Councils (1994b) *Report of the Welsh for Adults Joint Review Group*. Cardiff: WFC.

Welsh Funding Councils (1998) *Circular FE/CL98/38*. Cardiff: WFC.

Welsh Language Board (1997) *Strategaeth Genedlaethol Cymraeg i Oedolion/A National Strategy for Welsh for Adults*. Cardiff: WLB.

Welsh Office (1991) *Report by H.M. Inspectors on a Survey of Teaching Welsh to Adults in Gwent – Spring Term 1991*. Cardiff: Welsh Office.

Welsh Office (1995) *1992 Welsh Social Survey: Report on the Welsh Language*. Cardiff: Government Statistical Service.

Welsh Office (1998) *Learning is for Everyone: Green Paper on Lifelong Learning*. Cardiff: Welsh Office.

WJEC (1992) *Cymraeg i Oedolion: Y Ffordd Ymlaen/Welsh for Adults: The Way Ahead*. Cardiff: WJEC.

WJEC (1997) *Y Tiwtor: Cylchgrawn i Diwtoriaid sy'n Dysgu Cymraeg i Oedolion*, Rhifyn y Gaeaf 1997. Cardiff: WJEC.

Conclusion
Education Policy-Making and Devolved Governance in Wales, Past, Present – and Future?

RICHARD DAUGHERTY, ROBERT PHILLIPS AND GARETH REES

Introduction

This book brings together scholars working on the education system in Wales to reflect upon the key developments and themes that have influenced policies in Wales. A book on this subject is opportune: a chance to reflect upon the distinctive policy contexts, initiatives and imperatives which have emerged in Wales during the 1990s, but which also, as we saw in chapter 3 by Jones, have historical roots dating back over a century. Whereas recognition of this distinctiveness has increasingly permeated discourses on education in the UK national media (news coverage of education now often pointedly refers specifically *either* to England *or* to Wales), it has been less obvious in studies of education policy in the UK. For example, a recent publication entitled *Education Reform in the United Kingdom* (British Council, 1998), although containing a chapter relating to Scotland, does not contain an equivalent chapter on Wales. The main purpose of the book, therefore, is to map recent developments in education policy in Wales, and thereby to contribute to the wider debates on the nature of contemporary educational change in the United Kingdom as a whole and, indeed, more generally.

We are conscious that, inevitably, some dark holes remain which need illumination. For example, there is no chapter in this collection on gender issues in Wales and the overwhelming preponderance of male contributors is itself an interesting reflection of their current dominance within the Welsh education research community (see Betts, 1996; Salisbury, 1996). In addition, the preoccupation of contributors to this volume with the macro and meso levels has meant that there is little attention to another crucial area of education policy creation: the recontextualization of policy at the micro level *within* educational institutions. These provide interesting and fertile arenas for research in the future. Throughout the book, we seek, wherever possible and appropriate, to theorize about the origins and trajectories of policies and, in the process, we attempt to contribute to a better understanding of how education policies are conceived, as well as received. This involves considering the impact of a range of policy concepts, ideologies and movements, such as structural economic shifts, marketization and managerialism, which have influenced not only the United Kingdom over the past quarter of a century or so, but which have also impacted in Europe and the rest of the world (Ball, 1998). In seeking not only to describe some of the impacts of these global factors on education policies in Wales – and their interaction with distinctive cultural and social factors and imperatives inside Wales – we attempt to consider how they can best be explained and analysed in policy terms. Clearly, the general context of devolved governance is crucial here, not simply in terms of changes internal to the United Kingdom, but more widely in the European Union and elsewhere too.

Policy development in Wales

One of the most important reasons for bringing together a collection of this sort, therefore, is to explore the origins of policies, what Ball (1990) has termed the 'context of influence'. To what extent did the education policies of the late twentieth century originate from the central state (that is, Westminster and Whitehall) and apply, with minimal differentiation, to the 'England and Wales' context? Alternatively, in what ways were those policies recontextualized within the Welsh policy arena to produce characteristically Welsh policies? What role did institutional factors play in any process of mediation? Perhaps most significantly of all, to what extent were the impacts of educational policy reforms different in Wales from those in England? It seems apparent from the evidence presented in the book that it was the 'England and Wales' framework which dominated most of the education policy legislation of the period, and there were only elements of policy differentiation in

Wales. For example, the Education Reform Act of 1988 – passed almost exactly a century after the Welsh Intermediate Education Act of 1889 had first introduced a measure of distinctiveness to the education system in Wales – established some particular Welsh elements in relation to agencies, procedures and curriculum content. However, it must also be remembered that the 1988 Act, one of the biggest single legislative measures of the Thatcher era, in some ways strengthened, rather than undermined, Whitehall dominance over Wales. Some of the most significant elements of the legislation, such as the National Curriculum, assessment and monitoring systems, as well as funding arrangements, provided a new overall structure within which distinctiveness had to be argued for and conceded by London before it could occur in Wales. What this emphasizes, therefore, are the complexities of the education policy process within a constantly evolving system of devolved governance.

As Cox and Daugherty demonstrate in their chapters, however, a process of *mediation* within an 'England and Wales' policy context did take place too. Hence, an important dynamic within this policy context was the acceptance by central government policy-makers, including not only Whitehall civil servants but also Secretaries of State for Education, of the need to allow variants of English policies within clearly defined parameters. The contrasting ideological and political contexts of England and Wales provided interesting mediating influences here. This reflected differences in the value positions underpinning certain policy orientations, as, for example, concerning educational monitoring, accountability and performance. One significant feature of such policy mediation is described in chapter 8 by Egan and Thomas on the role of the inspectorate. Their evidence also illustrates a further theme touched upon by other contributors: namely, the greater propensity within Wales amongst those responsible for the monitoring, evaluation and shaping of policies to listen to the views of professionals.

Nevertheless, the dominant theme emerging from most of the chapters is that of actors within the Welsh policy process reacting to policies initiated elsewhere. There are a few exceptions to this broad generalization. Several policy developments during this period were exclusive to Wales, not only in terms of the chief characteristics but also in the sense of their policy origins. Obvious examples here relate to policies on language (see chapter 12 by

Morris) and bilingualism (chapter 6 by Baker) and the development of the Curriculum Cymreig in schools. Significantly, when distinctive policies such as these developed, they were usually in response to pressure-group demands and centred upon quasi-autonomous institutions. This points to the importance of institutional factors as a dynamic for Welsh education policies. The evidence in this volume enables us to recognize more clearly the complexity of the institutional frameworks within Wales prior to the establishment in 1999 of an elected National Assembly, as well as their relationships with each other, and with similar institutions outside Wales. In this respect, it is important to distinguish institutions of government, such as the Welsh Office, from quasi-governmental institutions with an independent statutory basis, but dependent upon government for funding, such as ACCAC or the WLB. The role of such institutions in mediating and reframing policy is a frequently recurring theme. Reference is made to actors within institutions responding to and working with the wider (national and global) picture of politics, economics and culture. Some chapters shed light not only upon the complexity of this process of mediation, but also upon its often contradictory impacts. This is well illustrated, for instance, by Jephcote and Salisbury's references to the disjuncture between the market model underpinning central government policy for further education and the hybridization process evolving through local hierarchies, networks and cultures. Inevitably, in a complex context of this sort, accommodation occurs at the institutional level between rival interests. This complexity is acknowledged in Fitz's highly instructive conceptual framework, which draws upon Giddens's account of the problematics of 'choice' and the creation of 'manufactured uncertainty' in postmodernity.

It is also important to consider the extent to which historical, cultural and ideological factors combined to give this complex process of policy mediation distinctive characteristics. The British political context of the 1980s and 1990s was crucial. For most of the period much of the populace in Wales felt effectively disenfranchised by the existence of Westminster governments committed to a combination of neo-liberal and neo-conservative policies. A direct parallel existed in relation to educational policy and the role of education professionals. In many of the chapters, particularly those on assessment, curriculum and the inspection, there is evidence of attempts being made to placate professional interests in Wales, as far as was possible within the externally defined political parameters. The same phenomenon is also evidenced in the way in which policy texts originating from London had their Welsh counterparts, often characterized by more conciliatory language and reference points.

The wider context

Accordingly, the specific features of education policy in Wales need to be understood in the broader context of education policy, both within the UK and internationally. Two such contextual dimensions are referred to briefly here: the trend, in Wales and elsewhere, to link education systems to the economies they are perceived as serving; and the new political context within the UK following the election of a Labour government in May 1997.

The major impetus behind the Conservative educational reforms of the 1980s and 1990s was the persistent diagnosis of declining standards in our schools and the wider inadequacies of educational institutions of all kinds (Ball, 1990). One of the principal focuses of this concern was the purported failure of the education system to provide adequately for the nation's economy. Unlike those in more 'successful' competitor economies, it was argued, young people in Britain tend to leave education early and, when they do, they generally do not have even the basic knowledge and learning skills, let alone the technical and social competences, to function effectively in the labour market. Hence, Britain's lack of economic competitiveness in relation to many of the other EU economies, the US and Japan or even the other dynamic economies of the Pacific Rim, is paralleled by an underperformance in the educational sphere too (for a critical discussion of some of these issues, see Avis *et al.*, 1996). As a number of the preceding chapters make clear, it was this kind of analysis which provided a significant part of the intellectual foundation for the emphasis in educational policies not simply on direct vocationalization, but also on enhancing achievement through curriculum and assessment reform, the more stringent monitoring of performance through 'league tables', the 'naming and shaming' of so-called 'failing' schools, and so forth (see, in particular, chapters 5, 7 and 2, by Daugherty, Gorard and Fitz). Moreover, these impacts were felt beyond the school system too. Further, higher and continuing education were all enlisted in the official cause of enhancing economic competitiveness, as chapters 9–11, by Jephcote and Salisbury, Williams and Humphreys and Saunders, all indicate. In Wales, these *general* diagnoses of educational ills took *particular* forms. Here, the argument was that the revitalization the economy after the traumatic decline of the staple industries – especially coal, steel and, less obviously, agriculture – required signal improvements in the skills and competences of the Welsh labour force. Influenced, no doubt, by the growing recognition of the importance of the regional level of economic governance within the EU, the sources of comparative 'best practice' were also specific to the Welsh context. Hence, if Wales was to be a successful, 'modern' economy, it would have to emulate the kind of education and training illustrated in, for example, the four European 'motor regions' (Baden-Wurttemberg, Catalonia, Lombardy and Rhones-Alpes). A number of Welsh Office initiatives – for example, *A Bright Future: Getting the Best for Every Pupil at School in Wales* (1995a) and *People and Prosperity: An Agenda for Action* (1995b) – thus prioritized the need to improve Welsh performance in schools and colleges and in the provision of vocational training, although the forms which these took frequently reflected – albeit in complex ways – the specificities of the Welsh policy community. Moreover, there was a widespread acceptance in civil society of these priorities and the diagnosis on which they were based. For instance, the Institute of Welsh Affairs recommended in its 1993 blueprint for the new millennium, *Wales 2010: Creating our own Future*, that by 1997 Wales should be declared 'Land of Life-Long Learning'. Similarly, the Wales TUC announced at its 1996 annual conference a joint initiative with the Wales CBI and the Welsh Training and Enterprise Councils (TECs) to improve the skills levels of Welsh workforce.

Examples such as these could, of course, be multiplied many times over. The point to emphasize, however, is that they embody a particular conception of the role of education, which is held to have a determinate relationship with the economy. To adopt the buzz-phrase of the moment, a 'learning society' is overwhelmingly conceived within this perspective as one where individuals are equipped with the basic knowledge and skills – technical and social – to function effectively within the labour market; and where, moreover, individuals are sufficiently flexible to engage in the recurrent training which is necessitated to meet the demands of changing production and work organization and the switching between occupations that this will imply. Necessarily, therefore, this involves not only excellent initial education, but also extended patterns of 'lifelong learning'. More specifically, Britain in general and Wales in particular fall some way short of achieving this ideal, as is illustrated by the unfavourable comparisons which are drawn with competitor economies. Therefore, the essential project for the policy-makers is to transform the quality and patterns of educational provision which will secure the achievement of a 'learning society' here at some point in the future (see the discussion of lifelong learning in chapter 11).

In this way, therefore, educational policies in Wales reflected precisely the same kind of 'pressures of economic circumstances' as those in England (and, indeed, elsewhere): a dominant discourse emphasized the economic necessity of educational reform. However, even here, there were also elements of a Welsh distinctiveness. As we have seen, the underlying diagnosis of economic ills necessarily reflected the specificities of the particularly precipitous decline of Wales's traditional employment base. Moreover, the educational policies which were devised to remedy these ills, whilst undoubtedly sharing a great deal in common with those in England, were developed and implemented in an institutional context which reflected the particular features of the Welsh policy arena. Mention has already been made of the distinctive relationships between policy-makers and professionals in Wales, which, for example, produced appreciable differences in policies with respect to school improvement (see chapter 7). Similarly, the wider institutional context was one in which relationships between educational institutions – and, in particular, the FE colleges and the funding councils – and those responsible for economic development – the Welsh Development Agency and the TECs – were appreciably closer than in the regions of England. In part, this reflected no more than the relative smallness of the Welsh policy arena. However, administrative devolution to Wales (unlike in the English regions) provided a context in which co-ordination between institutions was practicable and the role of the Welsh Office itself was undoubtedly very significant (Morgan, Rees and Garmise, 1999). It is also instructive to observe that these elements of Welsh distinctiveness have survived into the post-1997 era of New Labour. Indeed, the establishment of the Education and Training Action Group (ETAG) in the aftermath of the general election and its proposals for the reform of the post-16 education and training system not only reiterate the economic priorities for the education system, but also arguably provide an interesting example of policy in Wales clearly leading that in England (ETAG, 1999).

The perception of disenfranchisement felt in Wales (as in some other parts of the UK) during the Tory-dominated 1980s and 1990s mentioned above was based, essentially, upon the view that many of the social policies initiated during the period had minimal relevance to the needs of Wales. This might explain Labour's own conversion to the idea of devolution as a bulwark against repetition in the future. It may also explain the heady euphoria and optimism that greeted the election victory by Labour in May 1997. The reality, however, of the first few years of the Labour administration's record, as well as debacle over the Blairite desire to ensure Alun Michael's victory over Rhodri Morgan for the leadership of the Welsh Assembly, suggested that the 'honeymoon' period for New Labour ended even earlier in Wales than elsewhere.

It became evident, of course, both before and after the election, that much of New Labour's so-called 'Third Way' owed as much to continuity with previous neo-liberal policies as it did with anything radically 'new'. Thus, the 'Third Way' can be defined rather flatteringly as a combination of neo-liberalism and state socialism – a sort of market socialism (Giddens, 1998) – or merely a pragmatic, ideology-free response to the realities of pleasing a middle-class electorate and the severe fiscal restraints presented by the Treasury. Hence, the stress placed by recent analysts of Labour policies upon continuity; as Demaine (1999: 5) comments, 'new Labour appears intent on following a similar policy-line on education to that of the Conservatives when they were in office: albeit a line modified and adapted to the "real world"'.

An interesting issue to consider, therefore, in this concluding chapter is the extent to which Labour policies will more readily meet the needs of Wales. Hodgson and Spours (1999) describe new Labour education policies as 'Radical Centre' rather than 'Radical Centre-left' based upon three main principles:

- A 'traditionalist interventionist' approach to school standards with an emphasis upon basic skills.
- A 'voluntarist framework partnership' approach to lifelong learning based upon individual responsibility, information technology

and the development of a system of qualifications which recognizes a wider range of knowledge and skills.

• A more 'egalitarian approach' to social and educational inclusion which aims to focus more attention upon marginal groups, particularly through the widening of participation in education and training.

There is enough here to suggest a greater degree of optimism that there will be a closer correlation between the policy objectives and priorities of central government and the characteristic needs and interests of Wales. Thus, although New Labour's rhetorical emphasis upon 'traditional interventionism' ('standards'/'back to basics': see Welsh Office, 1997) suggest little has changed from the political priorities and tactics of previous Tory governments, New Labour's 'more egalitarian' approach – for example through a defence of comprehensive schools and discontinuation of GMS – are more in line with Welsh historical and ideological traditions. A crucial factor here, of course, is the extent to which the Welsh Assembly will be able to capitalize upon this potentially more conducive environment in the future, an issue that is discussed in the next section.

The changing context within Wales

The decision, following a referendum in September 1998, to establish an elected Assembly for Wales began the process of reshaping the political institutions of Wales. At the time of writing, it is too early judge the consequences for the making and implementation of education policy in Wales, but the prospect of change has stimulated a debate about what has been and what should be.

The opportunity to comment on an era of policy-making which was to come to end following the Assembly elections in May 1999 brought into the open some of the decision-making processes which could only be inferred from the evidence presented in this book. Those who have studied education policy in Wales in the pre-devolution era will not have been surprised to hear Ron Davies, Secretary of State for Wales until November 1998, explaining how, in his experience, policy decisions affecting Wales had sometimes been taken:

It was often over my cornflakes that I first became aware of changes in Government policy – innovations which, according to the theory of collective government, had been agreed with me. The practice was less than the theory required. I spent many happy mornings trying to decide whether we should follow the policy in Wales, if we could afford it, or whether we should construct a defence to explain why we weren't making an announcement in Wales on the self-same policy which was so eminently desirable in London. (Quoted by Osmond, 1999: 6)

In the same pamphlet, on *The Civil Service and the National Assembly*, Osmond anticipates the changing role of the civil service, responsible to the Assembly as a whole rather than just to the party in the power which has executive responsibilities. He suggests that 'the success of the devolution process will depend in very large measure on the way the relationships between the civil service, the Executive and the backbench members work out in practice' (p. 6) but warns that 'the danger will be of an over-dependence on the civil service' (p. 5).

Davies himself, in another pamphlet (Davies, 1999), has reflected on the lessons to be learnt – for the Labour Party, as well as for the government of Wales – from the experience over two decades of bringing about fundamental constitutional change. He also identifies three specific 'pressure points' for the Assembly. First, he points out that the devolution legislation provides a mechanism for the transfer of secondary legislative powers, but says nothing about how that mechanism might be used. A second 'pressure point' relates to the financing of the Assembly, within a UK and a European context. And the third concerns the extent to which the Assembly will be able to exercise its discretion when its priorities are considered against a background of priorities as seen from Westminster and Whitehall.

Whatever the uncertainties, all commentators are agreed that the assumptions and procedures which controlled policy-making in Wales until 1999 have been fundamentally changed, directly and indirectly, by the 1998 Government of Wales Act. As a 'senior Welsh Office civil servant', interviewed in 1998, put it:

Currently we are working for one Minister whose preoccupations are London- rather than Wales-centred. But once the Assembly is in being collective Cabinet responsibility will go out of the window. We are very close to being released from the straitjacket of thinking that Britain is a homogeneous community where policy diversity is a dangerous activity. (Quoted in Osmond, 1999: 6)

Into this new world of politics and policy-making in Wales has come a stream of ideas, arguments and proposals from individuals and organisations (see, for example, Jones, 1998; Jones and Reynolds, 1998) seeking to shape the agenda for post-devolution education policies in Wales.

The political parties also set out, in their manifestos for the Assembly elections, their policy priorities for education in Wales. The Labour Party manifesto stressed the claimed achievements of a UK Labour administration since the UK elections of May 1997 (Wales Labour Party, 1999). Looking ahead to the Assembly, the manifesto highlighted such policies as the extending of nursery education to three year olds and the implementation of the Education and Training Action Group's proposals for sixteen to nineteen year olds. As the party in power at Westminster, Labour was mainly concerned with the continued implementation of policy priorities already identified and, in some instances, partially implemented.

In contrast, the Conservative manifesto echoed themes well established as central to government policies in Wales, as in England, during the 1980s and most of the 1990s: parental choice, delegation of funding, private-sector involvement in state schools (Welsh Conservative Party, 1999). In other respects, for example in their unequivocal support for A levels, the Conservatives were in their more traditional role of defending the status quo. Only in its reversal of the policy that Welsh should be studied by all fourteen to sixteen year olds in state schools, a policy introduced by a Conservative government in the early 1990s, did the party's manifesto give rise to controversy during the election campaign.

The Welsh Liberal Democrats set out their education policies for the Assembly in the form of 'guarantees', fourteen of them in all. They ranged from the specifics of the school curriculum, stressing citizenship and the teaching of musical instruments, to aspects of the organization of education in Wales, including youth service development plans and a Wales Council for Lifelong Learning (Liberal Democrats Wales, 1999).

The most detailed, and arguably the most radical, of the party manifestos came from Plaid Cymru, the Party of Wales (Plaid Cymru, 1999). Its proposals were more concerned than those of the other parties with establishing new organizational and institutional structures, such as 'a network of comprehensive tertiary colleges' and an 'Education and Training Council for Wales'. From an integrated 'Educare' programme for children up to the age of seven to advocacy of a new, distinctively Welsh post-16 qualification, Plaid Cymru set out a full programme for transforming the education system in Wales. Following the May 1999 elections, Plaid Cymru, as the main opposition party in the Assembly (though 'opposition' is a term frowned upon in the brave new world of 'inclusivity'), with seventeen of the sixty seats against twenty-eight for a minority Labour administration, found itself potentially in a position to bring its policy agenda into the mainstream of Assembly policy-making.

Conclusion

The institutional framework established by the Welsh Assembly, together with the democratic mandate to provide it with authority, will clearly have an impact on the capacity of Wales not only to react to policy initiatives emanating from London, but also to play a proactive role in seeking to identify education policies which connect more directly to historical, cultural and regional imperatives. Tensions will continue to exist between, using Fitz's terms, 'territorial' and 'national' levels, but at the same time the democratic licence afforded by the Assembly provides policy opportunities.

Amid all this consideration of change, it is important to recognize some of the factors which will ensure continuity between the pre- and post-Assembly era. The primary role for the initiation of UK policies will still be with Westminster and Whitehall and any discussion of policies will still take place within the constraints imposed by central fiscal and budgetary limitations. On the other hand, writing in the immediate aftermath of the establishment of the Assembly, but before it has had an opportunity to establish its own agenda, we can speculate about some of the potential changes in relation to policy formulation which may arise from the existence of the Assembly.

First, the political culture initiated by the Welsh Assembly will have implications for education policy-making which have yet to be fully appreciated. For example, the Assembly has a relatively high proportion of women members – in marked contrast to the political and policy apparatus in the Welsh Office, Whitehall and Westminster – which may have interesting consequences for the ways in which policy is discussed, formulated and directed. Moreover, the fact that education policies will be discussed in an open, transparent forum will mean that there is potential, in theory at least, to formulate a more realistic connection between the policy apparatus and the wider community in Wales. The experience of the 1980s and 1990s showed that in many respects the ways in which education policies, for example on the school curriculum, were formulated was as significant as the policies themselves (Daugherty, 1997).

Second, the Welsh policy apparatus cannot be viewed in isolation. Wales, like the other parts of the UK, Europe and even, more recently, the Far East, will always be dependent upon the 'bigger economic picture', but the existence of a Welsh Assembly may provide more legitimate and more informed strategies to make a better attempt to deal effectively with the dislocation between education of the workforce and the economy than has been the case for most of the twentieth century. Although forging a more direct correspondence between the education system and the needs of the economy has had its historical tensions and difficulties, nevertheless, the potential capacity of the Welsh Assembly to respond to the economic climate with educational policy initiatives will be a crucial feature of its policy development.

Third, we can speculate about the ways in which the Welsh Assembly will influence the precise nature of education policies. Whereas the 1980s and 1990s were characterized, as we have seen, by policy borrowing with a strong injection of mediation, the presence of the Assembly is likely to prompt efforts to change some of the value positions underpinning educational initiatives originating from London. This will be particularly important when, as was the case in the 1980s and 1990s, there are sharp ideological differences between the politicians in power at Westminster and the political realities in Wales. There are strong grounds for suggesting that those education policies in Wales which have distinctively cultural connotations will be strengthened by the existence of the Welsh Assembly and will be far less vulnerable to the political vagaries of Whitehall. This has significant implications, too, for distinctively Welsh initiatives, particularly in the field of curriculum development. The prospect, for example, of achieving a Welsh *baccalau-réat* may be closer to being realized since the establishment of the Assembly (Jones, 1998).

Finally, linked to the above, we see considerable potential in the contrast between the political and ideological contexts in which education policy is initiated. Whereas we have made reference to the feelings of political and professional disenfranchisement which characterized education policy matters in the 1980s and 1990s in Wales, the Welsh Assembly provides at least the potential to initiate a more consensual form of educational discourse, politics and policy-making. There is potential here for the Assembly to build upon a legacy of conciliatory professional dialogue. Wales may provide a particularly conducive environment to 'bring teachers back in' to debates over policy and reform (Hargreaves and Evans, 1997). There is, however, little evidence of this occurring in a policy text published just prior to the Assembly elections for development and implementation in the new post-devolution political context (Welsh Office, 1999).

This book was never intended to provide lessons for policy-makers contemplating a new era. As the chapters by Gorard, Phillips and Fitz remind us, the relationship between the policy community and researchers is never likely to be an easy one, given their different priorities and agendas. Yet, as far as Welsh education policy matters are concerned, we see the role of the educational research community in Wales as providing some of the informed, objective and constructively critical framework within which debates over the merits and demerits of policies take place. Although a book of this sort cannot and should not seek to provide all the answers, it is hoped that it will at least contribute to an interesting and enlightened discourse on education policy matters in Wales in the future.

References

Avis, J., Bloomer, M., Esland, G., Gleeson, D. and Hodkinson, P. (1996) *Knowledge and Nationhood*. London: Cassell.

Ball, S. (1990) *Politics and Policy Making in Education: Explorations in Policy Sociology*. London: Routledge.

Ball, S. (1998) Big policies/small world: an introduction to international perspectives in education policy. *Comparative Education*, 34(2), 119–29.

Betts, S. (ed.) (1996) *Our Daughters' Land*. Cardiff: University of Wales Press.

British Council (1998) *Education Reform in the UK: Report for Overseas Offices*. London: British Council.

Daugherty, R. (1997) *A School Curriculum for a Future Wales*. Milton Keynes: The British Curriculum Foundation.

Davies, R. (1999) *Devolution: A Process Not an Event*. Cardiff: Institute of Welsh Affairs.

Demaine, J. (ed.) (1999) *Education Policy and Contemporary Politics*. London: Macmillan.

ETAG (1999) *An Education and Training Action Plan for Wales*. Cardiff: ETAG.

Giddens, A. (1998) *The Third Way: The Renewal of Social Democracy*. Cambridge: Polity Press.

Hargreaves, A. and Evans, R. (1997) *Beyond Educational Reform: Bringing Teachers Back In*. Buckingham: Open University Press.

Hodgson, A. and Spours, K. (1999) *New Labour's Educational Agenda: Issues and Policies for Education and Training from 14+*. London: Kogan Page.

Institute of Welsh Affairs (1993) *Wales 2010: Creating our own Future*. Cardiff: Institute of Welsh Affairs.

Jones, E. P. and Reynolds, D. (1998) Education. In J. Osmond (ed.), *The National Assembly Agenda*. Cardiff: Institute of Welsh Affairs, pp. 230–44.

Jones, G. E. (1998) *Growing Up at Last? Education and the National Assembly*. Talybont: Y Lolfa.

Liberal Democrat Wales (1999) *Guaranteed Delivery*. Cardiff: Liberal Democrat Wales.

Morgan, K., Rees, G. and Garmise, S. (1999) Networking for local economic development. In G. Stoker (ed.), *The New Management of British Local Governance*, Basingstoke: Macmillan.

Osmond, J. (1999) *The Civil Service and the National Assembly*. Cardiff: Institute of Welsh Affairs.

Plaid Cymru (1999) *Working for the New Wales*. Cardiff: Plaid Cymru.

Salisbury, J. (1996) *Educational Reforms and Gender Equality in Welsh Schools*. Cardiff: Equal Opportunities Commission.

Wales Labour Party (1999) *Working Hard for Wales*. Cardiff: Wales Labour Party.

Welsh Conservative Party (1999) *Fair Play for All: Your Voice in the Assembly*. Cardiff: Welsh Conservative Party.

Welsh Office (1995a) *A Bright Future: Getting the Best for Every Pupil at School in Wales,* Cardiff: Welsh Office.

Welsh Office (1995b) *People and Prosperity: An Agenda for Action*. Cardiff: Welsh Office.

Welsh Office (1997) *Building Excellent Schools Together*. Cardiff: Welsh Office.

Welsh Office (1999) *The BEST for Teaching and Learning: Building Excellent Schools Together*. Cardiff: Welsh Office.

Index